Project Management with dotProject

Implement, Configure, Customize, and Maintain your dotProject Installation

A complete beginner's guide to every aspect of setting up and administering your dotProject installation

Lee Jordan

BIRMINGHAM - MUMBAI

Project Management with dotProject
Implement, Configure, Customize, and Maintain your dotProject Installation

Copyright © 2007 Packt Publishing

All rights reserved. No part of this book may be reproduced, stored in a retrieval system, or transmitted in any form or by any means, without the prior written permission of the publisher, except in the case of brief quotations embedded in critical articles or reviews.

Every effort has been made in the preparation of this book to ensure the accuracy of the information presented. However, the information contained in this book is sold without warranty, either express or implied. Neither the author, Packt Publishing, nor its dealers or distributors will be held liable for any damages caused or alleged to be caused directly or indirectly by this book.

Packt Publishing has endeavored to provide trademark information about all the companies and products mentioned in this book by the appropriate use of capitals. However, Packt Publishing cannot guarantee the accuracy of this information.

First published: May 2007

Production Reference: 1270407

Published by Packt Publishing Ltd.
32 Lincoln Road
Olton
Birmingham, B27 6PA, UK.

ISBN 978-1-847191-64-9

www.packtpub.com

Cover Image by Vinayak Chittar (vinayak.chittar@gmail.com)

Credits

Author
Lee Jordon

Reviewer
Brian Kershner

Development Editors
Nanda Padmanabhan
Nikhil Bangera

Technical Editor
Shayantani Chaudhuri

Editorial Manager
Dipali Chittar

Project Manager
Patricia Weir

Project Coordinator
Abhijeet Deobhakta

Indexer
Bhushan Pangaokar

Proofreader
Chris Smith

Production Coordinator
Manjiri Nandkarni

Cover Designer
Shantanu Zagade

About the Author

Lee Jordan is a web developer with a large collection of web technology acronyms on her resume that sound like the names of laundry detergent and cause glazed expressions in school children. She designs and maintains internal and external enterprise-level websites and web-based applications as part of a project team for a privately held technical services company. Her work includes proposing, writing, and editing web content and user guides people actually read.

She began her career in 1997 as a web designer after graduating from Florida State University with a Bachelor of Fine Arts, where she swears that she missed at least one home football game while in the computer lab. Lee later convinced Seminole Community College to give her a Web Programming degree in 2003, even though her final project was a Java-based application that actually contained a usable help file.

Web development topics or whatever she can think of at the time are posted on her blog at `http://leesjordan.net`.

> To Nanda Padmanabhan, Abhijeet Deobhakta, and everyone else at Packt Publishing. Their patience, professionalism, and guidance throughout this project have made all the difference.
>
> To the creators and developers of dotProject whose focus and dedication to dotProject and the Open Source community is overwhelming.
>
> To my children for their hugs and curiosity. There are few things as humbling as trying to explain a technical topic to a six year old.
>
> To Brian Kershner for listening to my ideas being critical when I needed it.
>
> My husband Brian (not the same one, a different and unique Brian): Always, always, always.
>
> To my Mom and Dad. They encouraged me to read, read, read when I was growing up.

Table of Contents

Preface	**1**
Chapter 1: Introducing dotProject	**5**
What is a Project Management Application?	**5**
What are the Features Required of a PMA?	6
What is dotProject?	**7**
What are the Core Features of dotProject?	**8**
Core Features in Detail	9
Why dotProject is the Right PMA for You	**12**
Introducing ProjectRUs	**13**
Summary	**13**
Chapter 2: Installing dotProject	**15**
Prerequisites	**15**
Before you Install	16
LAMP, WAMP, or WIMP?	16
Web Server	17
PHP	17
MySQL	17
Windows	17
Browser	18
Mail Server	18
Fonts	18
Memory Limit	18
Installation	**18**
Backup First	19
Installing with an Online Control Panel	19
Browser-Based Installation	24
Secure your Installation with SSL	30
Troubleshooting	**31**
Database Installation Fails	31

Table of Contents

Using a Different Web Server/OS/Setup	33
dotProject Pages Display Differently for Me	33
JpGraph/Gantt Fonts Error	33
Summary	**34**
Chapter 3: dotProject User Basics	**35**
The dotProject Interface	**35**
User Menu	38
Help (Online)	39
The Todo List	44
Today	45
Main Navigation Bar	46
Companies	47
Projects	48
Tasks	49
Files	50
Contacts	51
Summary	**52**
Chapter 4: Getting Things Done	**53**
Managing Companies	**53**
Adding New Companies	55
Viewing Companies	56
View Company Tabs	58
Updating Companies	58
Adding a New Department	60
Managing Contacts	**62**
Downloading Contacts as a CSV	62
Adding New Contacts	64
Viewing Contacts	68
Updating Contacts	68
Managing Projects	**69**
Adding and Editing Projects	70
Best Practices for Creating Projects	72
Adding and Editing Tasks	73
Basic Task Creation	73
Task Dates Tab	75
Task Details Tab	76
Task Dependencies Tab	76
Task Human Resources Tab	77
Task Logs	77
File Management and Version Control	77
Adding New Files	78
Viewing Files	81
Updating Current Files	82
Editing Files	84
Summary	**86**

Chapter 5: Administering dotProject — 87
System Administration — 87
Language Support — 88
Adding a Language to dotProject — 89
Translation Management — 96
Preferences — 98
System Configuration — 98
General Settings — 99
User Authentication Settings — 106
LDAP Settings — 109
Email Settings — 111
Session Handling Settings — 112
Task Reminder Settings — 113
Default User Preferences — 114
Lookup Values — 116
Custom Fields — 118
Custom Field Notes — 121
Billing Code Table — 121
Module Management — 123
Installing Modules — 123
Activating Modules — 124
Re-Ordering Modules — 126
Administering Users — 126
Viewing Users — 128
Adding Users — 129
Editing Users — 130
Deleting Users — 130
Setting Permissions — 131
Roles — 132
Users — 132
Adding New Roles — 134
Administrative Roles — 139
Summary — 153

Chapter 6: Customizing the Look-and-Feel — 155
Setting User Preferences — 155
User Interface Style — 156
Finding Other Themes — 157
Custom Themes — 159
Altering an Existing Theme — 159
Changing Images — 159
Editing the Style Sheet — 164
Altering Existing Styles — 164
Changing Fonts — 164
Adjusting Links — 165
What Styles Should I Leave Alone? — 166

[iii]

Adding New Styles	**169**
Tips for Creating a New Theme	169
Customizing Module Text Strings	170
Summary	**172**
Chapter 7: Beyond Projects: Charts, Reports, and Extensions	**173**
More Standard Modules	**173**
Gantt Charts	174
The Combined Projects View	174
The Individual Project View	175
The ToDo View—New in Version 2.1.0	175
Project Reports	175
Generating Reports	177
Viewing Reports	177
Resources	178
Adding Resources	179
Forums	179
Calendar	181
SmartSearch	182
Backup	183
Add-On Modules	**184**
Installing Add-Ons	186
Eventum	187
Installing the Eventum Module	188
Using Eventum	191
Enabling Support Contracts in dotProject	191
Helpdesk	192
Installation and Configuration	193
Using Help Desk	194
Invoice	195
Using Invoice	195
TicketSmith	196
Using TicketSmith	196
Custom Modification and Integrations	198
Developer Resources	198
How do I Volunteer?	198
What should I Know?	199
Summary	**199**
Appendix A: Upgrading dotProject	**201**
Backing Up dotProject	**202**
Using cPanel Backups for Easy Manual Backups	204
Back Up the dotProject Database Automatically with Cron Jobs	205

Backing Up the dotProject Installation Files for Automatic Upgrades	208
Have a Rollback Plan in Place	209
Test the Upgrade in a Development "Sandbox"	209
Troubleshooting Upgrades	209
Database and Install Errors After Upgrade	210
Contacts Issues or User Details Lost During an Upgrade	210
Appendix B: Troubleshooting	**211**
Resolving Gantt Chart Errors	**211**
Method 1	212
Method 2	213
Individual Project/Task Gantt Display Error (Fonts)	213
Index	**215**

Preface

This is a comprehensive beginner's book on dotProject and deals with the basics of implementing and configuring dotProject. It is a simple guide to setting up an internal project management solution as quickly as possible, and at zero cost. All the examples in this book are fully practical and will help you to get things done with dotProject. To make sure that you create a site that fits in with your corporate identity, the book covers customizing dotProject to personalize the look for your pages.

This book illustrates an easy and effective method to handle projects with the help of extensive real-world examples.

What This Book Covers

Chapter 1 gives an overview of dotProject. This chapter explains the core features of a project management system, then it tells you why dotProject stands above your other choices and how it helps solve your project management woes.

Chapter 2 deals with how to get everything you need up and running on a development machine and helps you deal with configuration issues to set up a working dotProject site. It has walkthroughs for installing in three different ways and the last section helps you troubleshoot common problems.

Chapter 3 introduces the dotProject user interface and navigation system. It discusses standard navigation paths, navigation shortcuts, and tips on how to move around dotProject.

Chapter 4 covers the general modules used in dotProject and shows how to get things done: setting up and maintaining companies, contacts, projects, and file areas of dotProject from a user perspective. dotProject uses a sophisticated version control system for files, which this chapter covers in detail.

Preface

Chapter 5 examines all the areas of system administration within dotProject: language/translation management, system configuration, PostNuke and LDAP authentication, module management, and user administration including permission setup.

Chapter 6 focuses on customizing the look and feel of a standard dotProject system. We explore different ways to modify the appearance and settings of dotProject to better suit your needs—from playing around with the CSS and altering icons/images to modifying themes, we do it all in this chapter. At the end of this chapter, you will be able to personalize dotProject to suit your corporate standards.

Chapter 7 covers a host of advanced topics—we save the best for last! From a detailed overview of default dotProject modules, to working with dotProject reports and extending dotProject with add-ons, it describes the purpose and common functions of the standard core and optional modules; you will find something here to enhance your dotProject installation and push it a bit further.

Appendix A deals with the all-important topic of backing up your dotProject installation. This appendix presents a clear outline of what needs to be done and how to do it.

Appendix B deals with troubleshooting issues you might face while working with dotProject.

What You Need for This Book

You will need Apache web server (version 1.3.x or 2.x), MySQL server (version 3.23.x), PHP 4.1 or higher, and dotProject. 2.0.4 or later is ideal.

Conventions

In this book, you will find a number of styles of text that distinguish between different kinds of information. Here are some examples of these styles, and an explanation of their meaning.

There are three styles for code. Code words in text are shown as follows: "We can include other contexts through the use of the `include` directive."

A block of code will be set as follows:

```
A:link{
       color: #006600;/*was 08245b*/
       text-decoration: underline;/*was none*/
}
```

When we wish to draw your attention to a particular part of a code block, the relevant lines or items will be made bold:

```
BODY{
     background-color: #cc66cc;/*was #f0f0f0*/
     margin-top: 0px;
     margin-left: 0px;
     margin-right: 0px;
     margin-bottom: 10px;
     font-family: Osaka,verdana,Sans-Serif;
     font-size: 10pt;ss
}
```

New terms and **important words** are introduced in a bold-type font. Words that you see on the screen, in menus or dialog boxes for example, appear in our text like this: "clicking the **Next** button moves you to the next screen".

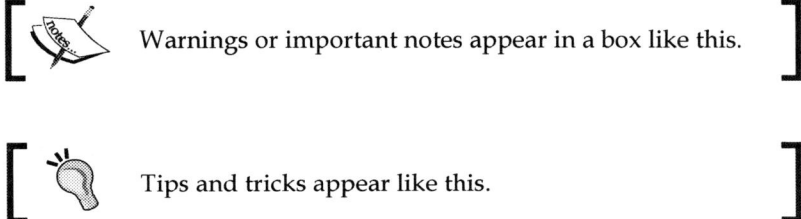

[Warnings or important notes appear in a box like this.]

[Tips and tricks appear like this.]

Reader Feedback

Feedback from our readers is always welcome. Let us know what you think about this book, what you liked or may have disliked. Reader feedback is important for us to develop titles that you really get the most out of.

To send us general feedback, simply drop an email to feedback@packtpub.com, making sure to mention the book title in the subject of your message.

If there is a book that you need and would like to see us publish, please send us a note in the **SUGGEST A TITLE** form on www.packtpub.com or email suggest@packtpub.com.

If there is a topic that you have expertise in and you are interested in either writing or contributing to a book, see our author guide on www.packtpub.com/authors.

Customer Support

Now that you are the proud owner of a Packt book, we have a number of things to help you to get the most from your purchase.

Downloading the Example Code for the Book

Visit http://www.packtpub.com/support, and select this book from the list of titles to download any example code or extra resources for this book. The files available for download will then be displayed.

 The downloadable files contain instructions on how to use them.

Errata

Although we have taken every care to ensure the accuracy of our contents, mistakes do happen. If you find a mistake in one of our books—maybe a mistake in text or code—we would be grateful if you would report this to us. By doing this you can save other readers from frustration, and help to improve subsequent versions of this book. If you find any errata, report them by visiting http://www.packtpub.com/support, selecting your book, clicking on the **Submit Errata** link, and entering the details of your errata. Once your errata are verified, your submission will be accepted and the errata added to the list of existing errata. The existing errata can be viewed by selecting your title from http://www.packtpub.com/support.

Questions

You can contact us at questions@packtpub.com if you are having a problem with some aspect of the book, and we will do our best to address it.

Introducing dotProject

dotProject is an open-source **Project Management Application (PMA)**, maintained by committed volunteers with the goal of providing a project management environment that is free for everyone. The volunteers use the term "project management environment" to describe their philosophy behind dotProject. To them, dotProject is not another collaboration tool or groupware application. They see dotProject as the forest and project information as the trees. dotProject is not just a place to put all the project documentation and contact information; it is the hub of all project activity.

This chapter will introduce you to dotProject, and covers the following:

- What a project management application is and why you need one
- What the core features of dotProject are
- Why dotProject is the right PMA for you
- How to find and get to know the dotProject community

What is a Project Management Application?

If you walked up to someone and asked them to quickly name a project management application they might say "Email," or "Microsoft Project", or "You mean our intranet, right?" Actually what they would probably do is stare at you blankly and say, "Huh?"

A project management application is an intimidating term for a simple concept: keeping an eye on all projects using a single program.

What are the Features Required of a PMA?

Project management applications should all contain certain core features to be useful to users. A PMA usually has the following characteristics:

- Projects are created in a central location, using a standardized process. All users involved in project planning and creation create and store their project information in the same place, the same way every time.
- Information about progress can be tracked using automatically created charts and alert systems. Color-coded time alerts and email notifications keep everyone involved in a project easily informed of the status of assignments.
- Projects can be categorized and tasks defined deeply or loosely. A user can create a project about a small task that has a short time frame, such as a minor site upgrade, or a large year-long project, that will require resources from multiple departments, many files, and a carefully planned list of activities.
- Measurement tools such as calendars, resource allocation, and time calculators assist users in managing projects. These tools should be easy to use and located close to where they are needed. A resource allocation tool should be accessible as a tab or window when a new task is created.

So are project management applications useful, or are they just something else to take up our time during the day? There are many benefits of using a project management application. The stakeholders and users have a centralized place for project information. Well-designed systems include some type of project team contact system, a place to store project files, version control, project status in graph or chart form, and a place to discuss project topics. Motivating project team members to add new projects and update information is the key to a system being useful.

The stakeholders of the project management system, be they the vice-president of the company or a department manager, should be champions of the application and encourage others to use it. Without their support, it may be difficult to persuade people not on the core project team to see updating the application as worth their time. Users need to be shown how it will actually save them time and be a tool for them to use.

Communication between project members is a crucial part of any project management system. Email works fine until someone is sick, goes on vacation, or leaves the company; the project information is trapped in email limbo. If a project management system was used, members could still email each other from within the system, but all the key information would be stored in a central location. Other forms of communication are available at any time: forums, file repositories, or task logs. Any serious PMA should provide communication tools such as these.

Chapter 1

What is dotProject?

dotProject enables you to create, track, and maintain your projects online. It provides enterprise-level project management tools that include contact management, an email notification system, and an online system to create and manage projects. The intuitive color codes indicate if you are headed for hot water. It is created, maintained, and developed by volunteers like you and me.

dotProject is free to use. The software license is BSD, GNU General Public License (GPL), which means it is free software provided as is with no warranty. The full license should be available in the folder where your installation of dotProject resides. You can learn more about this type of license at `http://www.gnu.org/licenses/gpl.html`.

When a user first logs in, they will see a personalized view of dotProject. The screen will display the events and tasks they are members of, including a full list of specific projects and tasks they are assigned to. The user can navigate to different areas as specified on the navigation bar, which will be displayed on the top or the left side of the screen.

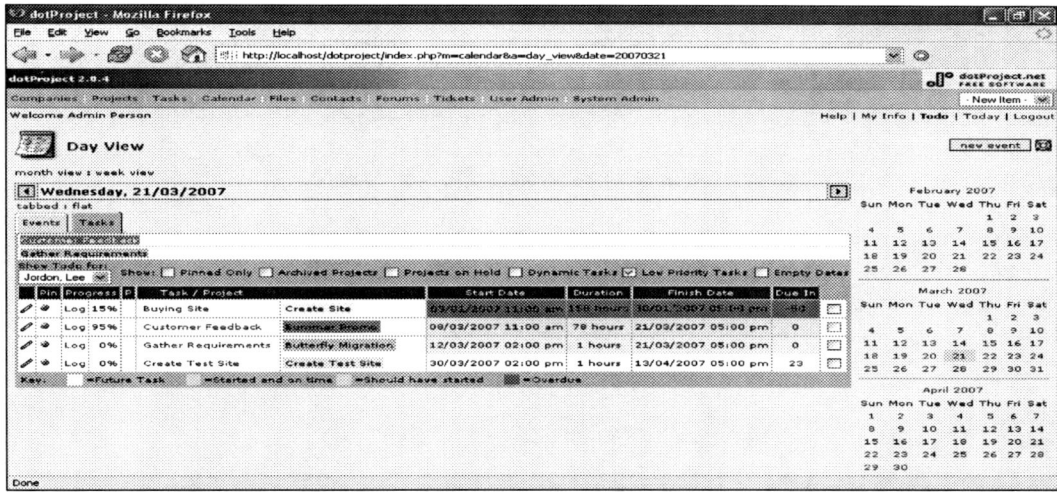

dotProject is an online project management application. You will need a browser and either intranet or Internet access.

[7]

dotProject is surprisingly versatile. A few of the many things you can do in dotProject are:

- Set up a project and its tasks
- Communicate with everyone on the project team from within dotProject
- See projects as Gantt charts
- Check task progress quickly with **Calendar** and **Events**

dotProject has great features for communicating with your contacts and resources. Even so, it is not intended as a groupware tool. Groupware is generally used to describe desktop or web-based applications that enable users to work collaboratively. There are often forums, chat environments, wikis, or email tools that are all-purpose in nature. Choosing a groupware over a focused application could be compared to offering a guest a wide variety of pies, cakes, and cookies for dessert when you know they have a deep and abiding love for cheesecake with raspberry and chocolate sauce.

dotProject is focused specifically on project management instead of being a generic groupware application. It does contain forums, calendar, and email functionality that are often associated with groupware tools, so that users can collaborate for the purpose of project management. The phrase, "for the purpose of project management" is the key difference between dotProject and groupware. The narrow focus on the needs of those involved in managing projects makes dotProject more useful to users than a generic tool. No project is too large or too small, whether you are trying to get the band back together or developing enterprise software projects.

dotProject is useful in many ways. There are features of dotProject that make using it a much more pleasant experience, like user-specific to-do lists and events: when a user logs in, they immediately see what project events they are involved in and what tasks are assigned to them.

What are the Core Features of dotProject?

The answer will actually depend on what your company uses dotProject for. A user with admin access has a great deal of control over what modules are active, displayed, or hidden, and who can use them. If a particular set of modules are not needed, they can be deactivated. There are 10 key features that make up the core of dotProject.

These are central to the dotProject philosophy of creating an environment for users:

1. User Management
2. Email-based Trouble Ticket System
3. Client/Company Management
4. Project Listings
5. Hierarchical Task List
6. File Repository
7. Contact List
8. Calendar
9. Discussion Forum
10. Resource-Based Permissions

 For more information pertaining to voxel dot net's ticketsmith please refer to the following link:
http://freshmeat.net/projects/ticketsmith/

Core Features in Detail

User Management: A simple feature, for tracking user activity, adding users, and managing users. User sessions showing date last logged in and other information are available.

Email-based Trouble Ticket System, (Integrated voxel dot net's Ticketsmith): A ticket-tracking system. Some use dotProject as a helpdesk or combination CRM (Customer Resource Management) tool.

Email notification for assignees: This feature is on by default whenever a new task is created. User assignees will receive information about the task they were assigned to unless you choose not to have the notification sent.

Client/Company Management: A digital rolodex of contact information that can be used to identify projects that directly affect customers or external clients. Basic default classifications and categories are already set up in the **Companies** module. A tabbed interface allows users to quickly see how many vendors, suppliers, and other types of companies are on the list. See screenshot overleaf.

Introducing dotProject

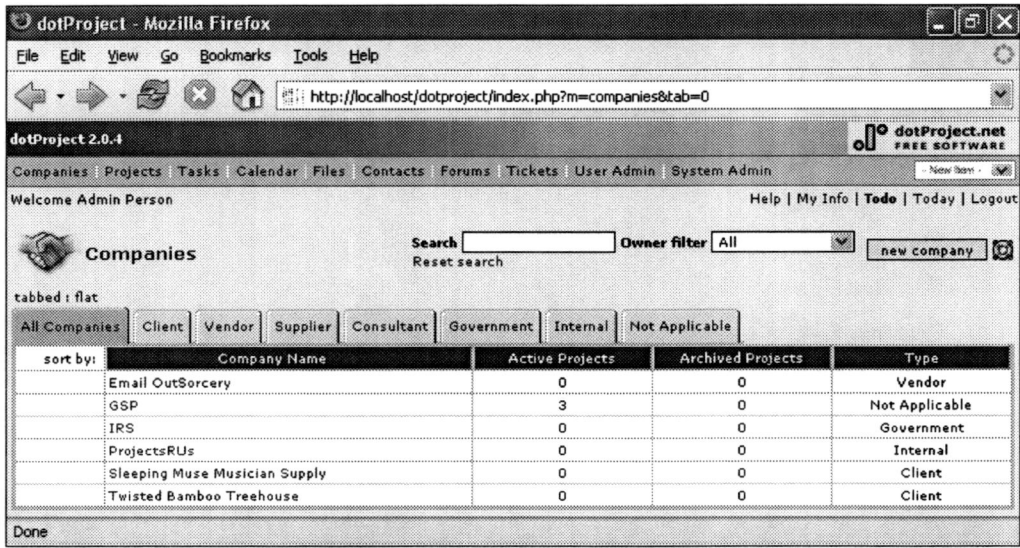

Project listings: Lists of projects are broken down by what state they are in, such as all projects, proposed, planning, in progress, on hold, complete, template, archived, not defined. You can quickly move from tab to tab to view the state of the projects. The number of projects listed in each state is in parenthesis on each tab.

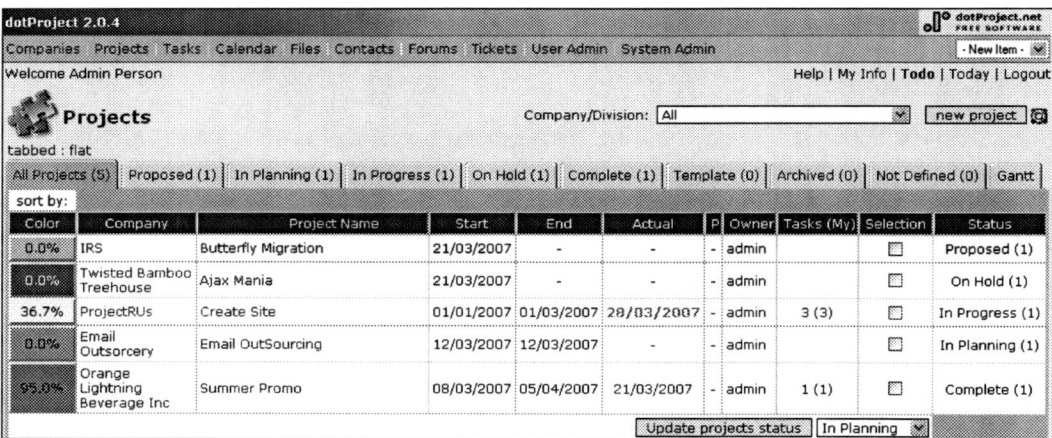

Layered project and task details: The minimum amount you need to know is displayed. Text links allow the user to drill down into the project or task for more information if required. Tasks can also be organized by precedence, dependencies, and time.

[10]

Hierarchical Task List: Tasks are organized in a hierarchy, not just arbitrarily listed. This is a very useful feature. Tasks can be dependent on other tasks.

Instant Color-Coded Progress: Instantly see if your project is in danger with intuitive color codes. If your task is highlighted with dark pink or red, it is past due.

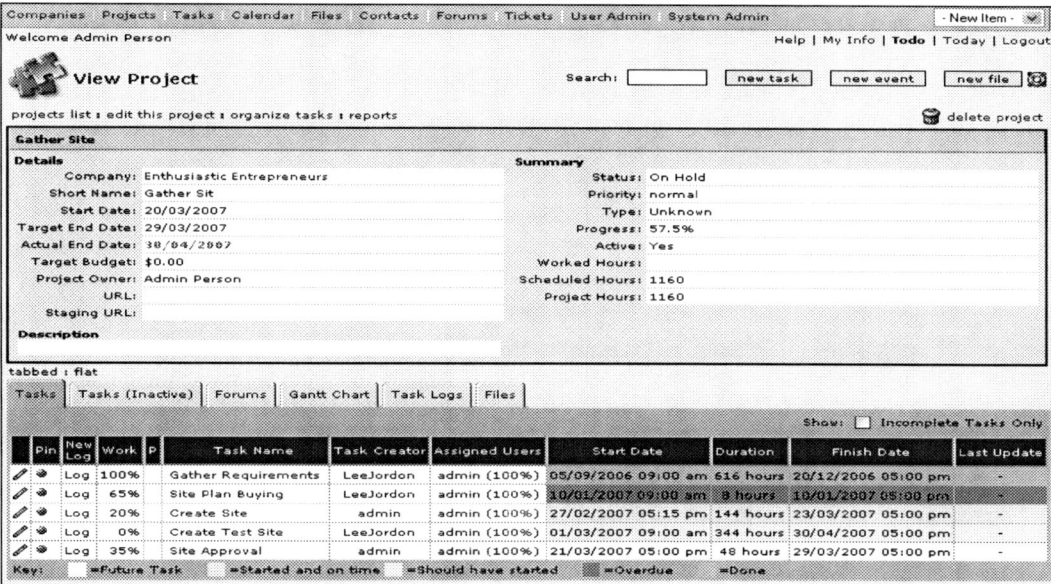

File Repository: The file repository is a central place to store project documents. They can be viewed from the central repository or from the project they are stored under. Files can be uploaded without being associated with a specific project. They will appear under the **All Projects** heading in the repository.

The file system strictly controls how files are downloaded and uploaded. All files can be assigned a version number. The check-in and check-out process can be confusing. We will spend some quality time covering it in Chapter 3, where I will help you avoid the embarrassing mistakes I have made using this feature.

Contact List: The contact list can be used intuitively within project listings themselves. This is a feature I am thankful for every time I have to edit or create a new task.

Calendar: The calendar has several display options, including a three-month mini-calendar view, a day view, week view, and a comprehensive month view. A full screen version of the calendar is only a click away on the navigation bar. There you can see a holistic view of all the projects and tasks. There is also a three-month mini-calendar that displays on the **Today** screen.

Discussion Forum: The forum module can be used to share project-specific news and information. It is integrated into dotProject. Everyone can view what is said in the forum. Threaded discussion forums can be created to discuss particular projects. All forums must be associated with projects. Forums can be moderated, and follow a standard post topic, reply, add new topic format.

Resource-Based Permissions: The permissions system in versions 2.0 and above is role based. It is granular, meaning there are many variations that can be used to specify access to the areas you want and to prevent access. Users can have read-only access to certain modules by role. Role-based permissions are intuitive. If most of the people using dotProject will be project managers, a project manager role can be created, and then individual users can be added to the system. Roles must be in place before a user is added. Think of it as a job. A job must be created, and then a person hired to fill the job position. This is a very important feature.

User-specific to-do lists and events: When a user logs in, they immediately see what project events they are involved in and what tasks are assigned to them.

Why dotProject is the Right PMA for You

So far we have examined what project management applications are, what they should do, and taken a high-level look at what features dotProject has to offer. Determining what project management tool best suits an organization calls for awareness of which features are critical and which are negotiable.

dotProject is the right choice for organizations that need a project management application that has no fees, has a generous license agreement, is stable, works on all the major browsers, has a supportive community, has permissions that are granular, and is scalable. It is open source, not a commercial application. There are no license fees, maintenance fees, or purchasing fees. For organizations on a tight budget, the price is right.

It has a history of integration with other popular open-source projects such as PostNuke. It's modular. Use only the modules you need. Don't want to use the **Forums** module? Disable it. It shares many advantages of other open-source, developer-maintained applications, in that it is relatively lightweight and can be customized by users or by contracting with its developers.

dotProject does have limitations. Its focused approach may turn off those looking for an all-in-one project development suite. There is no module for creating diagrams, for example. The ability of dotProject to integrate with other applications as part of a larger, customized group is a potential solution.

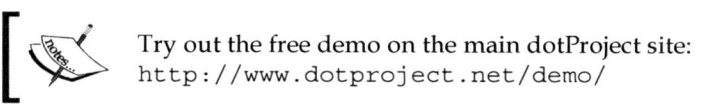

Try out the free demo on the main dotProject site: `http://www.dotproject.net/demo/`

Introducing ProjectRUs

Instead of creating projects arbitrarily as we move through the book, we will stick to "ProjectRUs", an imaginary project that will help us illustrate the concepts we learn. ProjectRUs is a technology company that has an extensive list of services, including consulting, Web development, Internet marketing and of course Project Management Services.

Even fictitious companies have employees, so in the course of the examples seen in the book; you will meet Lee Jordan, who moonlights as a System Administrator when she is not writing technical books. You will also bump into Happy UserPerson, happily designing some new modules for clients of ProjectRUs, and many others.

Summary

This chapter gives an overview about dotProject. dotProject can be easily set up within a day, yet has many complex attributes that a casual setup might miss. The true usefulness of this feature-rich application is both its surface simplicity and its hidden depths. We've defined what a project management application is and types of things they typically do.

Here we also demonstrated how dotProject fits in PMA landscape and what makes dotProject a popular tool. If we are in trouble and cannot figure out how to proceed with the tool, we can get assistance from the dotProject community, which has been introduced here. This book will gradually unfold the advantages of working with dotProject. And to do that we first need to install dotProject, which has been discussed in detail in the next chapter. We will start really getting things done with dotProject after that, covering the distinctive dotProject interface.

2
Installing dotProject

If you already have dotProject installed, you probably don't even need to skim this chapter, unless something has gone horribly wrong. We will cover the key information you need to know to successfully install dotProject, what to do if things are not working right, and how to avoid common pitfalls and hours of frustration.

This chapter will include:

- dotProject setup options including server, database, and browser issues
- Prerequisites for installation of the tool
- The process for control panels and browser-based installations
- Troubleshooting your installation

Installing dotProject is usually an automated process if your server and database are already installed and configured. dotProject is packaged with an installation wizard that walks you through the basic setup process. It is always wise to have an understanding of the process and the setup options before you begin.

Prerequisites

It is important to make sure that everything is ready and in place for dotProject to be installed. Let's go over what we need to have prepared for a successful installation of dotProject.

Before you Install

It seems redundant to review the requirements again, doesn't it? There are a few last-minute things to discuss, especially if a control panel installation is not possible. First, make sure that the software required to run dotProject is already installed. Installing a web server, MySQL, and PHP is beyond the scope of this book. There are many fine books and online materials that explain the installation of web servers, MySQL, and PHP in detail. The dotProject team recommends the following environment:

- Apache web server (version 1.3.x or 2.x).
- MySQL server (version 3.23.x).
- A downloaded copy of dotProject. 2.0.4 or later is ideal. The most recent stable release can be downloaded from SourceForge.
- MySQL should be set up first, so that a dotProject user can create temporary tables during installation. Specifically, the database user should have ALTER and DROP permissions.
- In the section on browser-based installation, we will go over how to deal with the config.php file. If your installation already contains a config.php file (not a config_dist.php file, etc.), then dotProject will assume you are trying to upgrade.

Your PHP installation should have register_globals set to OFF in order for dotProject to run in an optimized and more secure mode. The dotProject installer automatically detects the state of register_globals. dotProject will work with register_globals set to ON, but it is not recommended.

LAMP, WAMP, or WIMP?

There are several key requirements to run dotProject. You must have an active web server running PHP and MySQL, and an Internet browser. There are three main web-server setups that people running dotProject use. Which one you pick depends on what you already have and whether you have a preference for one over the other. If you use an Internet Service Provider (ISP) you may not have a choice on which to use.

- **LAMP** : Linux, Apache, MySQL, PHP
- **WAMP** : Windows, Apache, MySQL, PHP
- **WIMP** : Windows, IIS, MySQL, PHP

 LAMP is the most popular in the open-source community. Using LAMP provides an entirely open-source environment.

Web Server

Most web servers used today are either Apache or Microsoft IIS. Apache version 1.3.x or 2.x should be used. Your ISP or that clever person in the IT department knows which one your organization is using. There are always exceptions, so check the dotProject forums if you are using a different web server.

 Apache is the preferred environment for running dotProject.

PHP

To install dotProject 2.0, you must be using version 4.1 or higher of the very popular online programming language PHP. If you are using an Internet Service Provider, check your service details to see if PHP is provided. PHP can be downloaded from http://www.php.net/downloads.php. PHP 4.46 is the last stable version of PHP 4. PHP 5 is *not* recommended for use with version 2.0.4.

MySQL

dotProject uses the MySQL database system. You will need to have it installed before you begin as well. Version 3.23.x is recommended for use with dotProject. MySQL can be downloaded from http://www.mysql.org/downloads/. The dotProject team recommends that MySQL version 5 and above should not be used with version 2.0.4 of dotProject.

 The recent release of dotProject, version 2.1.0-rc 1 has been made more compatible with PHP 5 and MySQL 5; however, the changes incorporated does not take care of this completely. The features of this release are discussed in http://docs.dotproject.net/index.php/What%27s_New_-_2.1.0_-_rc1.

Windows

Using a bundled combination of PHP/Apache/MySQL is the best way to go if you do not already have them installed. This will save you the time and headache of installing them one at a time. The dotProject volunteers list the Apache2Triad available at http://apache2triad.sourceforge.net. Since there are limitations of dotProject being compatible with PHP5, version 1.2.3 is the download that is advisable.

Installing dotProject

Browser

dotProject works best with browsers that support **cascading style sheets** (CSS) and JavaScript. JavaScript and cookies should be turned on for full functionality. Most recent browsers such as Internet Explorer (version 5.5 or better), Mozilla 1.2, Netscape 7.x, and Firefox will work just fine. dotProject's PNG image files with alpha-transparency render best in Internet Explorer 6.0 and above. Internet Explorer 7 provides increased support for PNG image files.

Mail Server

As of version 2.0, sending mail is not a requirement. Administrators can set up the outgoing mail in the **Administration** panel.

Fonts

TrueType fonts are used for JpGraph, which is in turn used by the Gantt charts module. Most of the fonts JpGraph uses should already be installed on your system. All the fonts are not provided with dotProject because some of them have very specific licenses. If the Gantt charts module is insisting that font files are missing and you don't already have a spare copy of the files, search SourceForge or another reliable site for available fonts.

Memory Limit

The Gantt charts module can eat up your allocated memory. If the Gantt charts won't appear, and there is no error, chances are, you've reached your memory limit as set in the php.ini file. If your service is hosted, you will need to talk to your Internet Service Provider about increasing the memory limit set in your php.ini file.

Installation

There are two methods of dotProject installation:

1. Online control panel installation
2. Browser-based installation

The most recent versions of dotProject, 2.0 and later, are not meant to be manually installed. The online control panel method is very simple and usually takes between five and ten minutes. The browser-based installation generally takes a little longer, roughly ten minutes to an hour.

Which should you choose? If you already have an ISP who hosts your domain, they probably already provide you with an installation script for dotProject using one of the popular online control panels such as **cPanel** or **Plesk**. If they do not have the script available, they may be willing to install it for you if you make the request. dotProject can also be installed using a browser-based installation wizard. I recommend the online control panel installation for people who want a quick installation or are not technically inclined. The browser installation method is best for IT administrators or those who are comfortable installing web applications. If your only choice is a browser installation, don't worry; we will walk through one later in this chapter

Backup First

It is always smart to take back up of any crucial files or databases that might be affected by a new installation. Always have a backup plan when a new installation is about to be performed.

Installing with an Online Control Panel

Most control panel installations can be completed in a few steps. Be sure to write down or otherwise make a note of any file, folder paths, or other crucial information as you go. We will walk through a control panel installation using **cPanel/Fantastico**. If you have never used cPanel before, this is a great opportunity to get your feet wet. Your ISP should have provided you with a link to your cPanel when you first set up your service. You will need a user name and password provided by your ISP to log in to cPanel. Once you are logged in you will see a screen with icons for different online tools.

1. Log into your cPanel control panel.
2. Select Fantastico (double mouse-click). The Fantastico icon is usually located at the bottom right corner of the screen.

Installing dotProject

3. Scroll down the Fantastico screen until the **Project Management** category appears.

Left mouse-click on dotProject. There will be a short description about dotProject. Make a note of the version of dotProject available. The latest stable installation should be listed. The version of dotProject is in parenthesis by the new installation link. We will be using version 2.0.4 in the examples.

4. Click on the **New Installation** link to begin the installation process.

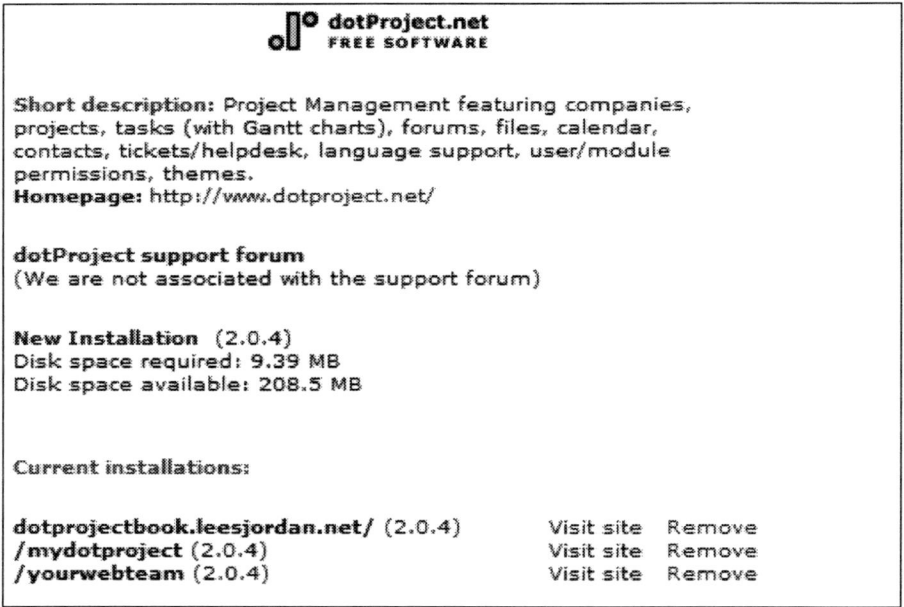

Type in the name of the subfolder, where your dotProject installation should be installed. If you leave it blank, then dotProject will be installed in the root folder of the URL path. For example, if I had left the folder field blank, the install tool would have placed the dotProject files directly in the public_html folder of www.leesjordan.net. I do not recommend leaving the folder field blank unless you already have a special URL set aside or are using a sub-domain.

Chapter 2

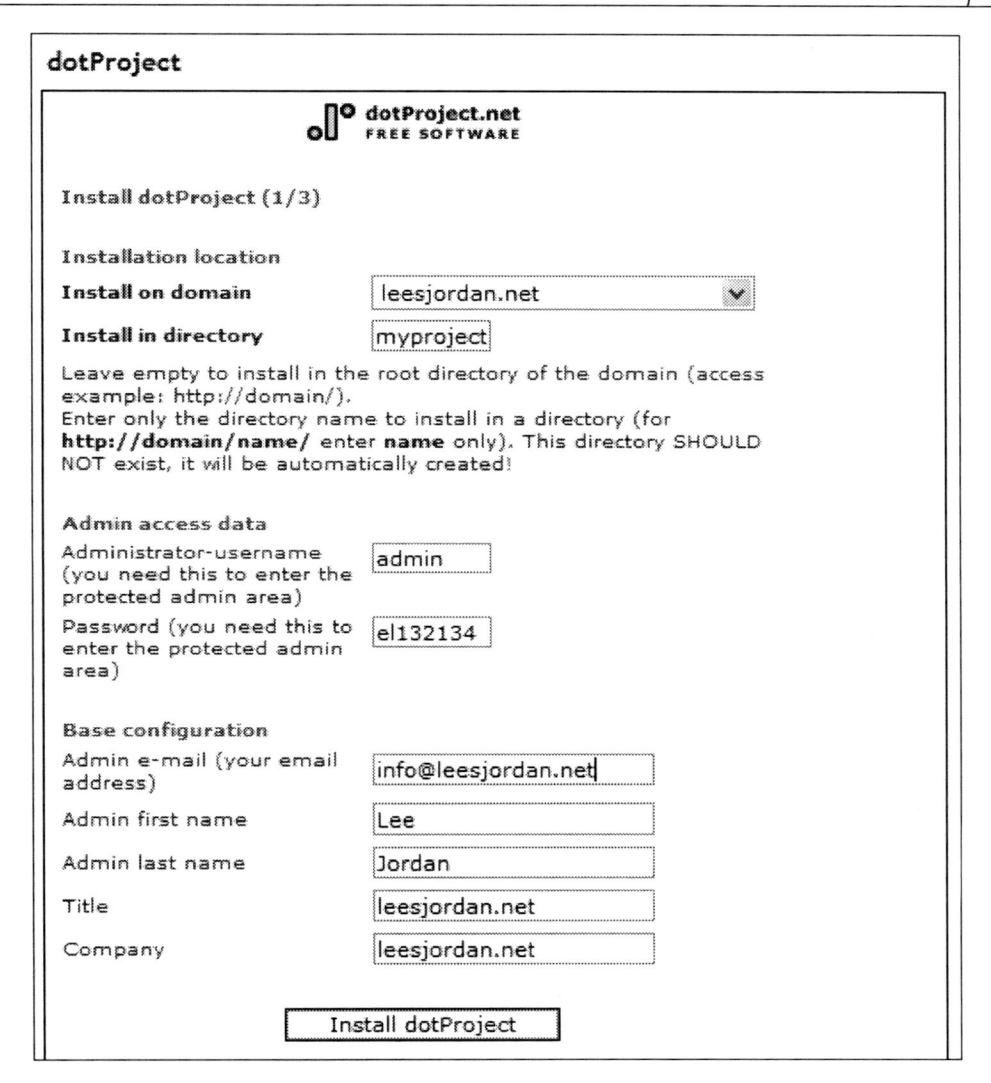

```
dotProject

                    dotProject.net
                    FREE SOFTWARE

Install dotProject (1/3)

Installation location
Install on domain        [ leesjordan.net         v ]
Install in directory     [ myproject ]
Leave empty to install in the root directory of the domain (access
example: http://domain/).
Enter only the directory name to install in a directory (for
http://domain/name/ enter name only). This directory SHOULD
NOT exist, it will be automatically created!

Admin access data
Administrator-username
(you need this to enter the    [ admin ]
protected admin area)
Password (you need this to     [ el132134 ]
enter the protected admin
area)

Base configuration
Admin e-mail (your email       [ info@leesjordan.net ]
address)
Admin first name               [ Lee ]
Admin last name                [ Jordan ]
Title                          [ leesjordan.net ]
Company                        [ leesjordan.net ]

                    [ Install dotProject ]
```

Enter the username for your dotProject **admin,** and the **Password**. You can add more administrators after dotProject is installed. Choose the username carefully. It is very difficult to change it.

5. Enter the email address of the dotProject administrator. A copy of the installation information will be sent to this email address.

6. Type the first and last name of the administrator.

7. Click the **Install dotProject** button when you are ready to continue.

Installing dotProject

8. The second installation screen gives you confirmation of the installation process so far. You should see information about your dotProject database, your subdirectory folder or other location where dotProject is being installed, and the URL from which dotProject will be accessed. Click the **Finish installation** button for the final installation screen.

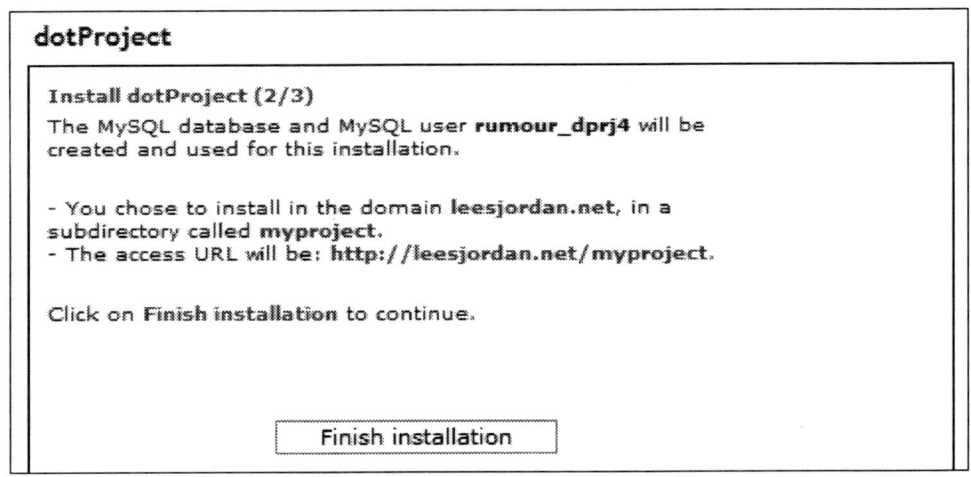

9. The first thing you should see on the final installation screen is information about your config.php file and data.sql file. They should both have been successfully configured. The username and password chosen on screen 1 should be listed again. Make note of them now if you haven't already. The administrator URL, which in this case is the same as the URL everyone will use, is displayed as well. The option to email a copy of the installation information is available. It is best to go ahead and send this information to a stakeholder or an alternative email address for backup purposes. If you choose not to send the information to another email address, then this is your last screen. Your installation process is done.

```
dotProject

Install dotProject (3/3)

/home/rumour/public_html/myproject/includes/config.php
configured
/home/rumour/public_html/myproject/data.sql configured


Please notice:

We only offer auto-installation and auto-configuration of
dotProject but do not offer any kind of support.

You need a username and a password to enter the admin area.
Your username is admin. Your password is el132134 The full URL
to the admin area (Bookmark this!):
http://leesjordan.net/myproject/




            Back to dotProject overview



        Email the details of this installation to:

              leejordan.webdev@gm
                 Send E-mail
```

An email confirmation screen will be displayed, after sending installation information to an additional email address.

```
dotProject

Email sent

Installation details were sent to leejordan.webdev@gmail.com.

Back to dotProject overview
```

Installing dotProject

10. Now it is time to check the URL where dotProject was installed and to make sure it is up and running. Type the URL into the browser. The login screen should appear.

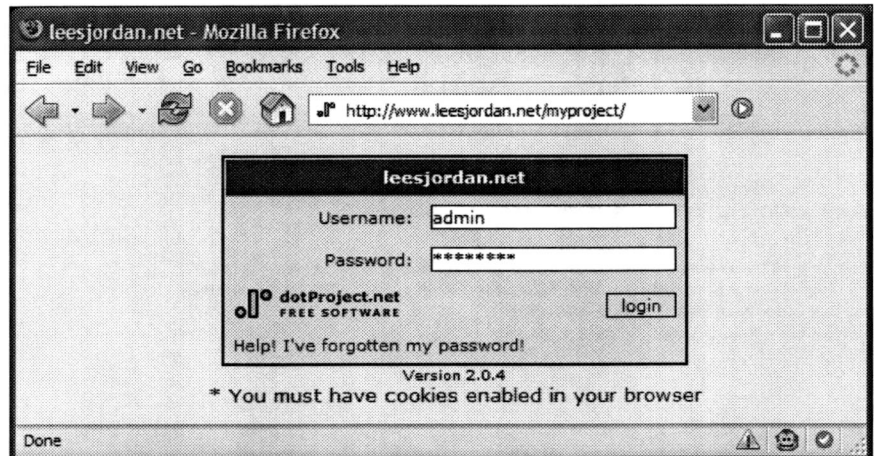

 Warning: If you want to install a version that is not provided by your ISP, you will need to download the version from SourceForge (http://sourceforge.net/projects/dotproject/) and follow the browser installation process instead.

Browser-Based Installation

How long will it take? A standard installation should take approximately 10 minutes to an hour. Does this seem like a large range of time? If things go well, the installation will go quickly. If corrections have to be made, it will take a little longer.

To prepare for installing dotProject, you will need:

- The latest stable version downloaded from SourceForge either as a tar.gz or zip package at http://sourceforge.net/projects/dotproject/.
- A web server as described earlier in the chapter.
- PHP 4.4 or above (but not 5) already installed on your server. If you have PHP 5 or greater, visit the dotProject forums if you run into any problems.
- A database ready for your dotProject installation, preferably MySQL.
- An Internet browser such as Firefox or Internet Explorer.

Carefully follow the instructions for installing PHP and a database on your server if they are not already provided by your service provider. If you do not know what version of PHP you have, you should be able to find out by running a `PHPInfo()` script. Be sure to delete the script after you have used it. Visit `php.org` to learn more about PHP if you are not sure how to do this.

Database management and PHP information should be available on your control panel, if your ISP provides you with one. The database and PHP must be installed before trying to install dotProject.

Hopefully no one has been scared off by the preparation necessary to manually install dotProject. Usually ISPs will already have PHP and MySQL available.

We're going to walk through the installation using the `zip` file. Those of you who want to use the `tar.gz` version just need to unpack the tar ball where you want your installation to be. Why are you advanced people even reading this chapter? Beats me. OK, while the gifted students show-off the rest of us will take it slow, and do the install step by step.

1. Unpack the `zip` file. By default it has the thrilling name of `dotProject`. You can do better than that, can't you? Yeah, I'll wait while you go ask permission. After you've chosen a name for your installation, we're ready to begin. Now for the easy stuff.

2. Fire up your FTP program and place the folder where you need it to go. If you are using a sub-domain, then you can install directly underneath it. If you are using a subfolder for your installation, place it under the `public_html` folder. Example: For this installation I am using the `browserdp` folder so the URL for my dotProject installation will be `http://leesjordan.net/browserdp/`.

3. After the files are uploaded, point your browser at the installation subfolder. For this example it will be: `http://leesjordan.net/browserdp/install/`.

4. The **Check for Requirements** screen will be displayed. It should look similar to the one displayed overleaf. Notice that under **Database Connectors** there are many red 'X's with the phrase **Not available.** It is a very long screen, and shows many optional configurations. The only requirement under **Database Connectors** is for the MySQL database to be prepared. If any of the mandatory requirements are not met, the installation will not be successfull. The `config.php` file can actually be uploaded after the installation is done.

Installing dotProject

Click **Start Installation** when ready.

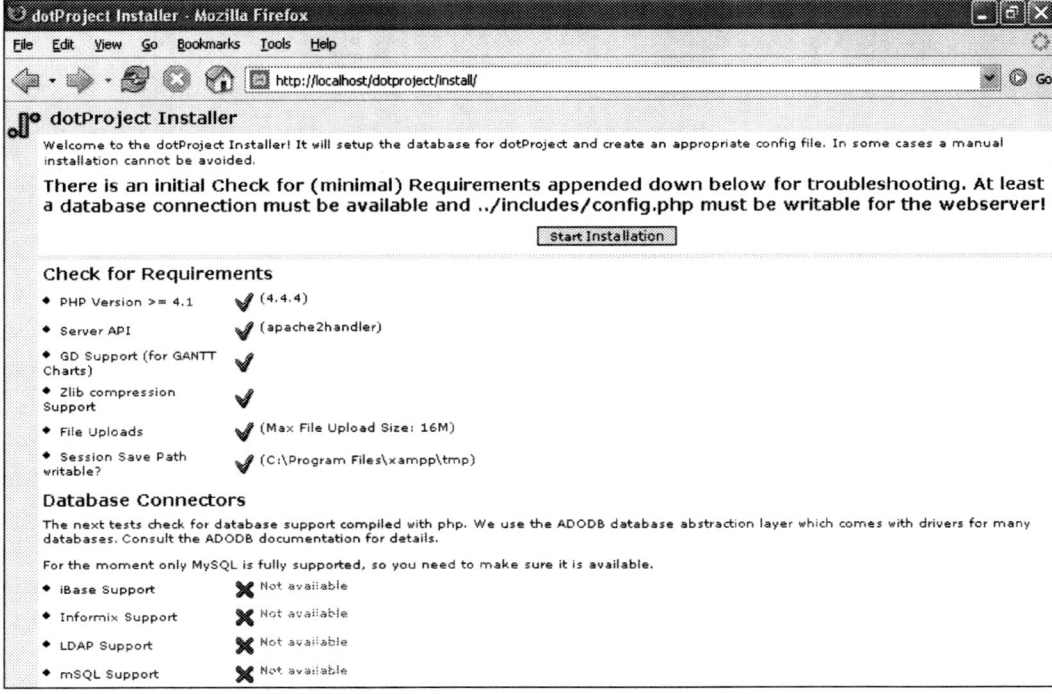

Enter the name of your database, the admin user, and the admin database user password. Click on **install db & write cfg** button. Be sure to have the drop existing database checkbox checked if you have a database you want to reuse. Make sure that the database name matches the one created in MySQL.

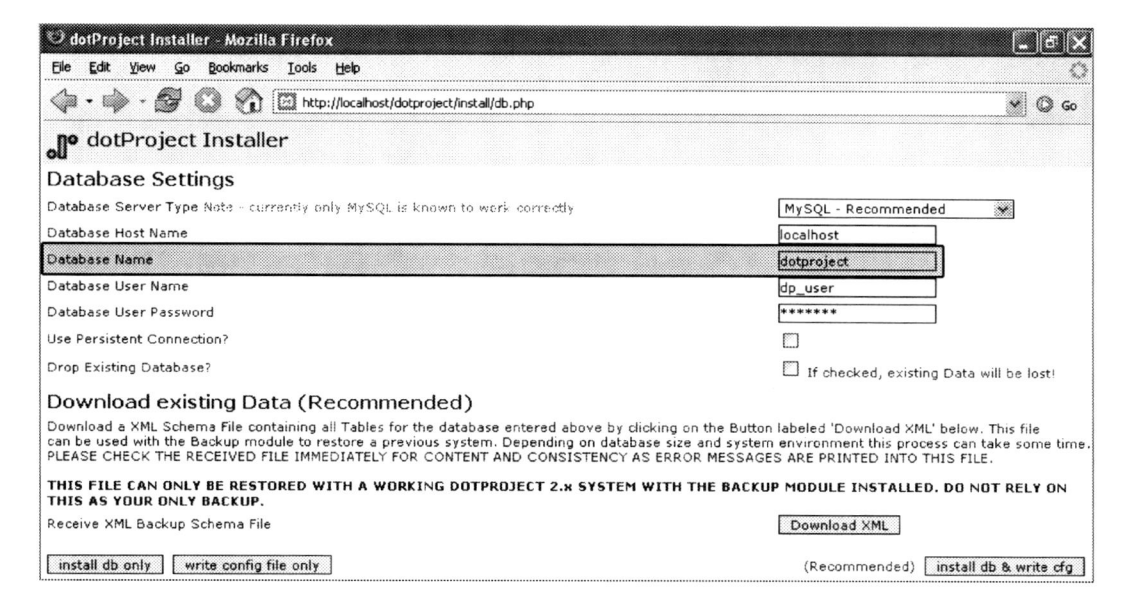

Installing dotProject

5. If your database was successfully created, a green success message **Database successfully setup** will be displayed. The `config` file creation feedback may display an error message in red. This is normal.

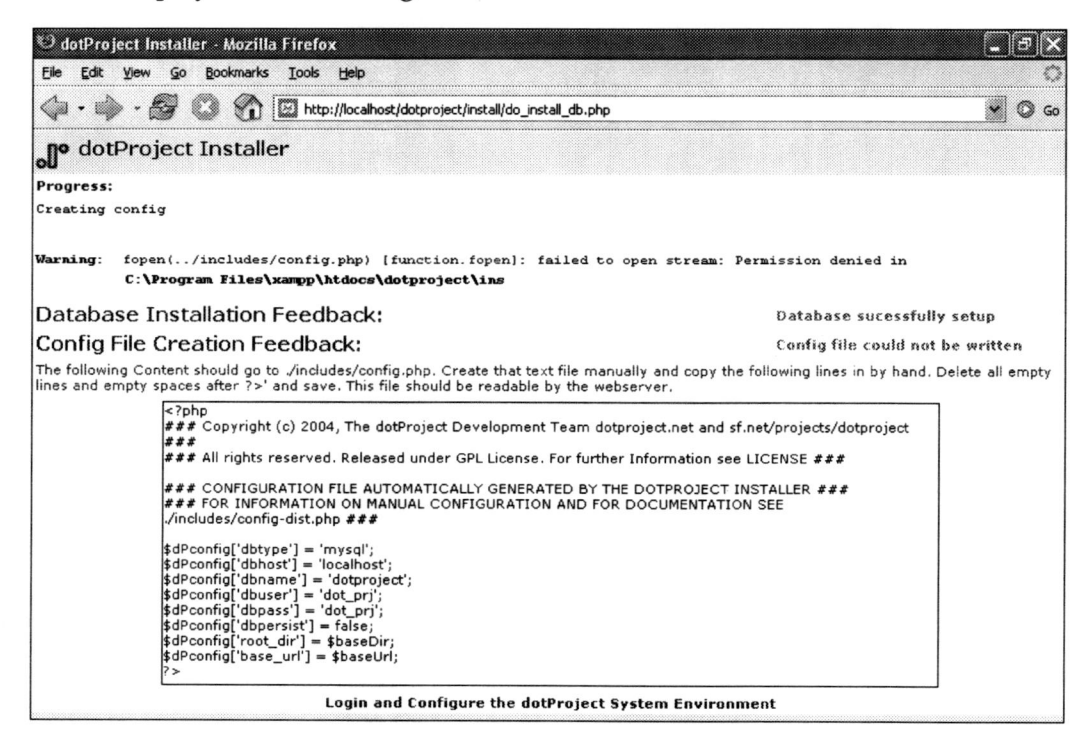

6. If the database setup was not successful, a screen like the following one will be displayed. Click the back button and double-check that you entered the database information correctly. Syntax is very important. The error screen looks like this:

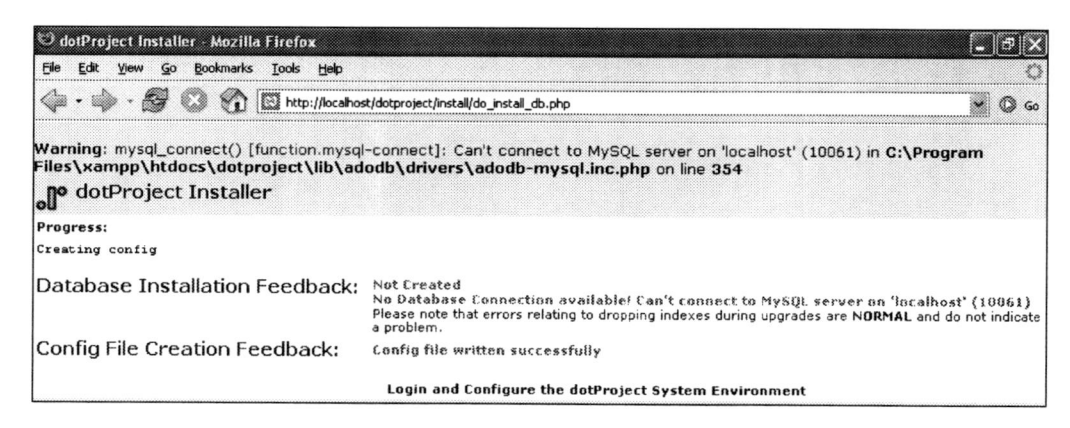

[28]

Still having trouble? See the troubleshooting section in this chapter for more help.

7. Copy and paste the configuration file text into a text editor such as Notepad and save it as `config.php`. Upload the file to the server in the `/includes/` subfolder of your dotProject folder.

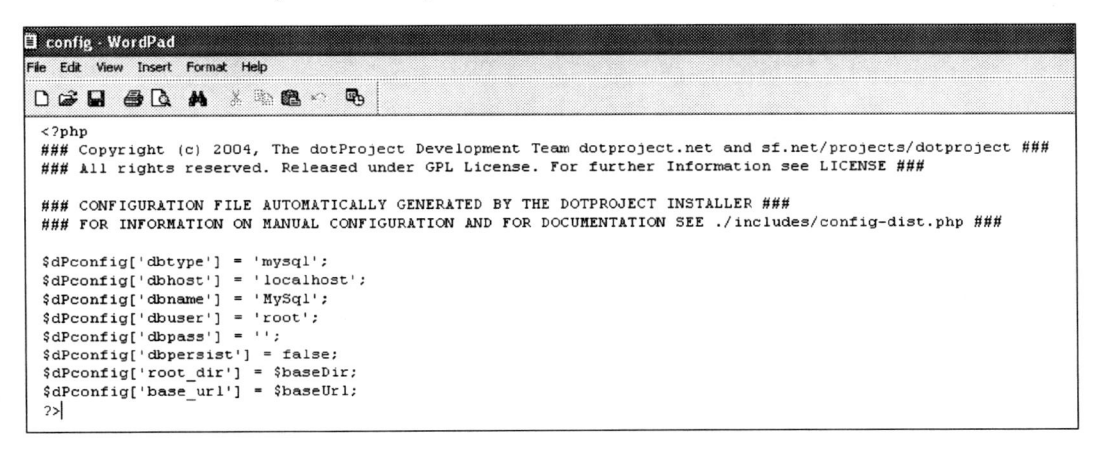

```
<?php
### Copyright (c) 2004, The dotProject Development Team dotproject.net and sf.net/projects/dotproject ###
### All rights reserved. Released under GPL License. For further Information see LICENSE ###

### CONFIGURATION FILE AUTOMATICALLY GENERATED BY THE DOTPROJECT INSTALLER ###
### FOR INFORMATION ON MANUAL CONFIGURATION AND FOR DOCUMENTATION SEE ./includes/config-dist.php ###

$dPconfig['dbtype']    = 'mysql';
$dPconfig['dbhost']    = 'localhost';
$dPconfig['dbname']    = 'MySql';
$dPconfig['dbuser']    = 'root';
$dPconfig['dbpass']    = '';
$dPconfig['dbpersist'] = false;
$dPconfig['root_dir']  = $baseDir;
$dPconfig['base_url']  = $baseUrl;
?>
```

The `config` file's properties should be set so that it is writable to the server or `755` should do it. After you have uploaded the configuration file, it is time to take a look at the installed application.

8. Open a new browser window and type the full URL of your dotProject installation. For this example we would type: `http://leesjordan.net/browserdp/`. A login screen like the one below should appear. The dotProject installation scripts create a default administrator username and password for you. Log in using the username as "admin" and the password as "passwd". You will want to change the password as soon as possible for security.

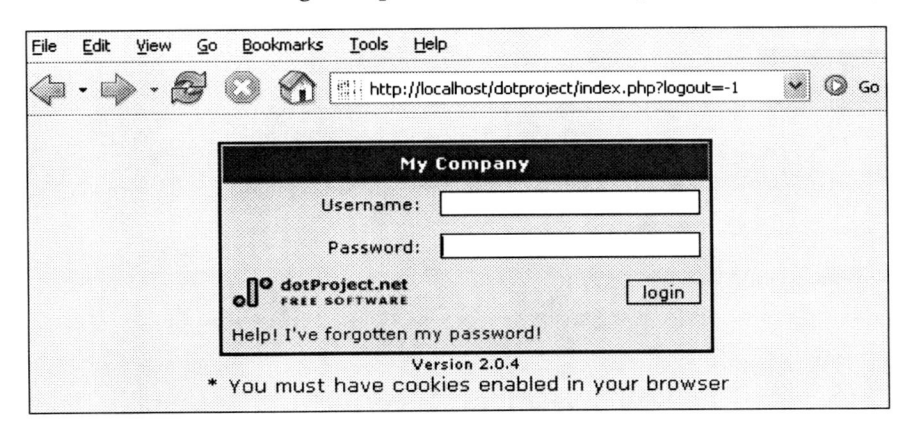

You should now be finished with installing dotProject. The next section covers secure install with SSL, an optional method.

Secure your Installation with SSL

Sensitive information is stored by many organizations on websites. If your company stores and/or shares project information, it may be necessary to encrypt it. Banks, medical organizations, government entities, or any other groups who have proprietary or private information can benefit from secured sites.

Using an SSL certificate will provide an encrypted, more secure way to access dotProject. Having an SSL certificate is not required for installing dotProject. Since there may be situations where a more secure installation is required, the dotProject volunteers have provided a code snippet for those using Apache servers. It is recommended that the SSL certificate be installed after dotProject. The installation of an SSL certificate is beyond the scope of this book.

Digicert, an SSL certificate provider, has detailed instructions for installation of certificates on many different servers. Visit http://www.digicert.com/ssl-certificate-installation.htm for more details Your ISP may already provide secured hosting as part of your service package. Contact them for more information if you are not sure. If you see a /httpsdocs/ folder when you FTP into your domain, then a secure folder has already been prepared for you.

The dotProject volunteers suggest that the following code be added to the end of the .htaccess file where the dotProject installation is located.

```
RewriteEngine on
RewriteCond %{SERVER_PORT} !443$
RewriteRule ^(.*) https://%{SERVER_NAME}/$1 [R,L]
```

The code snippet will cause requests for http://sitedomain/ to be redirected to https://sitedomain/ instead, where sitedomain is the location of your dotProject installation.

Example: If http://www.leesjordan.net/browserdp/ was changed to an SSL site, the following steps would need to be followed:

1. Obtain an SSL certificate.
2. Install the certificate.
3. Paste the code snippet above at the end of the web server's .htaccess file if using an Apache server.
4. The redirection should be to https://www.leesjordan.net/browserdp/.

Need more in-depth information about SSL for your situation? Verisign has a section of its site with a variety of information about SSL: `http://www.verisign.com/ssl/ssl-information-center/`.

Troubleshooting

You faithfully followed the installation instructions and something horrible happened. Or, you went ahead and tried to install dotProject without reading the instructions and now want to know how to fix what went wrong. We will take a look at the most common issues that can occur when installing dotProject.

Database Installation Fails

The installer will create a database if you have checked the **Create Database** box and the MySQL user you have nominated has sufficient permission within MySQL to do so.

If the user does not have permission, it will fail.

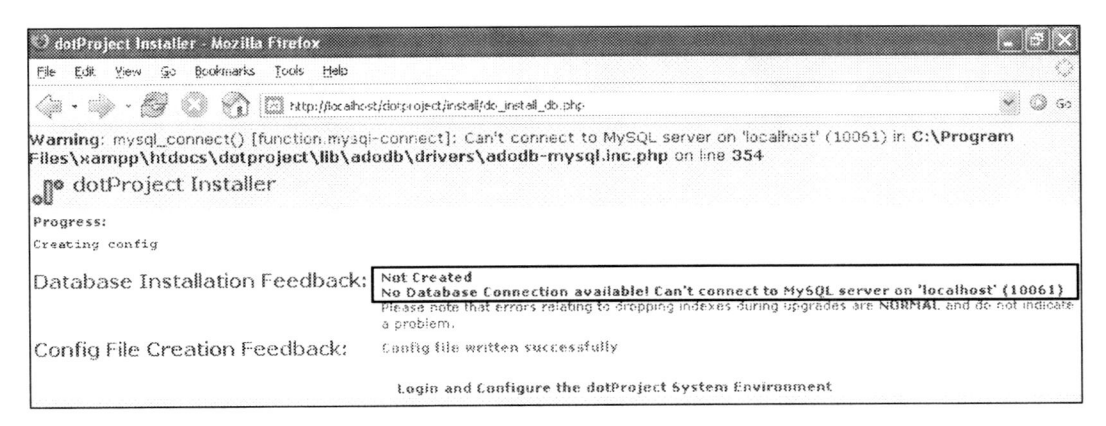

If the database already exists (i.e. you have used some other means of creating it), you do not need to check the **Create Database** box.

config.php Not Created

A `config.php` file must be in place for dotProject to operate properly.

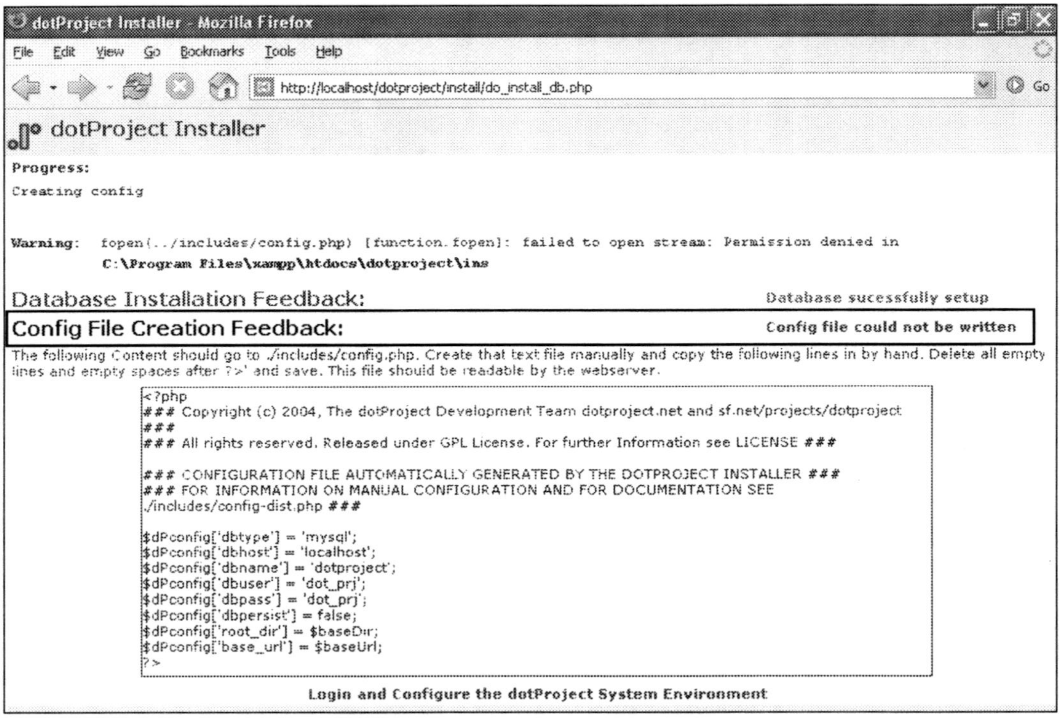
dotProject Installer - Mozilla Firefox
File Edit View Go Bookmarks Tools Help
http://localhost/dotproject/install/do_install_db.php
Go
dotProject Installer
Progress:
Creating config
Warning: fopen(../includes/config.php) [function.fopen]: failed to open stream: Permission denied in C:\Program Files\xampp\htdocs\dotproject\ins
Database Installation Feedback:
Database sucessfully setup
Config File Creation Feedback:
Config file could not be written
The following Content should go to ./includes/config.php. Create that text file manually and copy the following lines in by hand. Delete all empty lines and empty spaces after ?>' and save. This file should be readable by the webserver.
<?php
Copyright (c) 2004, The dotProject Development Team dotproject.net and sf.net/projects/dotproject
###
All rights reserved. Released under GPL License. For further Information see LICENSE
CONFIGURATION FILE AUTOMATICALLY GENERATED BY THE DOTPROJECT INSTALLER
FOR INFORMATION ON MANUAL CONFIGURATION AND FOR DOCUMENTATION SEE ./includes/config-dist.php
$dPconfig['dbtype'] = 'mysql';
$dPconfig['dbhost'] = 'localhost';
$dPconfig['dbname'] = 'dotproject';
$dPconfig['dbuser'] = 'dot_prj';
$dPconfig['dbpass'] = 'dot_prj';
$dPconfig['dbpersist'] = false;
$dPconfig['root_dir'] = $baseDir;
$dPconfig['base_url'] = $baseUrl;
?>
Login and Configure the dotProject System Environment

Since this file is not automatically included as part of the installation, it is recommended that the `config.php` code shown in steps 5 and 7 (under the section *Browser-Based Installation*) should be copied and pasted into a text file then uploaded to the server. This should be done before attempting to log in to dotProject. The PHP file shown in the section on browser installation should work fine as long as the **Database Name**, **Database User Name**, and **Database Password** information are modified. So, don't use the exact ones I used in the example. If you are using an online control panel to manage your database, it will usually append the same group of letters to each new database you create. For example, you can see during the installation that my database began with "rumour", which happens to be the name of my cat.

Using a Different Web Server/OS/Setup

Many different setups run dotProject successfully. Visit the dotProject forums at http://dotproject.net/vbulletin/ for installation help with a particular setup. Be sure to list all the details, including the operating system, web server, database, and programming language. Version numbers of these should also be included. Please read carefully about the compatibility of MySQL 5 and PHP 5.

dotProject Pages Display Differently for Me

Your dotProject installation pages do not look the same as the examples in this book. There are several different situations where this can happen.

What browser and operating system are you using to view dotProject? dotProject uses Cascading Style Sheets (CSS) files for presentation and formatting of most of the data. While most pages should display the same in all browsers, it is possible that there may be some differences between how they look on a Mac running Safari and for a Windows XP user running Internet Explorer 7.

What theme is being used as the default theme? The classic dotProject default theme is being used in this book. There are other themes available, which will alter the way dotProject looks.

The skin or "look" of dotProject can be further customized by altering the files in the styles folder. Back up any files before you attempt to make changes. We will discuss customizing dotProject in further detail in Chapter 6.

JpGraph/Gantt Fonts Error

An error message displays when the user attempts to go to the **Todo** section of dotProject or view Gantt charts. The actual error will depend on the web server and system configuration, but it will probably look similar to this:

```
JpGraph Error
Font file "/usr/X11R6/lib/X11/fonts/truetype/arial.ttf"
is not readable or does not exist.
```

Errors of this type usually occur when the font file cannot be found. dotProject does not install the fonts for JpGraph by default. This issue is discussed fully in Appendix B of this book.

Summary

In this chapter we installed dotProject in several different ways and covered what to do when things go wrong. The quickest way to install dotProject was using a control panel. Installing dotProject using the browser took more time, and required a little bit more technical know how. Now you should be able to install dotProject successfully using a control panel or a browser. This chapter also delves into common installation issues and how we can elude them.

At the end of this chapter, dotProject has been successfully installed. The user interface and navigation system will be covered in Chapter 3.

3
dotProject User Basics

To understand the tool better and increase our proficiency, we will start with examining the interface and navigation components of dotProject in this chapter. dotProject uses a graphical user interface, commonly called a **GUI** (pronounced *gooey*), that includes image and text links for navigation. There are many different ways to get to the more popular features in dotProject. We will talk about navigation shortcuts and tips as well as the standard navigation paths.

This chapter will include:

- A detailed look at the dotProject interface
- How to use the navigation menus
- Tips on getting around in dotProject

The dotProject Interface

Let's take a look around. Logging in to dotProject shows the **Today** screen in **Day View** mode by default. Unfortunately, there is no way for users to set their own unique default screen at this time. The actual default page you see after logging in will be different if your system administrator has altered the default setup. For example, the administrator could set the default sub-module to be **Todo**. The **Todo** screen will then display every time users log in. Why did the developers of dotProject make the **Today** screen in the **Day View** mode the default view? Most users who log in to dotProject will be working on project tasks as part of their regularly scheduled work.

> **Modules = Sections**
>
> The different sections of the dotProject application are divided into modules. Modules are self contained mini-applications that can be disabled, activated, and configured to customize dotProject.
>
> Each menu item shown on the main navigation menu is a dotProject module.

There is no one central "home" screen for dotProject. Instead, each modular area has its own section. The core areas can all be accessed using the main navigation menu located on the top or left, depending on the dotProject theme being used.

> **Too many tasks displayed?**
>
> If there are too many tasks on one screen, we can check select boxes to filter tasks.

The actual navigation links you are able to see will depend upon the user rights assigned to you by the administrator of your dotProject application. We will discuss the default interface in this chapter. Most users will see the following menu items listed on the navigation bar: **Companies**, **Projects**, **Tasks**, **Files**, **Contacts**, **Forums**, and **Tickets**. Users with administrative rights will also see the **User Admin** and **System Admin** menu items.

dotProject looks similar to a website. There is a "header area" for a company logo or banner, a top navigation area, and a content area known as the work pane in the central portion of the page, which changes depending on what section of dotProject the user is in.

The header area, top navigation area, and the user menu do not change from section to section in dotProject. They will be the same on every page. The work pane will change depending on what section of the dotProject application the user is in.

A dynamic menu is displayed below the work pane heading of each page. This menu will change depending upon what page the user is currently on or what access rights the user has been given. On the screenshot opposite the **Day View** screen is displayed. Dynamic content such as the choice of **month view** or **week view**, the current date, and tabs for different sections of the work pane are shown. The **Tasks** tab is the active area displayed. This dynamic content area stretches from below the page title heading **Day View** to the end of the content area window.

Chapter 3

The user can view tasks assigned to them and control what tasks are displayed using the selection boxes. Tasks can be edited by clicking on the pencil icon to the left of each task. The tasks or companies can be viewed by clicking on their titles. See the following screenshot:

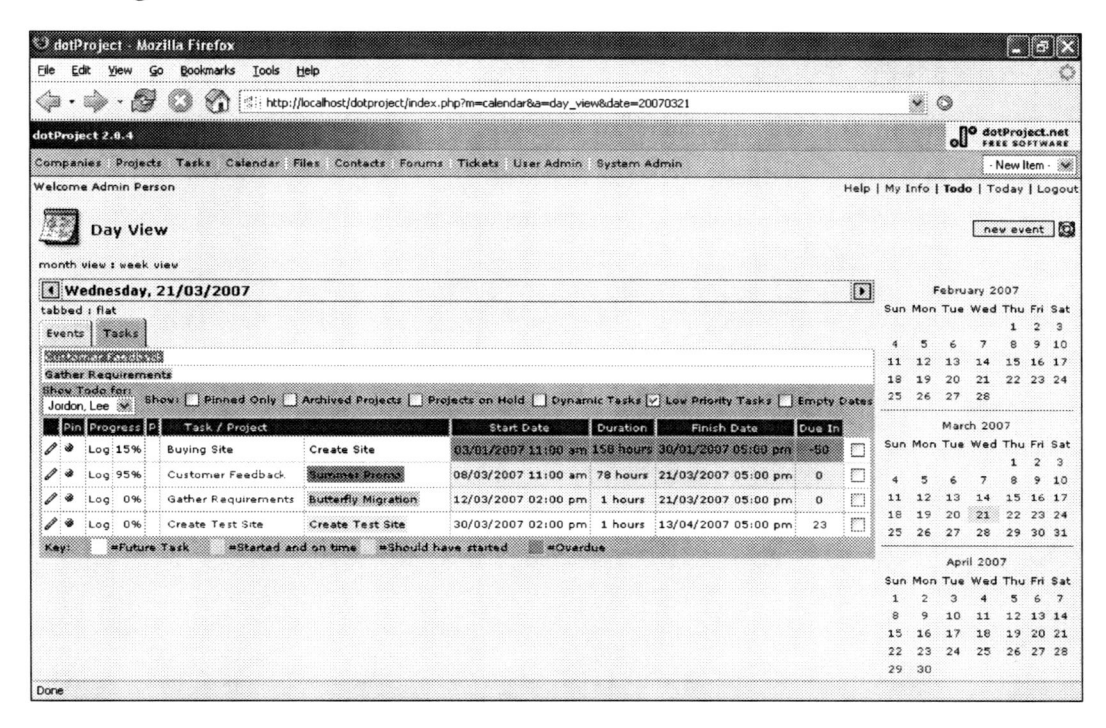

> **Get to Assigned Tasks Quickly**
> Click on the **Task** name or on the pencil icon to the left of the task.

Need to create new items such as **Companies**, **Contacts**, **Files**, or **Tasks**? There is a quick-start drop-down menu in the uppermost right corner. All items that a user has permission to access will appear in the drop-down menu. A user menu is in the upper, right corner of the screen. The user menu provides quick links to each user's personal work and preferences within dotProject. We will discuss it in more detail in the next section. The **new event** button shown below the user menu is a contextual button that will change depending upon the screen a user is on. On the projects screen it will become the **new project** button. The small, circular life preserver icon is a way to reach the help menu. The work area begins just below the section title on every dotProject screen.

[37]

User Menu

The user menu provides a quick way for users to go to different screens containing information just for them. The main navigation system is for areas central to all users, while the user menu displays mainly information of particular concern to that user. With the exception of the **Help** link, all the other user menu links are that user's personal area of dotProject.

There are four links in the user menu by default:

- **Help**: Links to online help with dotProject.
- **My Info**: User information such as name, department, birthday, email, and other contact details.
- **Todo**: Tasks assigned to the users and Gantt chart items. The user's own tasks are shown by default. Other users' tasks can also be viewed using the drop-down menu if the user has access.
- **Today**: **Day View** displaying tasks and events assigned to the user. The **Day View** is shown by default. A month or week view is also available to view.

The user menu is available from anywhere in dotProject. It is always one click away from any screen the user is currently in.

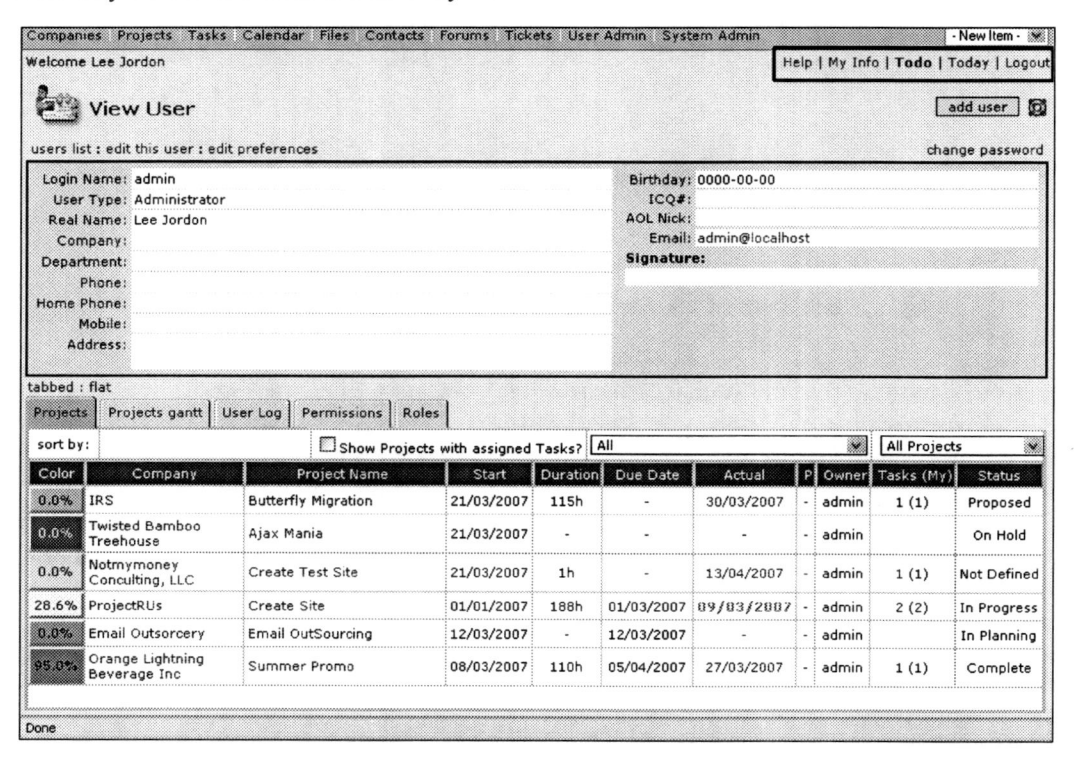

> **Change Password**
> You can change your dotProject password by clicking on the **change password** link on the right side of the **View User** screen

Help (Online)

The help screen appears as a pop-up window or as a content page within dotProject. It lists different online resources available to dotProject users. The **Help** screen is available from the main navigation menu, the user menu, and by clicking on the life preserver icon just below the user menu. The help icon looks like a floatation device and has a red background.

The **Help** screen, also known as **dotProject Online Assistance**, lists five main sources of information about dotProject.

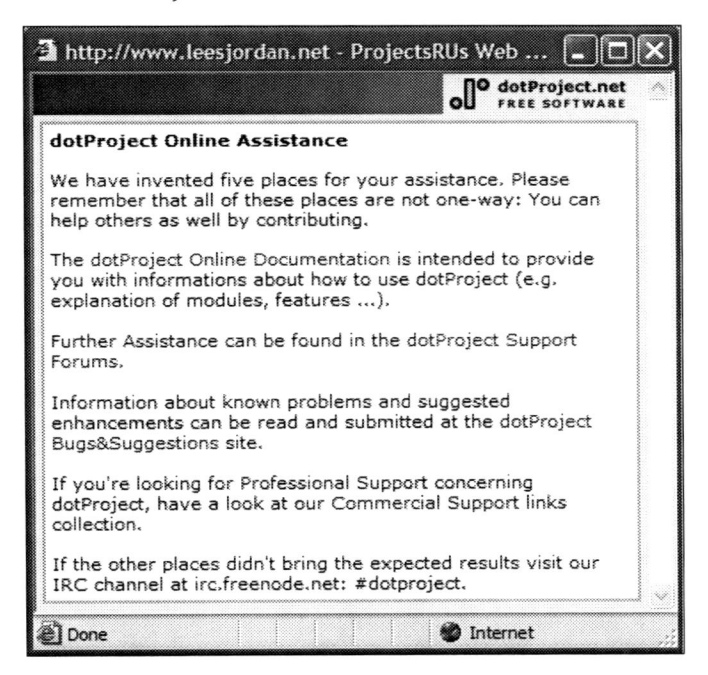

> **Find help fast on dotProject Forums**
> The dotProject user community is your best bet when looking for help with dotProject issues. Visit `http://www.dotproject.net/vBulletin/` to search and participate in the dotProject community forums.

My Info

The **My Info** screen, also known as the **View User** screen, shows information specific to the user such as their user name, company, department, IM, email, and other contact information. Only the **Real Name** and **Email** are required fields, while the others are optional. There is also a quick overview of **Projects** available on the bottom section of the screen, with different filters.

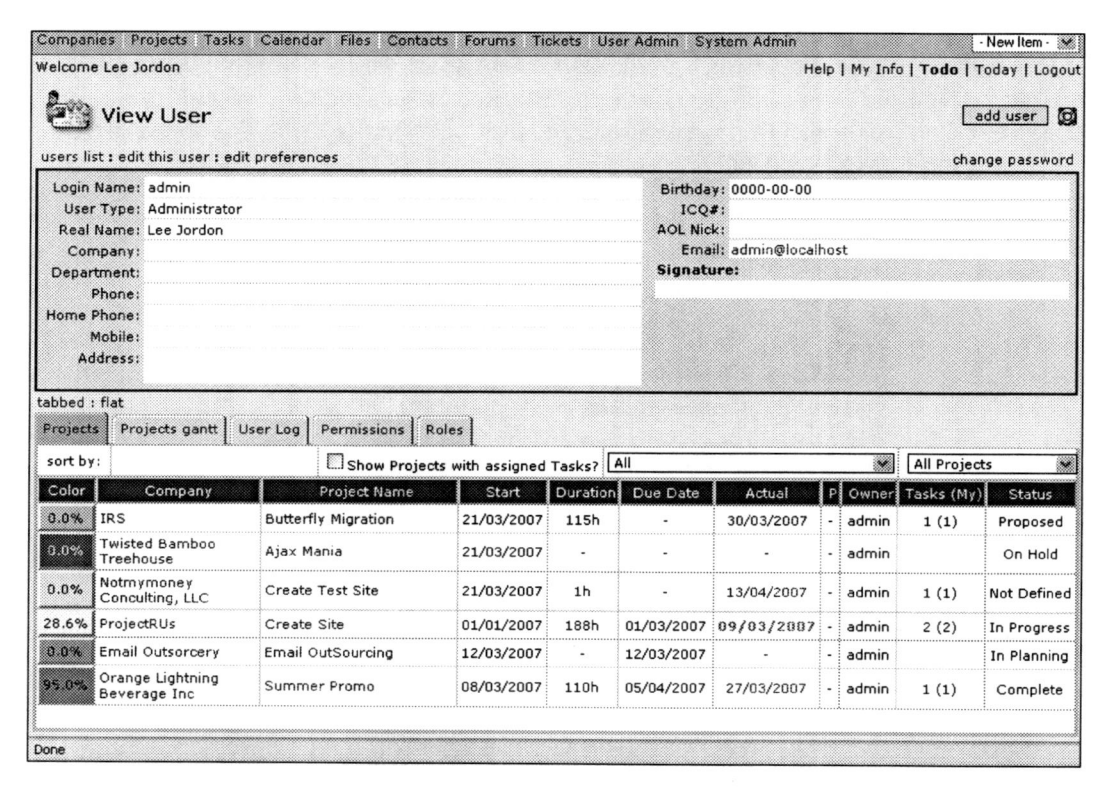

Users can also change their personal preferences as long as the system administrator has given the user edit access. How can a user check their permissions access? Clicking on the **Permissions** tab will display what rights a user has in dotProject.

A typical user has access to non-admin modules: **Companies, Projects, Tasks, Calendar, Files, Contacts,** and **Forums**. Below we can see after clicking on the permissions tab for **Happy UserPerson** that **Happy** can see all non-admin modules (referred to as **allow**). **Happy** can also **Add, Edit,** and **View** the **Companies, Projects, Tasks, Files, Contacts, Forums,** and **Events** tabs. **Happy** cannot add new users, since that is an administrative function and **Happy** does not have access to any administrative modules. Permissions will be discussed in depth in Chapter 5.

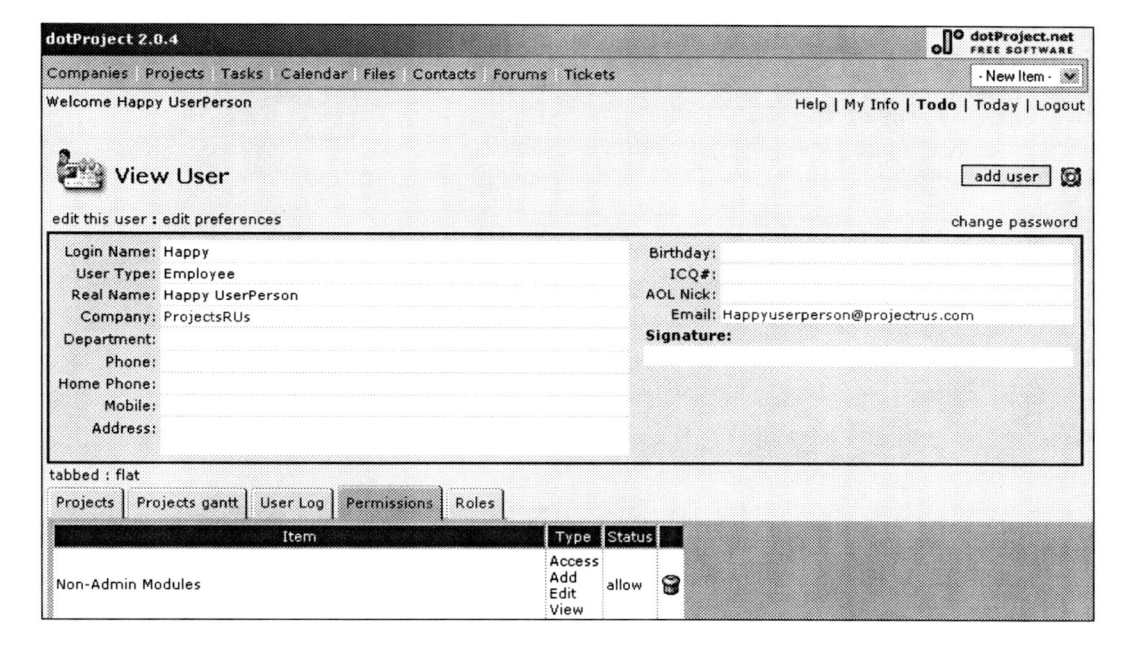

dotProject User Basics

Edit User Preferences (for Users)

Want to change your date format? Set your tabbed box view to flat or tabbed on all your screens? Change the notification settings for **Tasks**? Liven up the GUI style? The **edit preferences** option will give the user the options shown in the following screenshot:

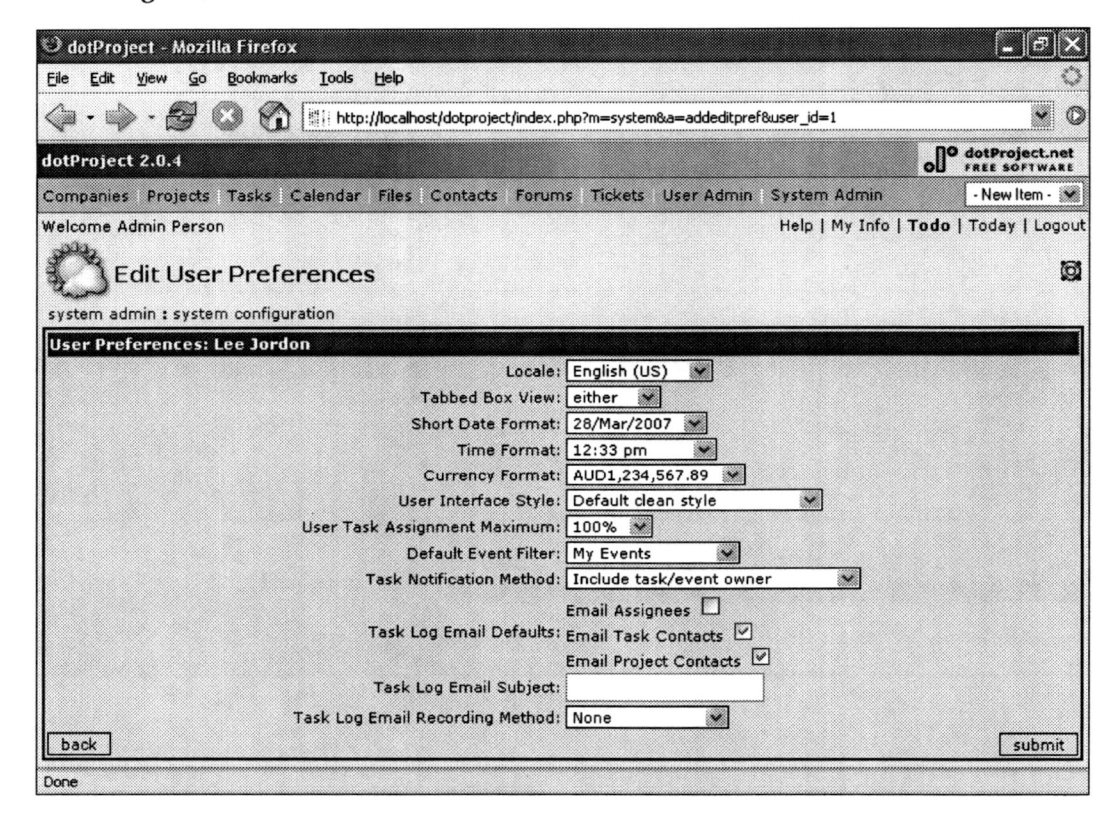

- **Locale**: Choose from several versions of English including US (American) and AU (Australian). Other languages will be available if the language packs have been added to the dotProject installation. This is covered in detail in Chapter 5.
- **Tabbed Box View**: Users can view tabs, a flat link view, or either. This does not change the links themselves. It changes how they appear.
- **Short Date Format**: Choose from several different formats for dates.
- **Time Format**: Twelve hour (hour:minutes), twenty-four hour (hour:minutes), and twenty-four hour detailed (hour:minutes:seconds).
- **Currency Format**: Choose from several different international currencies. The choices will depend upon the language packs installed.

- **User Interface Style**: The phrase "user-interface style" refers to the appearance of dotProject including the icons, images, and colors that are displayed as part of the graphical user interface.
- **User Task Assignment Maximum**: When tasks are created and project workers (called resources in the task module) are assigned, the default assignment is 100% for each person. If you have limited availability, setting a lower maximum will help keep you from being over-assigned in tasks.
- **Default Event Filter**: Users can specify the default events they want to be notified of.
- **Tasks**: Users can specify default notification details for all tasks.
- **Task Notification Method**: Choose whether to automatically include the task/event owner when a task or event is changed or created.
- **Task Log Email Defaults**: A checkmark by the three email options below cause an email to be sent to them when a task log is created.
    - Email Assignees
    - Email Task Contacts
    - Email Project Contacts
- **Task Log Email Subject**: Enter a default subject for all task-log emails if desired.
- **Task Log Email Recording Method**: A record of the email information can be appended to the task log.

When the changes to the **User Preferences** screen are complete, click the **submit** button.

When we click on the submit button we go back to the **View User** screen, where we see a confirmation stating **Preferences updated**.

> **Access Denied?**
> Don't have permission to do something you need to do in dotProject? Contact your dotProject administrator for access.

What happens when a user tries to do something they do not have permission to do? Let's find out. **Happy UserPerson** is a typical dotProject user. He has access to add new projects and tasks, but not to add users. When Happy attempts to add a new user by clicking on the **add user** button on his **View User** screen, the following error message is displayed: **Access Denied - You have attempted to access an item in dotproject without the sufficient permissions to do so. Please contact the dotproject System Administrator.**

Yes, dotProject shouldn't display buttons or links users cannot use, but as a safety measure, the warning message is displayed and the user is unable to perform the action they attempted.

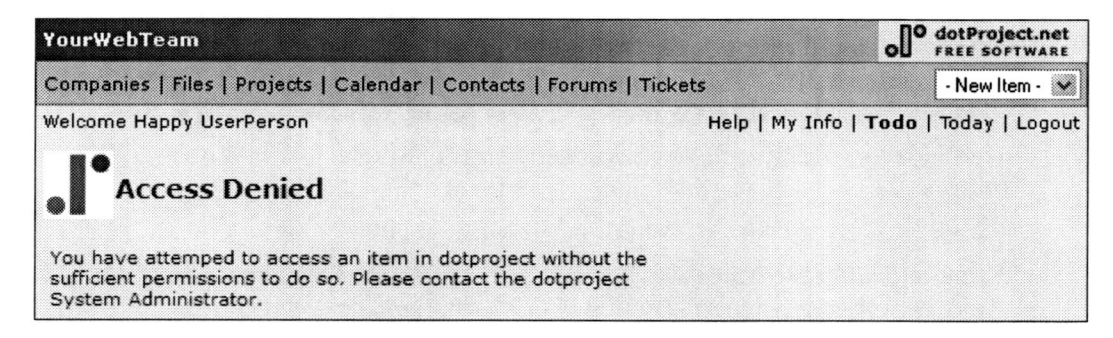

The Todo List

There are two main tabs on the **Todo** list: the **My Tasks** tab and the **My Gantt** tab. Both tabs give users a quick way to see what tasks have been assigned to them, when they are due, and whether the task is on schedule. The **My Tasks** tab provides users with a choice of which tasks they prefer to view. Clicking on the selection boxes above the tasks will change the tasks shown. Clicking the pencil icon to the left of a task will open the edit screen for that task.

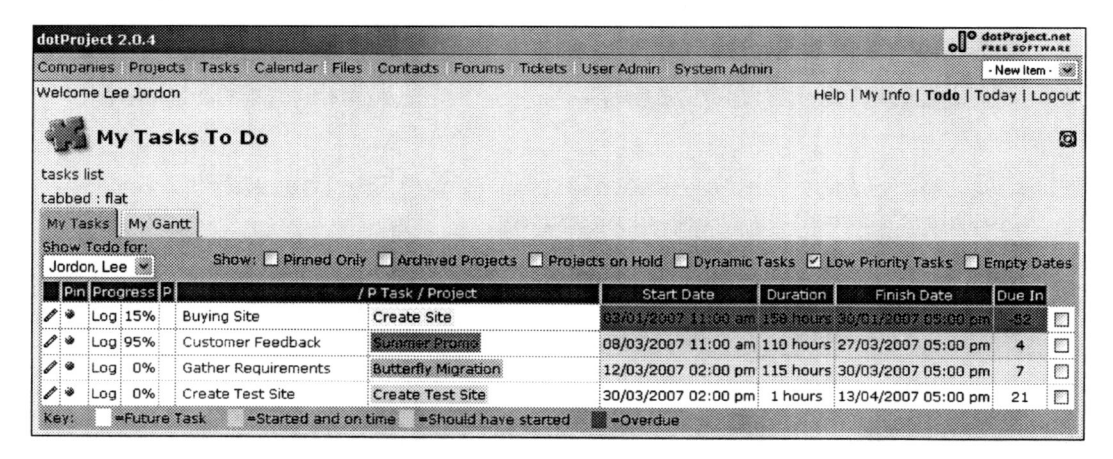

> **Filter the tasks**
>
> Clicking any of the select boxes above the tasks list on the **My Tasks** tab will filter the task view. Multiple boxes can be selected. The boxes shown to the right of each task do not have a function on this screen.

The round dots to the left of the pencil icon are used to flag or "pin" tasks. This is a way for users to visually mark the tasks. A link to the log for each task is listed next, along with completed percentage under the **Progress** heading. **Tasks** and **Projects** are listed by their name. Each is a link to view that specific task or project. The **Start Date**, **Duration**, **Finish Date**, and hours **Due In** are displayed next. To the extreme right is a checkbox that updates task on the **Task List** screen. It is not used on the **My Tasks** tab.

The **My Gantt** tab displays tasks in a visual format independent of projects. Users can view their tasks and the tasks assigned to other users in the form of a graphical chart with optional choices for dates and other display information. The Gantt charts may take a few seconds to load.

Users may experience a JpGraph font error when clicking on the **Todo** tab. That is what happened to me after I installed dotProject. Fixing this issue can be done by those with administrative access and is covered in Appendix B of this book.

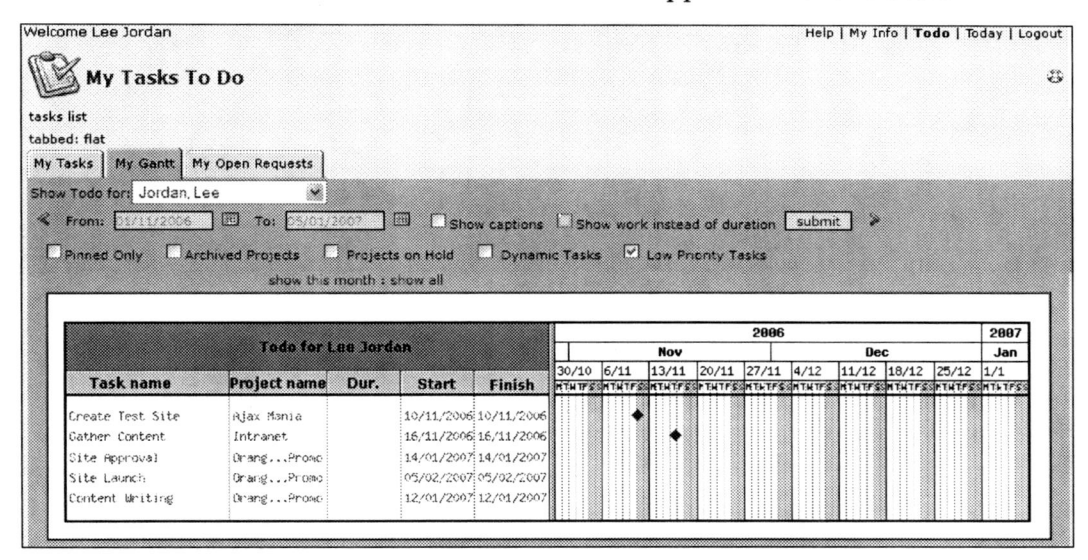

Today

The default view when you log in to dotProject is the **Day View** of the **Today** section, also listed as **Today** on the user menu. Users can choose from a **month view** and **week view** as well. It displays **Events** and **Tasks** the user has assigned to them in a tabbed menu format. Task progress, title, project title, dates, and duration can be viewed at a glance. Users can edit a task, if they have the rights to do so, by clicking on the pencil icon next to the task. Task information is highlighted according to the color key at the bottom of the task list. The colors are intuitive: green is on-time and red is overdue. The color coding is consistent throughout dotProject.

dotProject User Basics

A three month mini-calendar is available on the right side of the screen, as illustrated in the following screenshot:

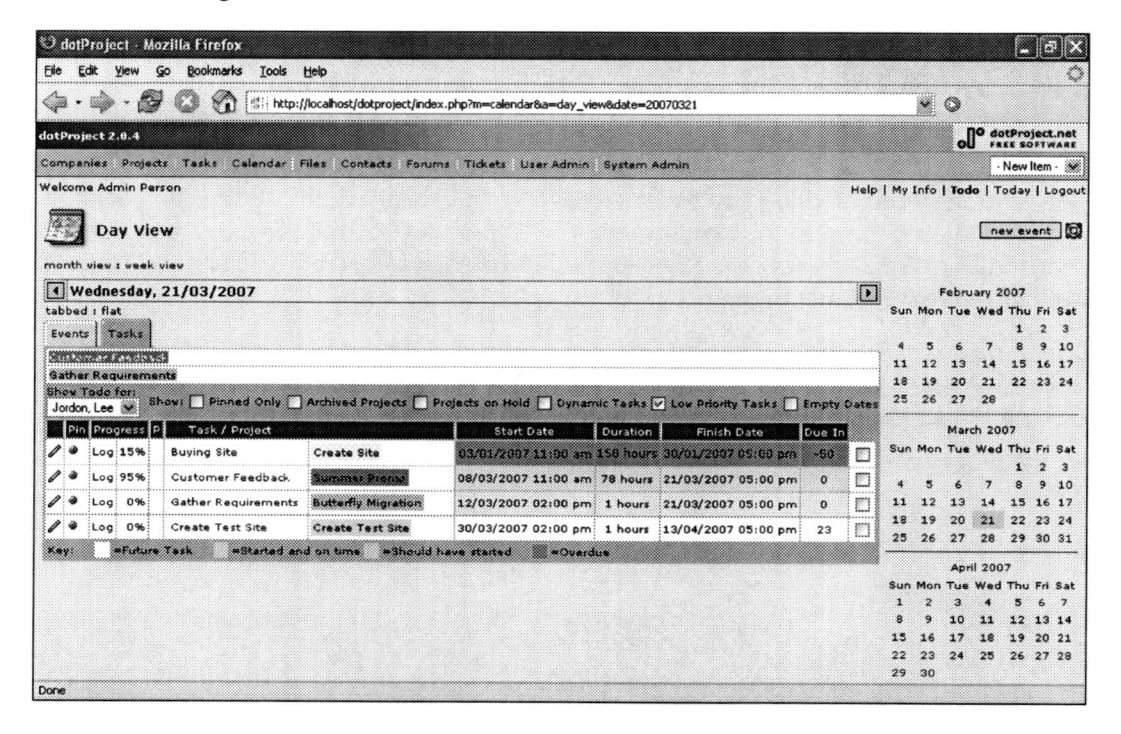

Main Navigation Bar

The navigation bar usually appears at the top of the screen by default. There are dotProject templates and system administration settings that allow this to be changed. The menu items covered are those that are turned on for most dotProject installations.

What do the terms **Companies**, **Projects**, and **Tasks** mean? As has been stated before, dotProject is a Project Management Application. It uses terms specific to project management. A company in dotProject is an organization or group. It can be a customer, client, vendor, contractor, donor, or any other entity.

> **Changing Company**
>
> If the word **Company** is awkward for your group, it can be changed using a hack proposed by Karen, a dotProject administrator on the dotProject community forums. We will discuss changing the company by hacking the Translation Management module in Chapter 6 of this book.

The term **Project** in dotProject refers to a group of scheduled work being performed in a series of steps with a defined long term goal. Saving money for the down payment on a house is a long term goal that can be broken down into smaller tasks, such as set up direct deposit for savings account, create a budget, and so on.

> **Tasks are Parents too**
>
> Tasks in dotProject can have smaller "child" tasks. The "parent" task is usually a milestone (defined date or goal); the child task is an important step towards completing the parent task.

Tasks in project management are smaller portions of work that when combined together make up a project. Tasks can be projects themselves if the overall project is large enough. Writing a book can be both a task and a project. The book can be a task as part of a larger project to provide documentation for a product. The steps needed to plan, write, edit, and print the book are tasks.

> As with all other areas of dotProject, what the user can do depends upon the permissions set up by their system administrator.

Companies

The **Companies** link on the main navigation menu will take you to the **Companies** screen. The user will see the companies they have permission to see. This is especially important to know if you have a customer who has access to dotProject. The customer will see their company only listed. The **All Companies** tab is chosen by default. Users can view the company name, number of projects, and company type at a glance. Companies are shown according to the user's access rights. A user can search, filter by owner, add a new company, or view companies based on what type they have been categorized as by clicking on different tabs. We will discuss the tabs in detail in the next chapter.

The following screenshot gives a view of what the **Companies** screen will look like:

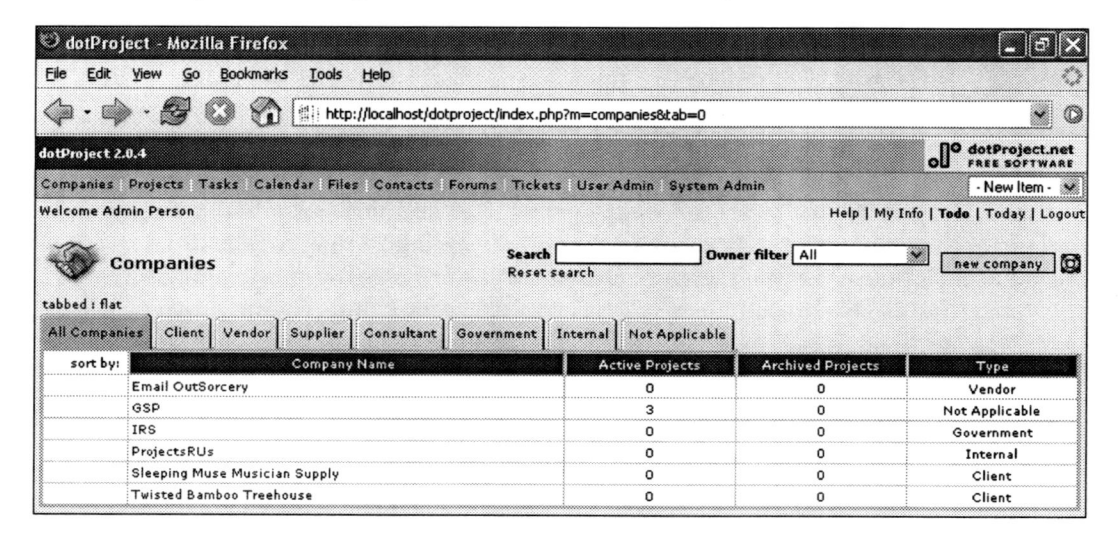

Projects

Clicking on the **Projects** link in the main navigation menu will take you to the **Projects** screen. The projects are organized by status into tabs. The **All Projects** list will be chosen by default.

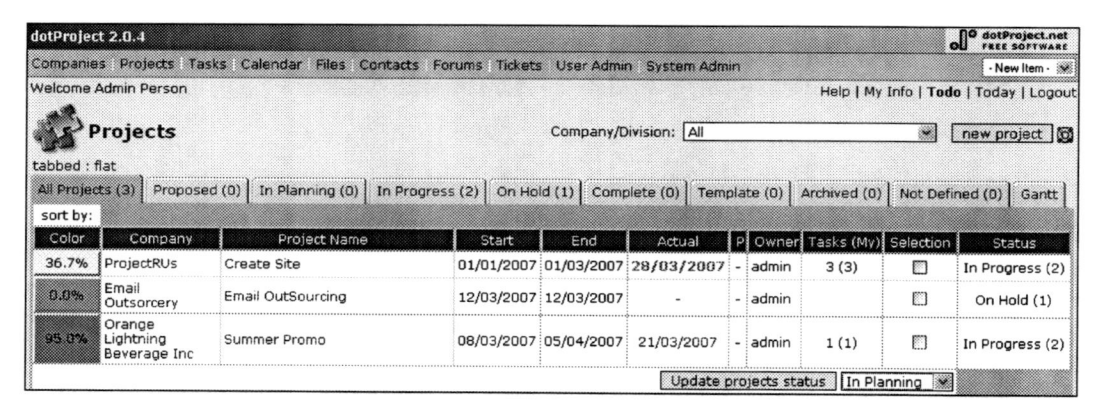

Clicking on a **Status** tab will show you only the project(s) with the same status. The projects shown can be filtered by **Company/Division** using the drop-down list on the right side of the screen.

Chapter 3

> **What's your Status?**
> Status in dotProject is the state of the project. Just like water goes through a cycle of different physical states of solid, liquid, or gas, a project has a status life cycle composed of states such as planning, proposed, and complete.

New projects can be created from the **Projects** screen by clicking on the **new project** button on the right. Online help is available by using the icon on the right. Below the projects list is the **Update projects status** button. By checking one or multiple projects in their selection row, a project or group of projects can be quickly updated.

Tasks

The **Tasks** link goes to the **Tasks** screen. **Tasks** is a more generalized screen than **Today** or **Todo**. It shows tasks assigned to different users with filters and submenus. The screen displays tasks by user. Notice the search box to the right of the screen heading. Different users can be selected with the user drop-down list. The **Company** drop-down list is set to **All Companies** by default. The **Task Filter** is set to unfinished tasks by default.

Below the **Tasks** heading is a submenu. It will display individual user lists, inactive tasks, and tasks per user. Clicking on a submenu link will cause a new screen to display. The filters will not be available on the submenu screens.

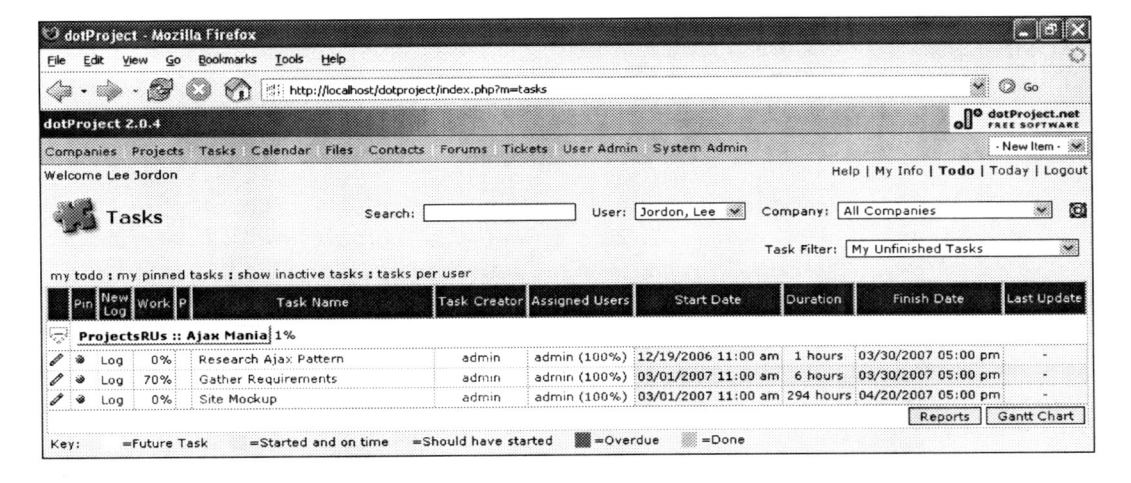

[49]

dotProject User Basics

The **Reports** button below the task list goes to a **Project Reports** screen. Users can choose from a variety of reports to run. These will be covered in more detail in Chapter 4.

A Gantt chart is also available by clicking the **Gantt Chart** button. The following screen shows the type of Gantt chart that will be displayed.

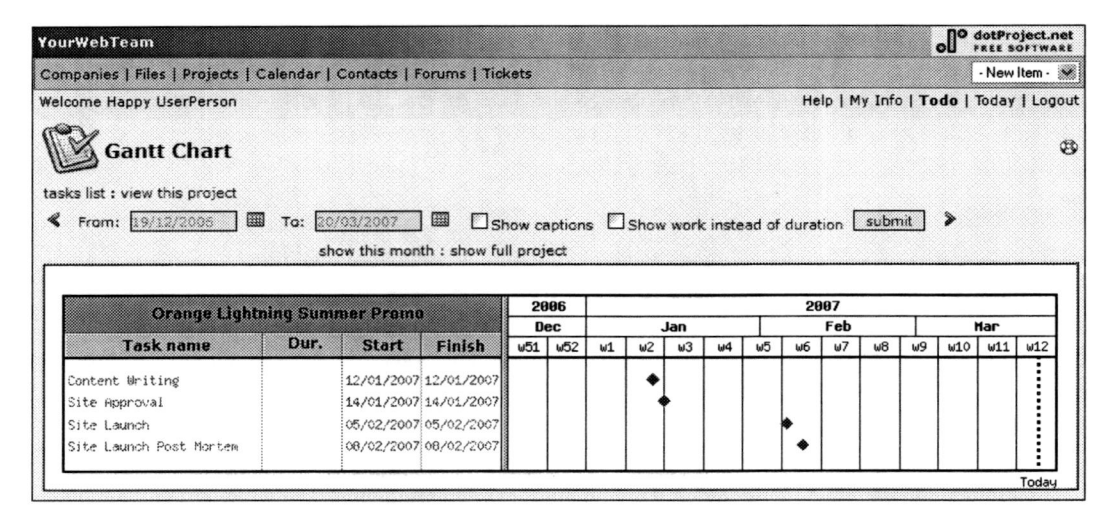

Files

The **Files** repository is displayed when the **Files** link is chosen. The **Files** screen also uses a tabbed menu. Users can choose from a list of **All files**, **Unknown**, **Document**, and **Application** (see the screenshot in the following page).

Most common file types such as spreadsheets, documents, images, code snippets, and text files can be uploaded into dotProject. These include the following file formats: xl, csv, pdf, doc, txt, png, jpg, gif, and php. Compressed files can also be uploaded when file size is a concern. Files that are compressed will not be available for preview in the browser window. Users can preview most file types in a browser window, check a file out to revise or review the content by downloading it to their computer, and search for files. Files that are downloaded must be checked back in before they can be checked out by other users. The disk symbol next to each file listing changes according to whether a file is checked out.

Chapter 3

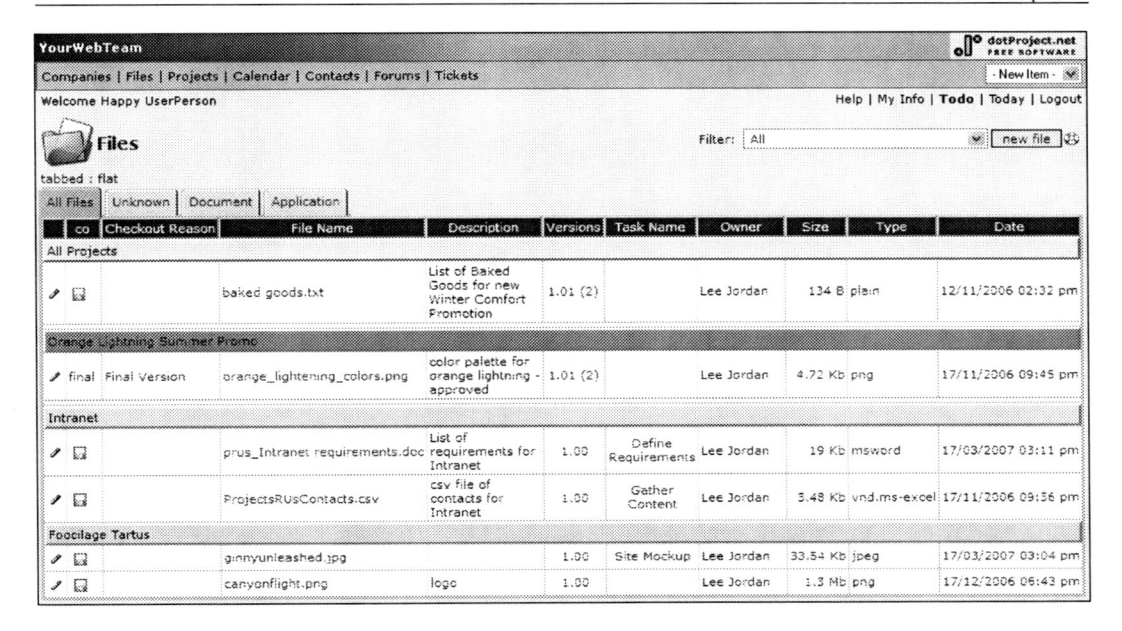

[screenshot of Files repository interface]

> **Check it out, check it in**
>
> When I first started using the file repository, I had no idea that downloading a document prevented anyone else from editing it, until the project manager called me and wanted to know why the file had been checked out for over a week.

The **Files** repository is discussed in detail in Chapter 7 of this book.

Contacts

The full **Contacts** screen is shown when the **Contacts** link is clicked. All contacts that the user has rights to see will be displayed as seen in the screenshot overleaf.

> **Contacts can be Private**
>
> Contacts created by the user can be set to private on the **Edit Contact** screen by selecting the checkbox next to the **Private Entry** field.

[51]

dotProject User Basics

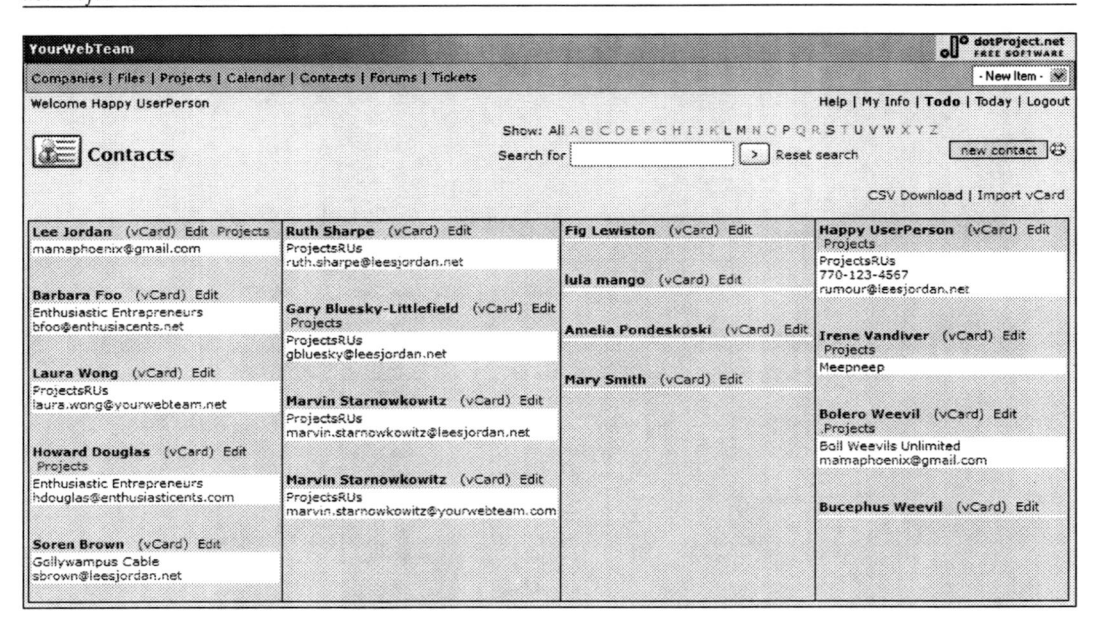

The filter is set to "All" by default. Contacts can be viewed by an alphabet link-list or searched for. Users can edit the contact list as long as they have edit rights. Clicking on the **Edit** link next to a **Contact** will open up the **Edit Contact** screen. Using the **Edit Contact** screen is covered in Chapter 7 of this book.

Summary

This chapter covered how to navigate to different areas within dotProject, and what navigation options are available to most users. We have highlighted the two main navigation systems, the main navigation menu and the user menu, and have explored deeper.

The **Help** menu is available from any screen using the **Help** link on the user menu, the life preserver icon, or the **Help** link on the main navigation menu. The user menu can be accessed from any dotProject screen and it has information based on user permissions. The rights to the menu items are reserved based on the user permission rights. The main navigation menu contains a series of links leading to different sections of dotProject.

In the next chapter we will probe further into each tab. Now that we have covered where to go, we are ready to get things done.

4
Getting Things Done

We want to make progress and achieve results by getting things done. dotProject gives users a central place to share and manage all project-related information. No more wondering if Ken in Marketing got a copy of the latest project tasks. Most users will find this chapter helpful in their day-to-day use of dotProject.

Chapter 4 will cover setting-up and maintaining the **Companies**, **Contacts**, **Projects**, and **File** areas of dotProject from a user perspective. We will look at examples based on real-world situations in project planning and maintenance. Remember, project management is a big topic, so in-depth project planning is beyond the scope of this book.

This chapter will include:

- Managing **Companies** in dotProject
- Managing **Contacts**
- Managing **Projects** and **Tasks**
- The dotProject **File** Repository
- Time-saving tips

The sections in this chapter are divided on a functional basis, so the user can quickly find the information needed. Most of the forms used by dotProject are easy to use, but there are some quirks and some special areas that we will discuss in detail.

Managing Companies

Why list companies first? It turns out that in dotProject, you must have at least one company in order to create projects. External companies should be added if they are related to projects. This makes it easier for the users to know whom to contact. **Departments**, **Files**, **Users**, and other information can all be managed from the individual view **Companies** screen. First we need to make sure we have a company added before we add any projects related to it.

Getting Things Done

> **Why the term "Companies"?**
>
> Why not use a more generic term such as group or organization? The original developers of dotProjects are business people themselves. dotProject's initial audience was businesses looking for an open-source project management solution. We will walk through a hack to change the phrase "Companies" to a more flexible term in Chapter 6.

When we visit the **Companies** page of the **ProjectsRUs** dotProject installation, notice a list of companies has already been added. **Search** and the **Owner filter** dropdown allow the user to further control what companies are listed on the screen.

The **ProjectsRUs** company is listed under the **All Companies** tab and the **Internal** tab.

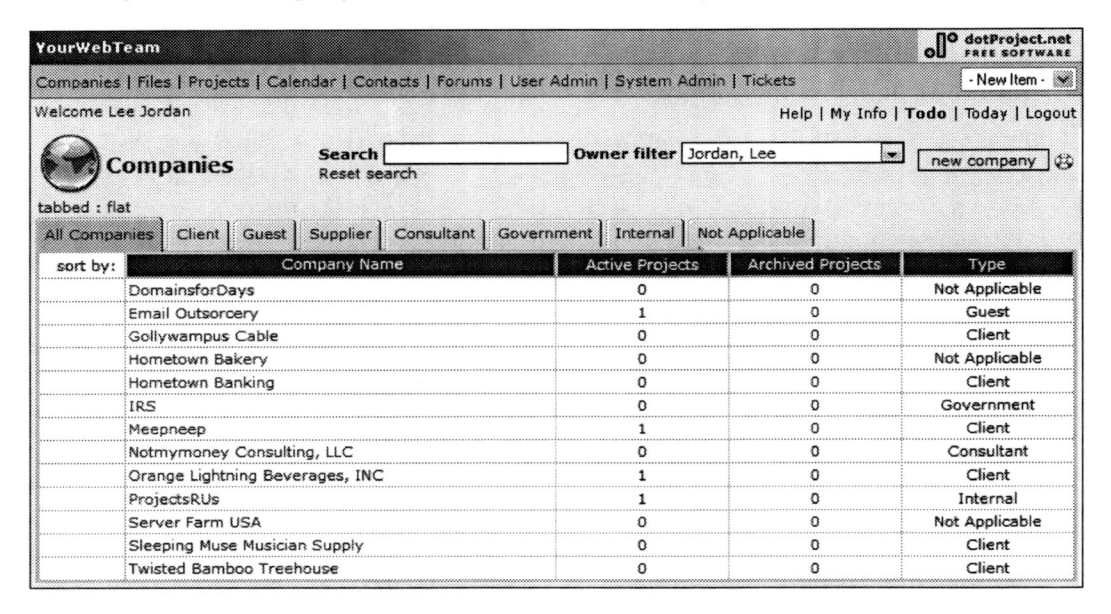

Company Name	Active Projects	Archived Projects	Type
DomainsforDays	0	0	Not Applicable
Email Outsorcery	1	0	Guest
Gollywampus Cable	0	0	Client
Hometown Bakery	0	0	Not Applicable
Hometown Banking	0	0	Client
IRS	0	0	Government
Meepneep	1	0	Client
Notmymoney Consulting, LLC	0	0	Consultant
Orange Lightning Beverages, INC	1	0	Client
ProjectsRUs	1	0	Internal
Server Farm USA	0	0	Not Applicable
Sleeping Muse Musician Supply	0	0	Client
Twisted Bamboo Treehouse	0	0	Client

dotProject installations do not contain any companies by default. The first company added is the internal company. The **Companies** screen just after installation is shown in the following screenshot:

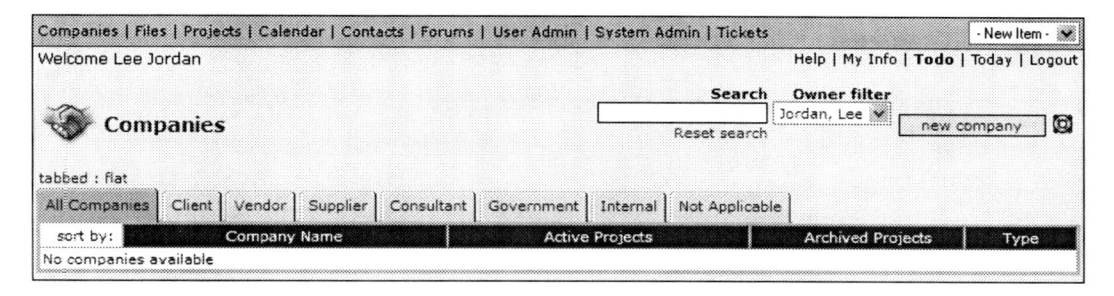

Adding New Companies

New companies are added by clicking on the **new company** button located on the right side of the **Companies** list screen. When the **new company** button is clicked, an **Add Company** form will appear as shown in the screenshot overleaf.

> Which comes first—The Contact or the Company?
>
> **Contacts** can be added without any **Companies** listed in a dotProject installation. **Companies** can be added without any **Contacts** also. The best practice is to create the basic company, add contacts to the **contacts list**, then edit the company information as needed. This way each contact will be tied to a company.

Only the name of the company is required. Filling most of the form is simple data entry. Type in the URL of the company's website if one exists. It can then be tested by clicking on the **test** link next to the form field. The **Company Owner** field will show a drop-down list of people already entered into the dotProject contact list. If the company owner or contact person is not already listed, you may want to add them to the **Contacts** list. Click on the **submit** button to finish the process.

Getting Things Done

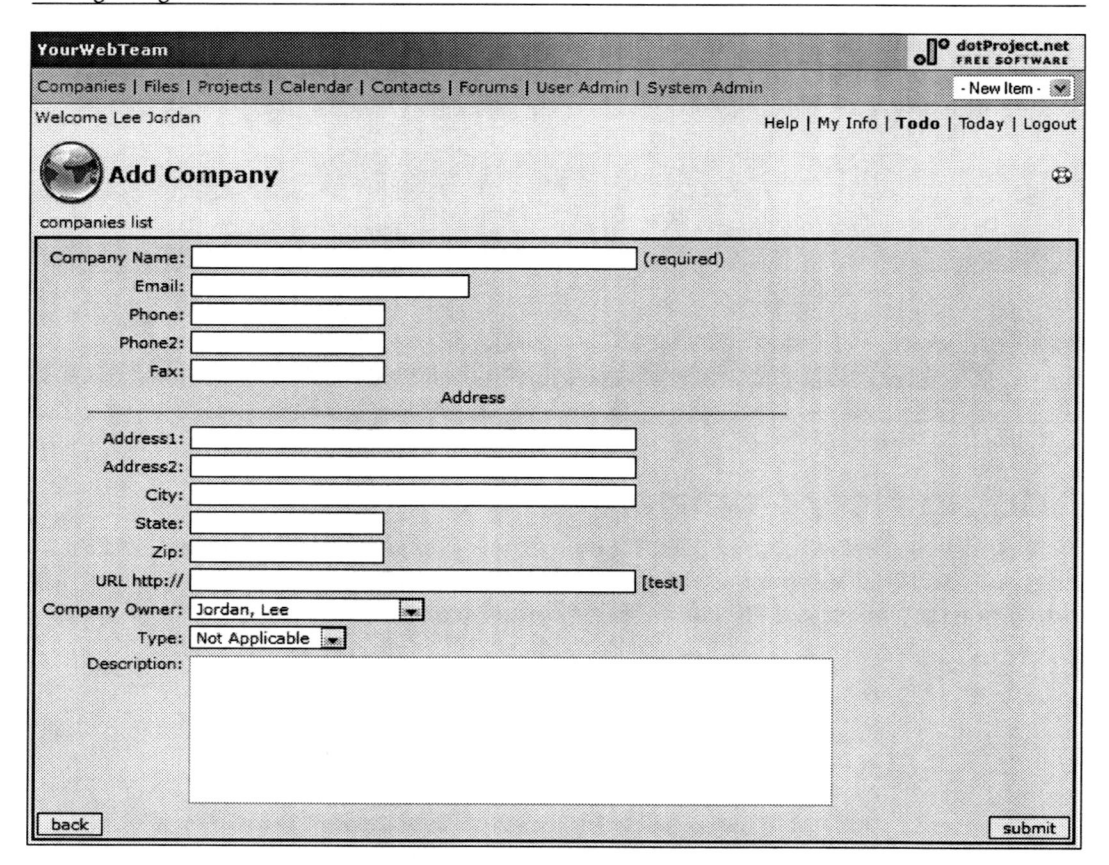

> Although the **Company Owner** dropdown does not have a "none" option, if no name is actively chosen from the dropdown before clicking the **submit** button, the **Company Owner** field will be blank.

Viewing Companies

Individual companies can be viewed by clicking on their listing in the **companies list** on the main **Companies** page or by clicking on the tab (name of the tab as defined under **Type** tab) adjacent to the **All Companies** tab. Company **Type** is an optional way to identify different types of companies in dotProject.

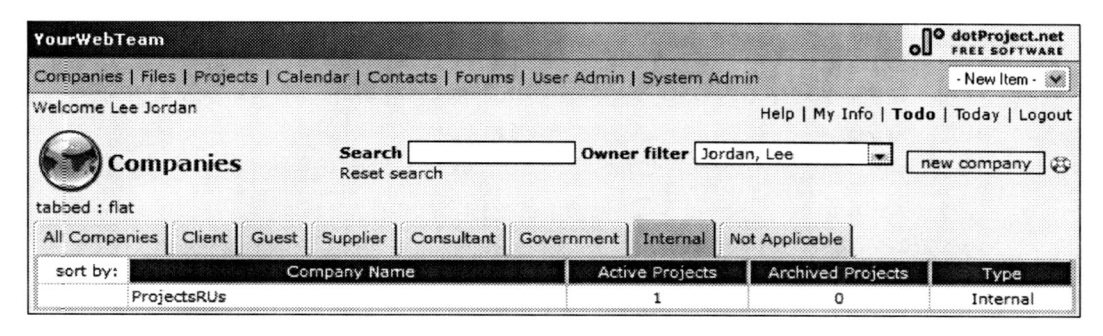

To view **ProjectsRUs**, either click the name on the main **Companies** list or click the **Internal** tab and then the company name.

> **Internal Companies**
>
> An internal company is usually the organization or group who has installed dotProject. A company can have multiple additional branches or companies within itself. These should all be given the **Internal** dotProject company type.

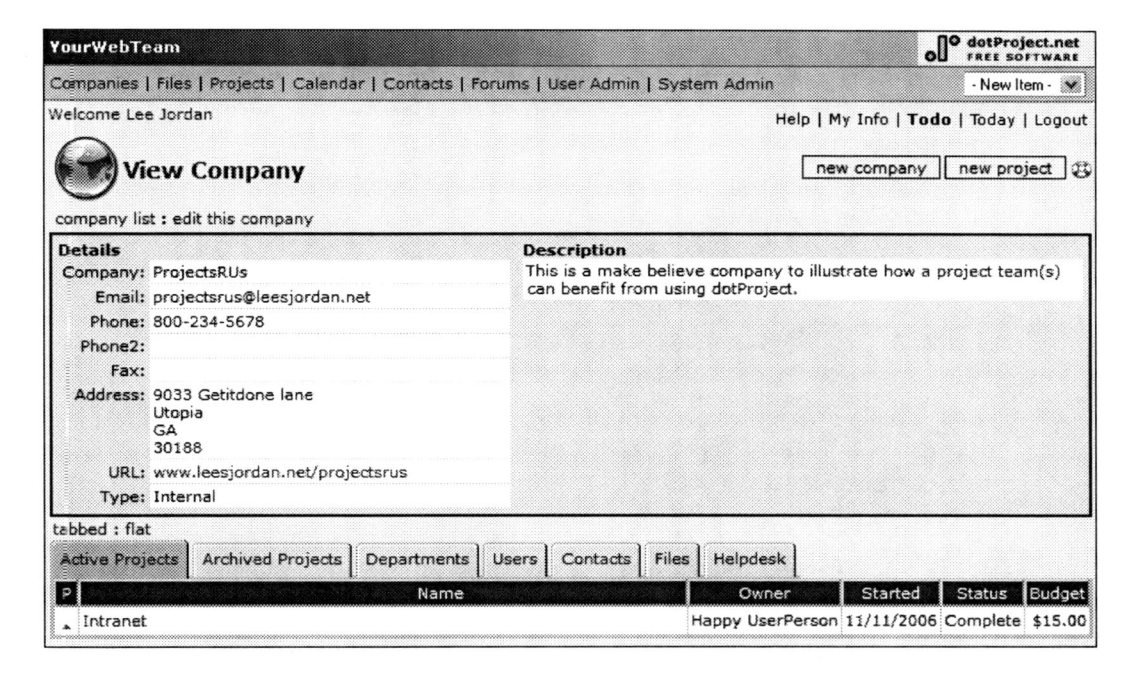

The **View Company** page has many options.

- Links to the **company list** and **edit this company** are directly below the page title.
- New companies can be created using the **new company** button on the right.
- The details section gives basic company information that was entered when the company was created.
- The description section gives an optional paragraph about the company.
- Below the box with company information is a series of navigational tabs: **Active Projects**, **Archived Projects**, **Departments**, **Users**, **Contacts**, and **Files**.

View Company Tabs

The tabbed section of the **View Company** page allows users to manage information tied to the company from one central area. The break down of what each tab does is as follows:

- **Active Projects**: Shows a list of all active projects related to the company. This is a quick way to see what active projects are associated with the company, without having to visit the projects area.
- **Archived Projects**: List of all archived projects of the company are shown on this tab. It is another way for managers and project workers to view project information related to a specific company.
- **Departments**: Lists all departments and allows new departments to be created in the company.
- **Users**: Lists all users assigned to the company. Detailed user information can be viewed by clicking on the user name.
- **Contacts**: Lists the name and email address of all contacts that are part of the company. New contacts can also be added.
- **Files**: Lists all files associated with the company. Files can be attached to all projects or a specific project. It is recommended that you already have a project and task set up before attaching files.

Updating Companies

Information about **Companies** does not stay the same. Phone numbers change, new departments are added, and companies move. The information changes over time. dotProject provides a form-based screen for updating information about individual companies at any time. The **Edit This Company** screen can be accessed from the **View Company** screen in dotProject.

We are going to walk through updating a company step by step. The **ProjectsRUs** company needs to be updated. There are no departments. Other information should be added as well, to better organize the internal contacts.

Preparing to Edit

To edit the **ProjectsRUs** company:

1. First click on the company name on the **Internal** tab if you are not already on the **View Company** screen.
2. The **View Company** screen will appear. Different information can be edited depending on what links or tabs are chosen.

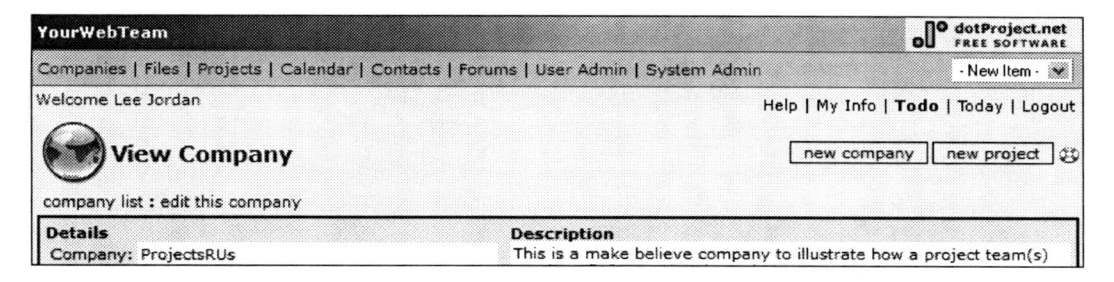

What can be edited?

- All general company information, including the company name.
- Departments can be created.
- Contacts can be added.
- Files can be attached.

The step-by-step examples will be organized by topic. The section *Updating General Company Information* will cover the different fields of information that can be updated, as well as tips on the form itself. We will cover what to do when a company has no departments listed in the *Adding a New Department* section. Managing contacts will be discussed after adding departments. Files will be covered later on in the *File Management and Version Control* section of this chapter.

Updating General Company Information

Choose the **edit this company** link under the page title. The **Edit Company** screen contains the same form as the **Add Companies** screen. Refer to the *Adding New Companies* section earlier in this chapter for step-by-step instructions on making changes to company information.

Getting Things Done

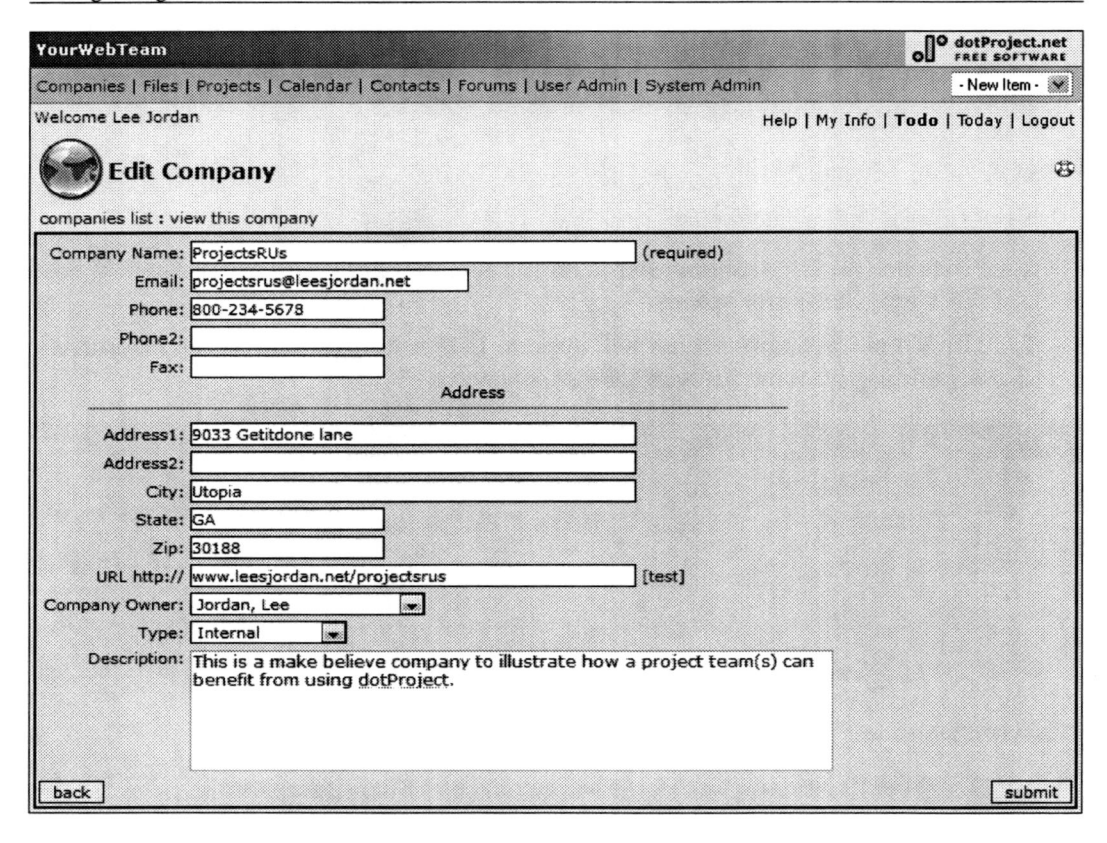

Adding a New Department

New departments are easy to add to dotProject. The only required field is the department name. If departments are being organized in a hierarchy, add the highest-level departments first, then the ones below them. Be sure to select the **Department Parent** for departments lower on the hierarchy.

1. Click on the **Departments** tab below the details box. Choose the **new department** button on the right.

2. The **Edit Department** screen will appear. The companies list or the individual company can be returned to by clicking on the links below the **Edit Department** title.

3. Type the name of the new department into the **Department Name** field. This field cannot be left blank. In the example opposite, **Project Management** has been typed into the field.

4. Enter the rest of the department information in the fields if it is available. If there is no more information to enter, click the **submit** button at the bottom left corner of the screen.

5. The **Department Parent** dropdown allows the user to make the new department a sub-department of another department.

6. The **Owner** field is where the manager or person responsible for the department can be chosen if one exists on the user list.

7. The last field gives the user the option to enter a description of the department.

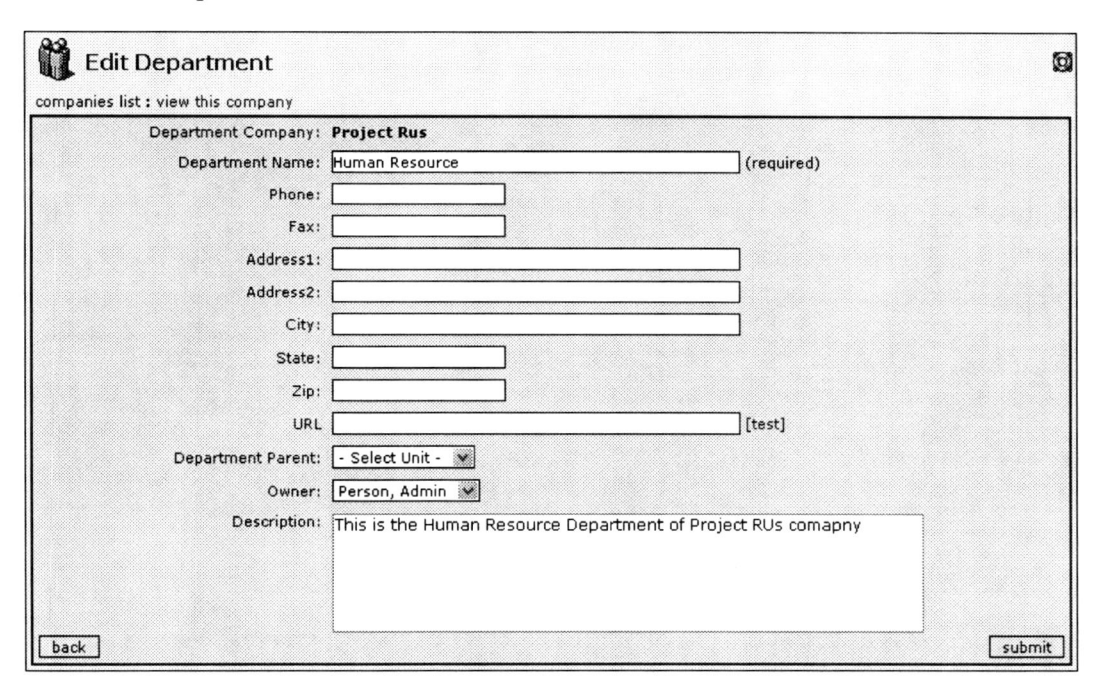

8. Clicking on the **submit** button will return the user to the **Departments** tab on the **View Company** page.

Each new department will appear on the departments list under the **Departments** tab. To edit a department, click the notepad and pencil symbol to the right of the department name on the list. The **Edit Department** screen is exactly the same as before. The department name and all other fields can be altered. To view a department, click on the department name. The **View Department** screen will appear with a similar format to the **View Company** page. The only tab below the details area will be the **Contacts** tab.

Getting Things Done

Managing Contacts

Contacts can be internal, such as employees, or external such as clients, vendors, and contractors. Maintaining the contact list is an important part of successfully using dotProject. Assigning tasks and notifying others on the project team is easier if an accurate list is maintained. The administrator or head of the project managers usually maintains this list, though most of the time users have access to add more contacts. The actual rights you will have will vary depending on those granted to you by the administrator.

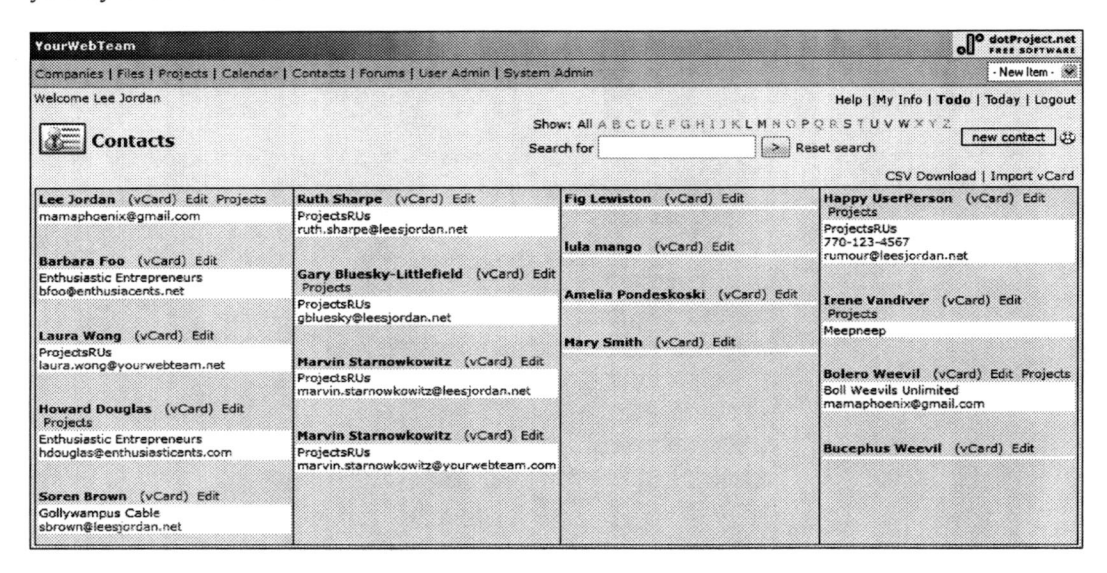

> The entire contacts list can be downloaded as a .csv file. The file can then be opened in a spreadsheet program or used for other purposes. Importing a .csv file may be available as an option in future releases.
>
> vCards can be imported one card at a time. This can speed up the process of including detailed contact information. vCards are contact information of individuals stored in an email or address book program. Think of them as virtual business cards.

Downloading Contacts as a CSV

The dotProject **Contacts** module provides a time-saving way to store and manipulate contact information. User contact files can be downloaded in CSV format and saved as a spreadsheet. This data can then be added to a database, imported into another application, or kept as a backup file, or added to an existing spreadsheet, or document.

CSV stands for **Comma Separated Values**, a phrase that refers to the way each data item is separated from other data by commas. We will download a CSV and view it in Microsoft Excel as a spreadsheet.

1. Click on the **CSV Download** link on the main **Contacts** screen.

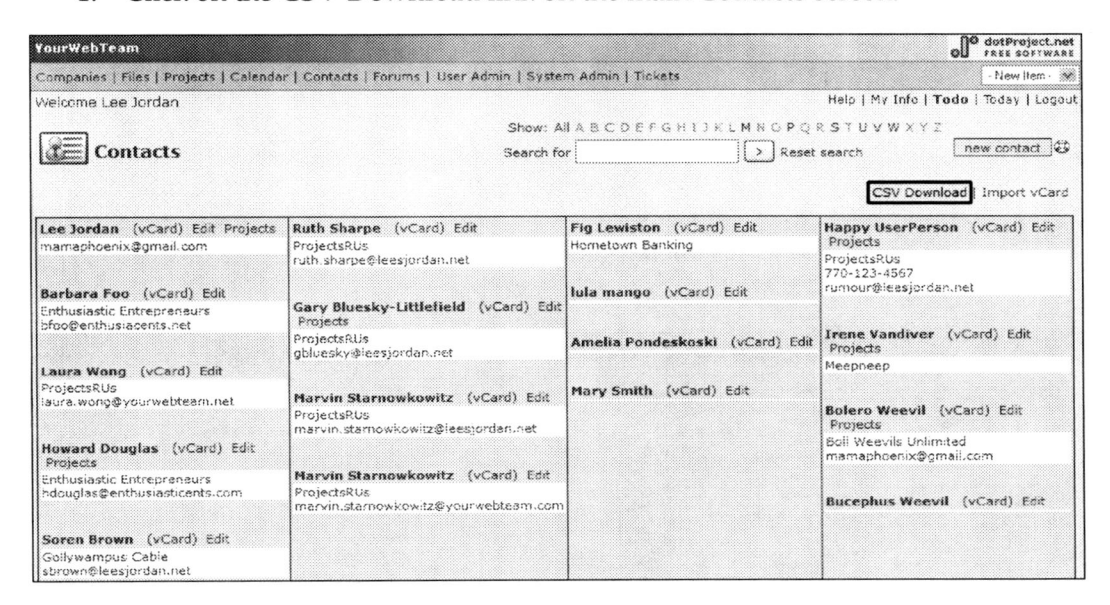

2. A dialog box will appear prompting you to choose whether to open the file or save it to disk.

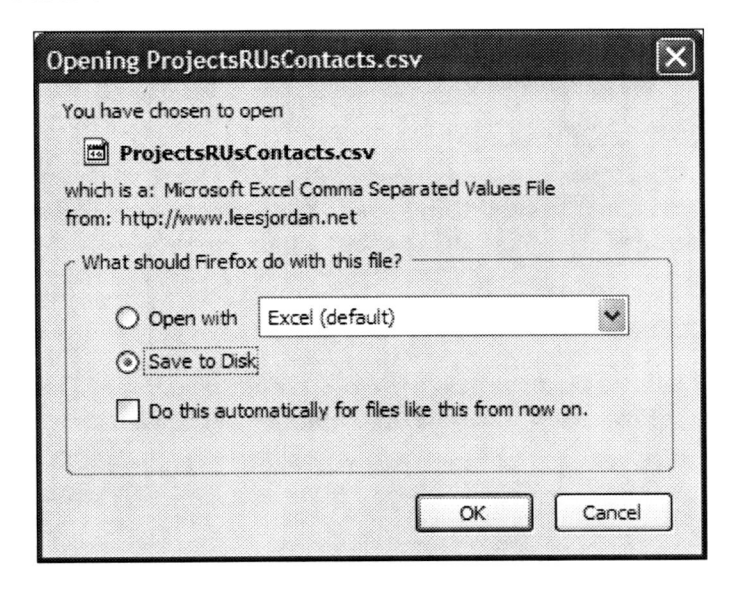

Getting Things Done

3. Click on the **OK** button to save the file.
4. When the download is complete, open the file. It will be automatically saved to display in your default spreadsheet program. The downloaded file as it appears saved on a computer desktop is shown in the following screenshot. Note the lowercase "a" followed by a comma that shows the file format.

5. View the file. Notice it displays the contact information in a structured spreadsheet format.

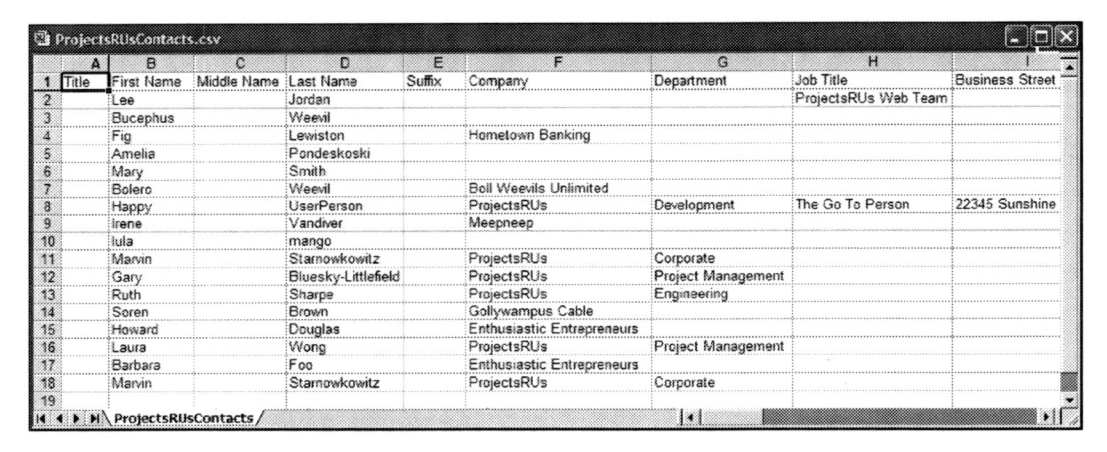

Adding New Contacts

New contacts can be added from many screens in dotProject, wherever there is a **Contacts** tab or link. This makes adding a new contact easier for users. We will go directly to the **Contacts** screen in dotProject using the main navigation bar.

The **Contacts** screen shows all public contacts and the user's private contacts. Links to view a vCard, edit the contact, and view their projects are grouped with each contact.

1. Click the **new contact** button to the right of the search box and you will see the **Add Contact** form as shown in the following screenshot.
2. Type in a first name, and then a last name in the fields marked. These are required fields. If you leave either of them blank and click the **submit** button, an error message will appear.

3. When all the contact information is entered, click the **submit** button.

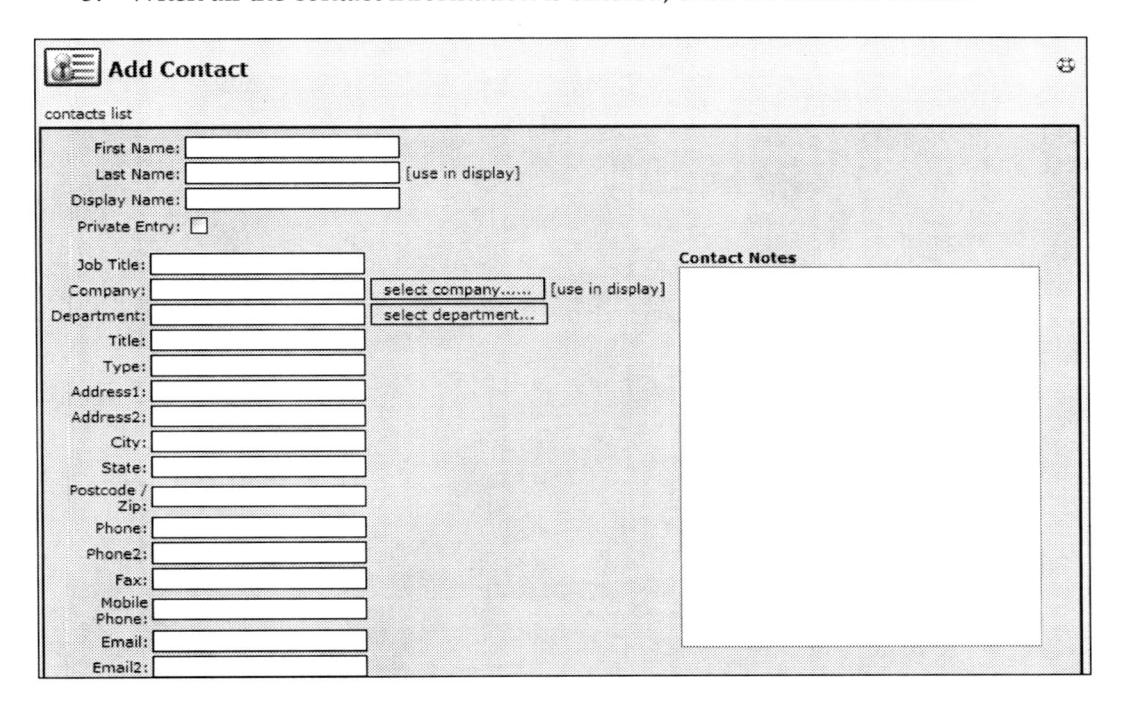

Adding a Contact as a vCard

Users who have taken the time to store contact information in an address book will want to save time by uploading their contacts as **vCards**. The actual process will vary depending upon the address book or email program used. We will upload a **vCard** from Microsoft Outlook in this example.

1. Click on the **Import vCard** link on the main **Contacts** screen. The **Import vCard** screen will appear.

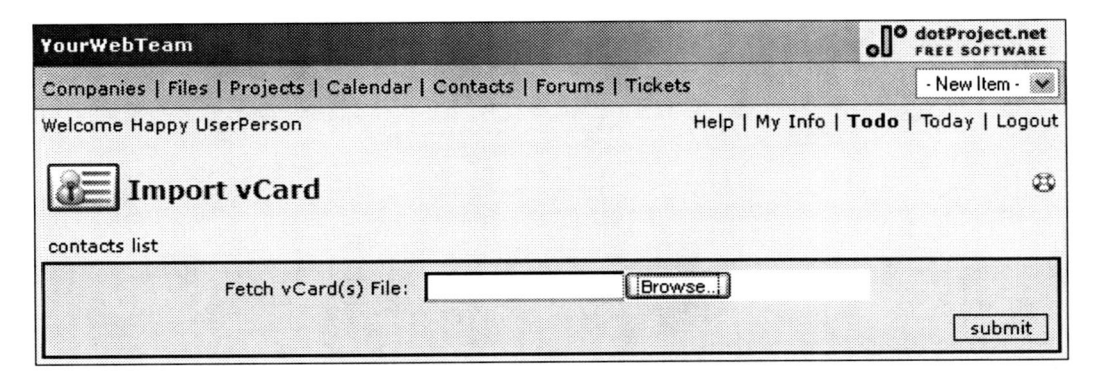

2. Click on the **Browse** button to locate a .vcf file on your computer. When vCards are saved, they should be in .vcf format.

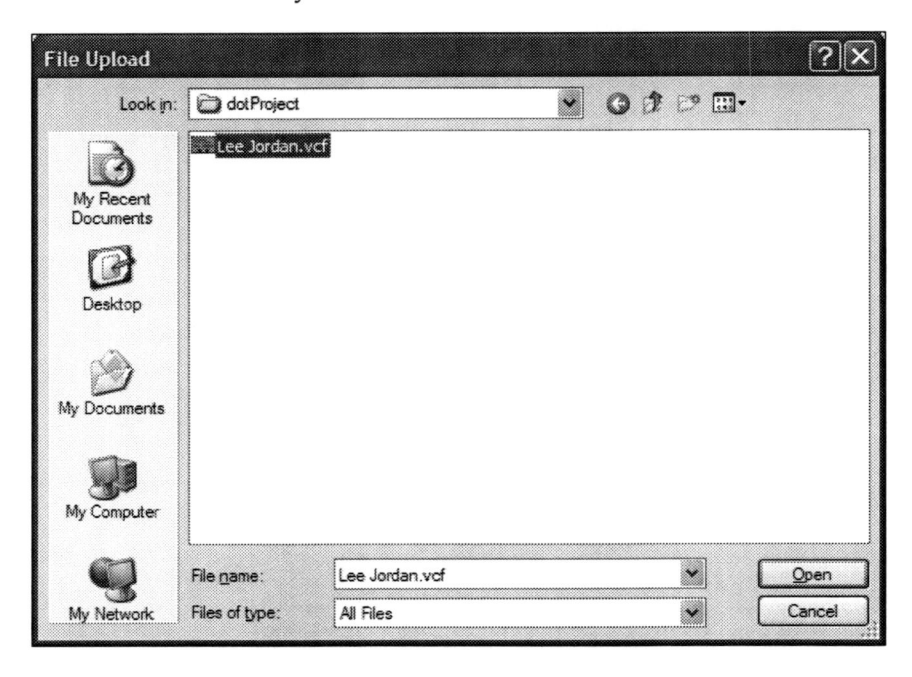

Click **Open** to load the file location into the import screen.

3. The path to the vCard file has now been added. Click on the **submit** button to complete the import.

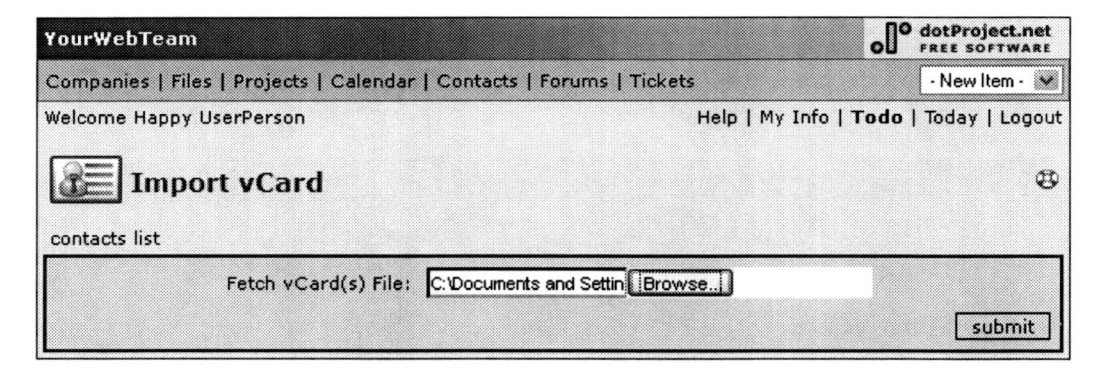

4. The **Contacts** screen will display a success message. The contact has been added to the lower section of the contact list. Notice that the name is the same as another contact. Multiple contacts with the same name can be added with no conflict.

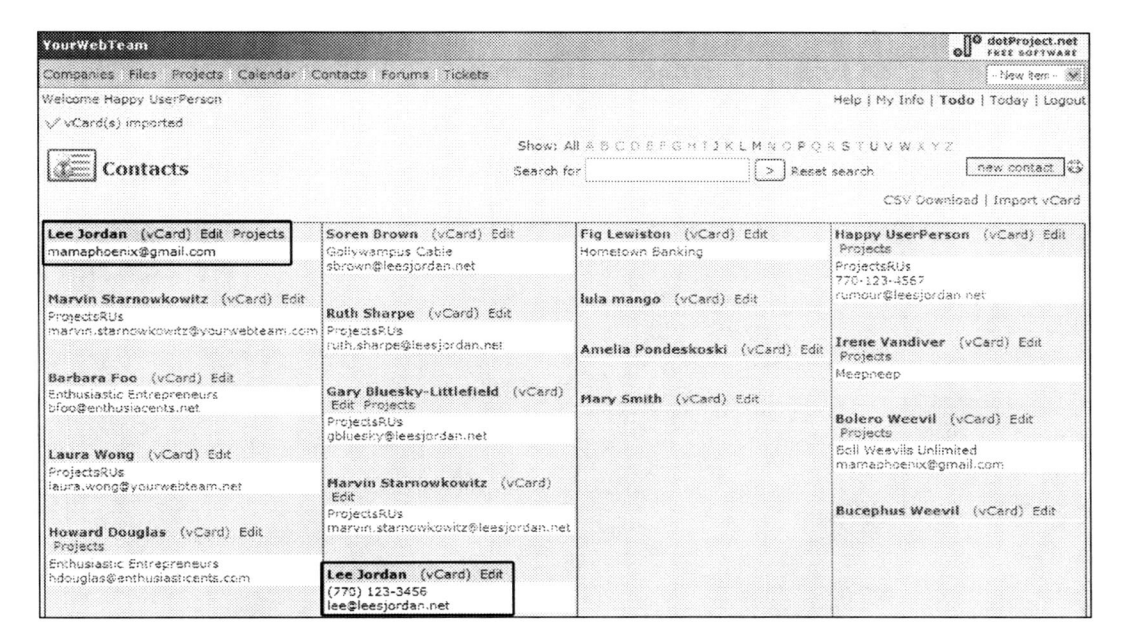

> **Save contacts as vCards**
>
> You can also save dotProject contacts as vCards by clicking on the (**vCard**) link next to their name on the **Contacts** screen.
>
> Learn more about vCards and using them from:
>
> Microsoft : How to use the vCard feature in Outlook:
> `http://support.microsoft.com/kb/290840`
>
> Apple: Addressbook 4.0 Importing and exporting vCards:
> `http://docs.info.apple.com/article.html?path=AddressBook/4.0/en/ad995.html`

Getting Things Done

Viewing Contacts

Clicking on the name of a contact will cause the **View Contact** screen to appear. The options to return to the contacts list or edit the contact appear below the page title. New projects can be created by clicking on the **new project** button on the right-hand side of the screen. The current contact can be deleted by clicking on the **delete contact** link on the right-hand side. Information about the contact is displayed in a long, simply formatted text list.

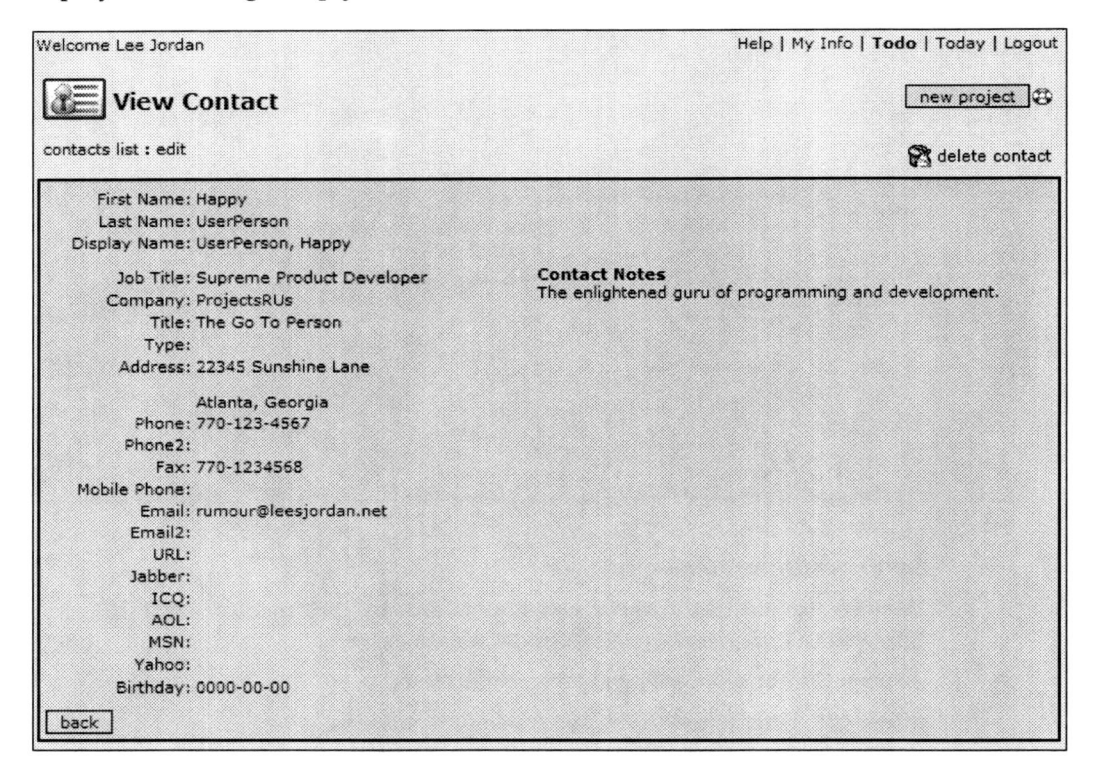

Updating Contacts

To edit a contact, view the contact or click on the **edit** link next to the contact name on the contacts list. The **Edit Contact** screen contains the same type of form as the **Add Contact** screen. **Contacts** can be deleted on the edit screen using the **delete contact** link on the right-hand side.

Chapter 4

Managing Projects

This is the central purpose of the dotProject application. Projects can be created with many details and optional field entries, or with the bare minimum of information. This section will cover the best practices for creating and editing projects. Tasks are smaller projects that fit under the umbrella of a project. Tasks are usually extremely focused on one goal, such as creating documentation for the new version of a product.

The projects view on the **Projects** screen can be altered in three different ways:

1. Sorting the projects list by **Color, Company, Project Name,** etc. by clicking on a title header under the **sort by** tab.
2. Selecting one of the nine project status tabs.
3. Filtering by **Company/Division** using the drop-down list above the tabs.

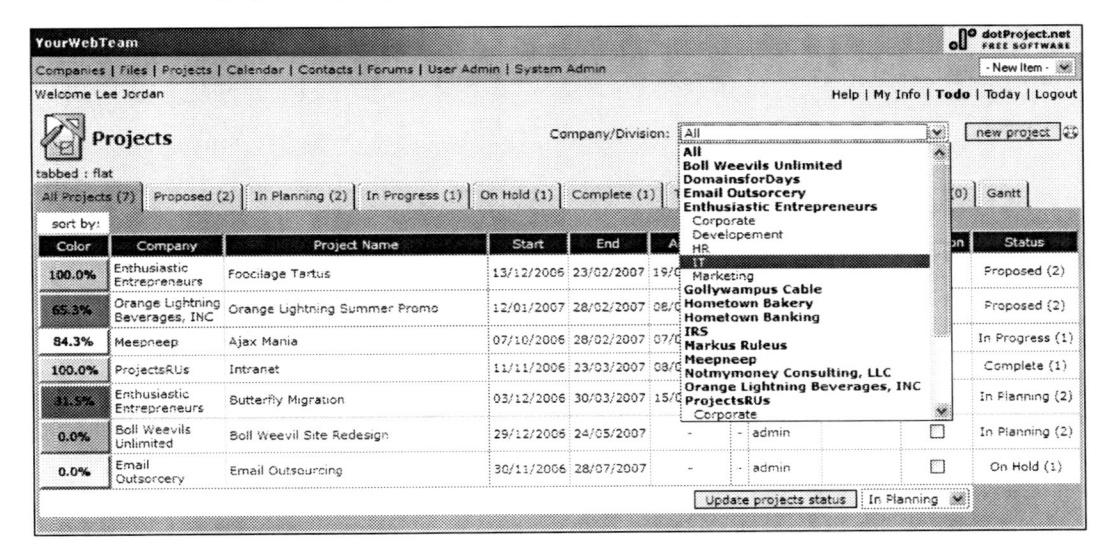

> **Keep to the Color Code**
>
> Projects can be given unique color codes when edited or upon creation. Color coding makes project identification easier. Projects that are part of a particular grouping or a much larger company goal, or for any other logical reason can all be given the same color code. Sorting the project list by color will then display all the projects with the same color code in sequence. The color code can be edited by the system administrator in the **System Lookup Values** area. This will be covered in Chapter 5 of this book.

[69]

Getting Things Done

Single and multiple project status can be quickly updated by selecting the checkbox in the project row under the **Selection** heading, choosing the new status from the drop-down menu below it, and clicking on the **Update projects status** button to the left of the drop-down menu.

Adding and Editing Projects

Projects can be added from the main projects list or when viewing a company. We are going to create a new internal project for ProjectsRUs.

1. Click on the **new project** button and the **New Project** screen will appear. The only required fields are the **Company**, **Priority**, **Short Name**, **Color Identifier**, **Project Type**, and **Status**. All other fields, including the **Project Name** are optional. It is best practice to include a unique project name.

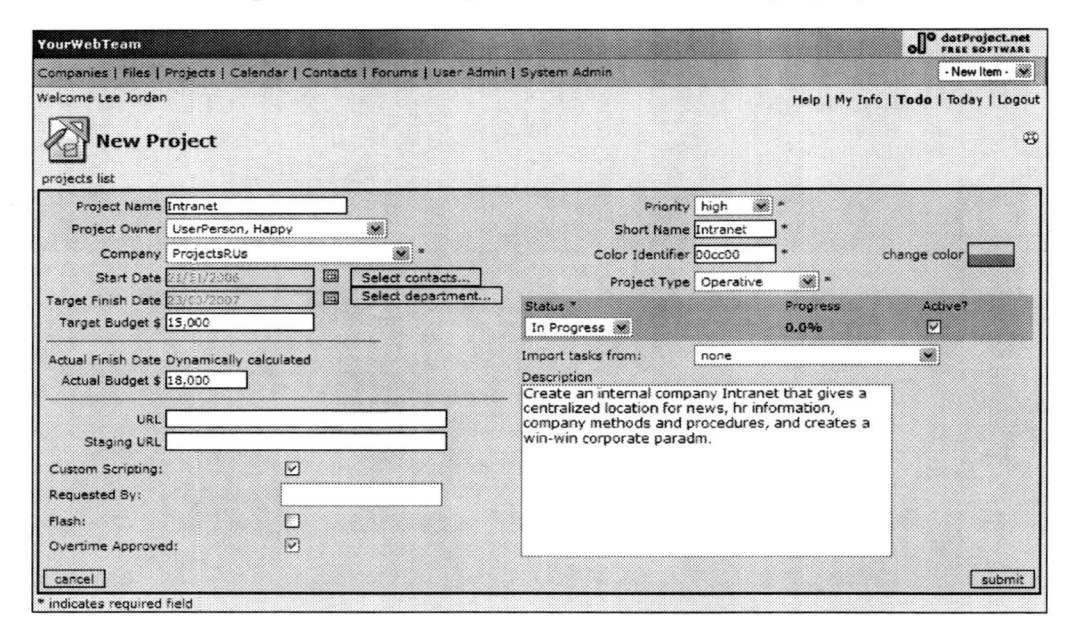

2. Each project should have a unique name. We are adding a project, titled "Intranet". We could also have given it other titles like "PRU Intranet" or "Company Intranet Initiative", or "Intranet 2.0". The first twelve characters of the name entered will automatically be used to create a short name, which acts as a nick-name for the project.

3. The project priority can be **normal**, **low**, or **high**. The default is **normal**. Choosing high will cause a special arrow symbol to show in the "P" column of the listed project. The actual options can be changed by the system

[70]

administrator in the **System Admin** section. Priorities are system wide, and cannot be personalized to an individual company or project.

4. The **Company** must already have been added to the company list to appear in the drop-down list.

5. The **Start Date** is chosen by clicking on the calendar icon. A new window will pop up. Clicking on a date will add it to the date field and return to the **New Project** screen. The **Target Finish Date** is chosen the same way.

6. **Color Identifier** shows the color code in hexadecimal format. Users familiar with HTML will recognize the default color FFFFFF as white. The color can be changed by clicking on the color box next to the **change color** link. A color box will appear. The best practice is to use the pre-set colors defined by the system administrator. Users can also choose from the **Color Selector** by clicking on a color. An alternative method is to enter a different hexadecimal code in the **Color Identifier** box manually on the **Add Project** screen.

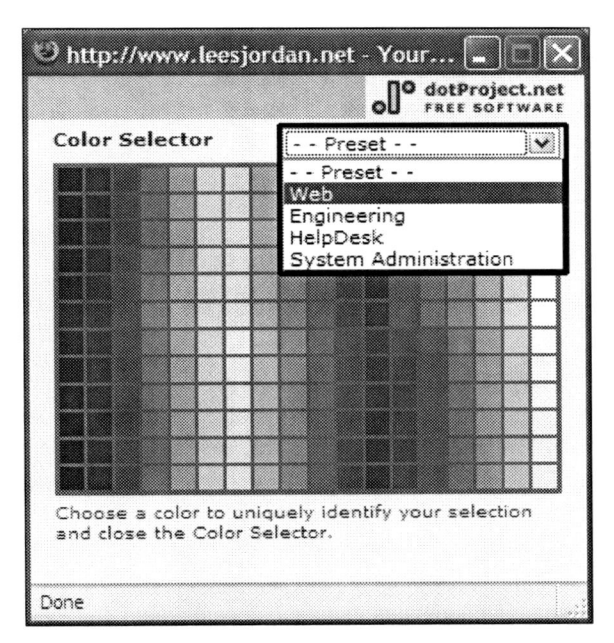

> A hexadecimal color code is a set of six hexadecimal characters (numbers and letters) that each represent a unique color. White is always #ffffff. Black is always #000000. The color code indicates to the Internet browser or application what color should be displayed. The actual appearance of the color may vary slightly depending upon the user's screen, browser, or operating system.

7. The **Status** drop-down box is the main way that projects are organized. A project's status represents its place in the project life cycle. The status chosen determines how the project is sorted in the **Projects** list. The options are **In Planning, Proposed, In Progress, On Hold, Complete, Template**, and **Not Defined**. The status chosen will sort the project under a tab of the same name on the **Projects** screen.
8. **Import Tasks From**: Tasks can be imported from another project, reducing repetitive work when projects share some of the same set of tasks.
9. **URL** is a text field where the IP address or website of a project can be added.
10. The **Staging URL** is the test site for a project, if any exists.
11. **Description**: Enter a brief text description of the project goals or purpose.
12. Click on the **submit** button once all the new project information has been entered.

Best Practices for Creating Projects

The best practices for creating projects will help us to work swiftly and save time; we will cover the art of creating projects in a few steps:

- Use a unique project name.
- Have your contacts and the associated company already entered into dotProject.
- **Short Name** will suggest a short name. It can be altered by typing in the text field.
- Click on the **change color** link or the color box next to it to choose a unique color for your project or group of projects. It is useful to set up a color scheme for projects that are part of a larger company objective or goal.
- If you already have a list of standard tasks in a project, you can copy them to another project to use the same tasks again.

> View the project before adding a new task to avoid duplication. dotProject does not require unique project names. This can cause duplication unless the project team agrees to use unique names for projects.

Adding and Editing Tasks

A project needs tasks to make it effective. Tasks are key units of work. They are often classified as milestones or smaller goals on a project timeline. If this book was defined as a project, then the first draft of each chapter could be broken down as a task. The actual decision of how exactly to break a project into tasks can be complicated, but a general rule of thumb is to take a time-sensitive and functional approach. Projects can usually be broken down into a series of steps that lead to the goal and completion of the project.

Adding and editing tasks is done on the same screen, using the same structure as with the **Companies** and **Departments** screens. Tasks can be edited by viewing a task and then choosing the **edit this task** link. Adding a task is usually done from the **Project** where the new task is needed.

The project "Intranet" needs tasks added. The following example will show how to fill out the different task areas easily and efficiently. There are many tabs: **Details**, **Dates**, **Dependencies**, and **Human Resources**. Each tab has unique functions that define the task in greater detail. It can be overwhelming to a new user. The complexity has the advantage of giving users better control and focus on the actual progress of their project.

Basic Task Creation

The procedure for creating a **Task** is as follows:

1. **Task Name**: Enter the **Task Name** in the text box. This is a required field. Be clear and descriptive, so the title will make sense on a list.

2. **Status**: Select a status from the drop-down menu. The choices are active or inactive. Unchecking the **Active** select box will set the overall status of the task to **Archived** and place it under the **Tasks (inactive)** tab. The task will not automatically display on a user's **Todo** or **Today** task lists if it is inactive. Users will have to choose to display inactive tasks by selecting the **Show: Archived Projects** checkbox on the **Todo** or **Today** screen.

3. **Priority**: Determine the **Priority** of the task: high, low, or normal. The default is normal. Normal and high priority tasks will display automatically on the assigned user's **Todo** and **Today** task lists. High priority tasks have a red arrow in the **P** column. If a task is low priority, it will not display on the user's **Todo** and **Today** task lists unless the user checks the **Low Priority Tasks** select box to show them.

Getting Things Done

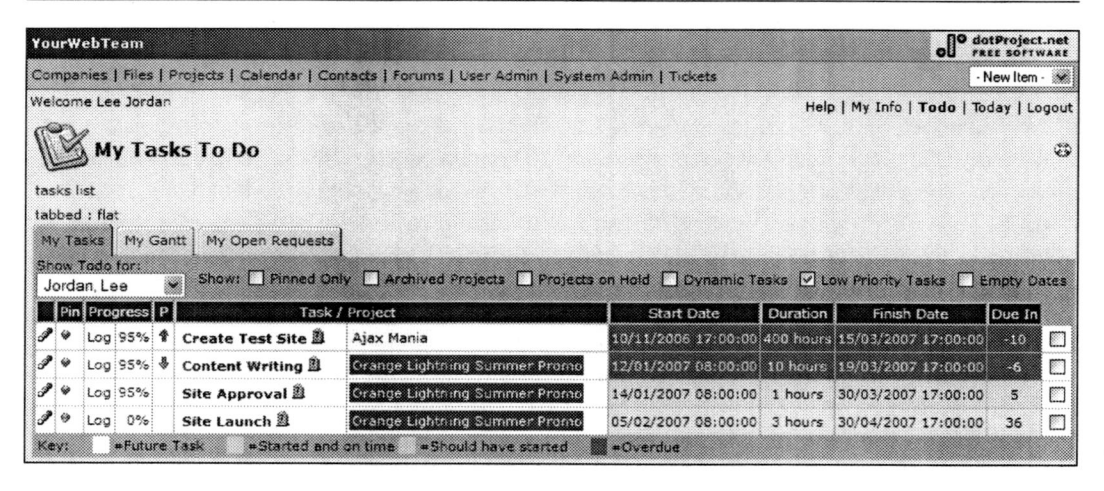

4. **Percentage Complete:** The progress of the task is a drop-down list that allows the user to display the percentage of work already done. If the task is already in progress, go ahead and estimate how close it is to completion. Changing the percentage will affect the overall calculation of the project's completion status.

5. **Project Milestone:** Is the task a project milestone? Some project management teams only want tasks that are project milestones documented. Whether all tasks are included is an issue to be decided on within your project team.

6. The **Dates** tab: The next important information to include is a valid end date. Scroll down if you need to and click on the **Dates** tab. The dates section will appear in a blue box below the tabs.

7. **Select a finish date:** There are two ways to select a finish date. The first method is more precise. Click on the small calendar square next to the **Finish Date** field to choose a valid end date. A monthly view calendar will appear.

8. Click the date or navigate to the month needed using the arrows by the month title. The date must be on or after the start date. We will learn more about **Dates** tab in the following section.

9. **Early Submit:** If you are done, and do not want to enter any more information, click on the **save** button as shown in the following screenshot. The progress and duration information displayed may be inaccurate.

Chapter 4

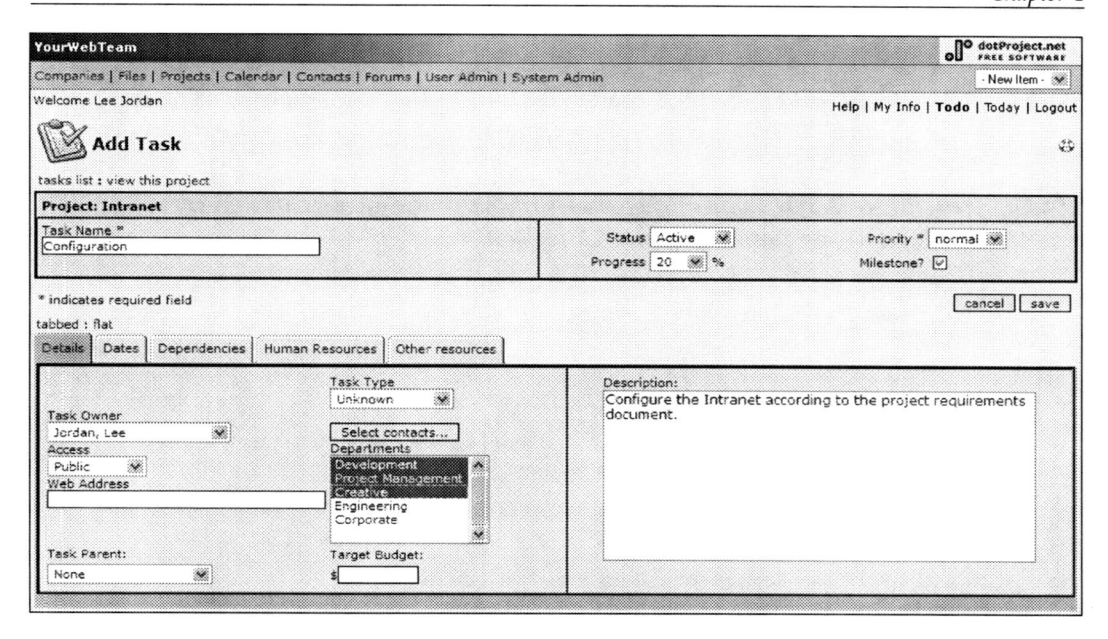

Task Dates Tab

We need to add more information, so let's continue:

- Duration: To select the duration of the task, type in the number of hours or days the task is expected to take. It is also possible to let dotProject calculate the duration or finish date for you.

- To calculate the duration automatically, make sure to have the finish date chosen and click on the **Calculate Duration** button.

- Working Hours: If the daily working hours are different for your team, you can adjust them on the **Dates** section as well. The date format and range of time is controlled by the system administrator.

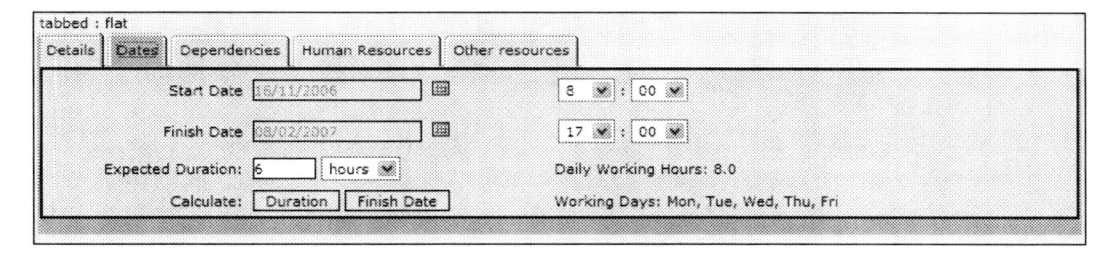

[75]

Task Details Tab

- The **Task Owner**, related departments, and other basic information are defined here. The active user who created the task is selected as the task owner by default.
- **Task Type**: **Task Type** choices are limited to **Administrative, Operative,** or **Unknown**. The default status is **Unknown**.
- **Access**: The task creator can restrict access to the task. The choices are **Public, Protected, Participant,** or **Private**.

> **Public** tasks will be viewable to all users who have access to the project.
>
> **Protected** tasks are viewable to users assigned to the task or for those in the same company as the task owner.
>
> **Participants** are defined as those assigned to the task. If participant access is selected, only users assigned to the task can view the task.
>
> **Private** tasks are viewable only by the task owner.

- A **Web Address** or URL for a task can be entered if appropriate.
- **Task Parent**: Some tasks in more complex projects are sub-tasks. Tasks can be arranged in a hierarchy by choosing task parents.
- **Target Budget**: If a budget has been set for the task, the amount can be entered here.
- **Description**: A brief text description of the task can be entered. This will be viewable from the main page of the task.

> The dotProject developers have stated that dependencies are still a work in progress. They work best in situations where all tasks have a start and finish date assigned.

Task Dependencies Tab

- **Dependency Tracking** is off by default. Turn **Dependency Tracking** on only if it is needed.
- The **Dynamic Task** option is used when there are child tasks that will refer to the current task as a parent. The parent task will then derive its start date, finish date, and duration time from the child tasks.

- **Do not track this task**: Clicking on this checkbox will remove it from the set of dependencies, even if the other dependency settings are on.
- **Set task start date based on dependency**: Checking this box will cause the start date to be recalculated based on the tasks before it. Leaving this checkbox empty means the start date will be recalculated only when the task before it is marked as completed and the end date is reset as part of the task log.
- Make a task dependent: Tasks can be selected from the **All Tasks** box by clicking on the task box and using the arrow keys below the boxes to move a task to the **Task Dependencies** box.

Task Human Resources Tab

The **Human Resources** tab lists the available users on the left in a box by the same name. The task creator is listed in the **Assigned to Task** box on the right by default. Notice the percentage is listed as 100%. To change this, select the task creator name and click on the left arrow below the boxes to return the user to the **Human Resources** box. Unfortunately, this is the easiest way to have control over the percentage of work on a task the user will perform.

1. To assign a user to a task, select the user name, the percentage, then click on the right arrow.
2. A brief email message can be added to send to all users.
3. The **notify assigned users of task by email** checkbox is selected by default. Uncheck the box if you do not want the assigned users to be emailed about the task.
4. If the task has not already been saved, click on the **save** button. The task can be edited at a later time as needed.

Task Logs

Task logs are brief updates about the progress of a task. They are a quick way for everyone on the project team and task assignees to track the activity within a task.

File Management and Version Control

dotProject uses a sophisticated and often confusing version control system for files. Many different file types can be stored in the **File** repository, including images, PDF documents, snippets of code, and Microsoft Office documents. The confusion usually occurs during the document checkin/checkout process.

We will discuss:

- Adding new files
- Viewing new files
- File repository icons
- Updating current files

Adding New Files

Files are associated with tasks and projects in dotProject. The **Files** screen allows the user to filter the files list by project, as well as view all files, **Unknown** file types, **Documents**, and **Applications**. The color code of each project is prominently displayed in the files list. The pencil and notepad symbol takes the user directly to the **Edit File** screen. The floppy disk icon with an orange arrow means the file is available for checkout.

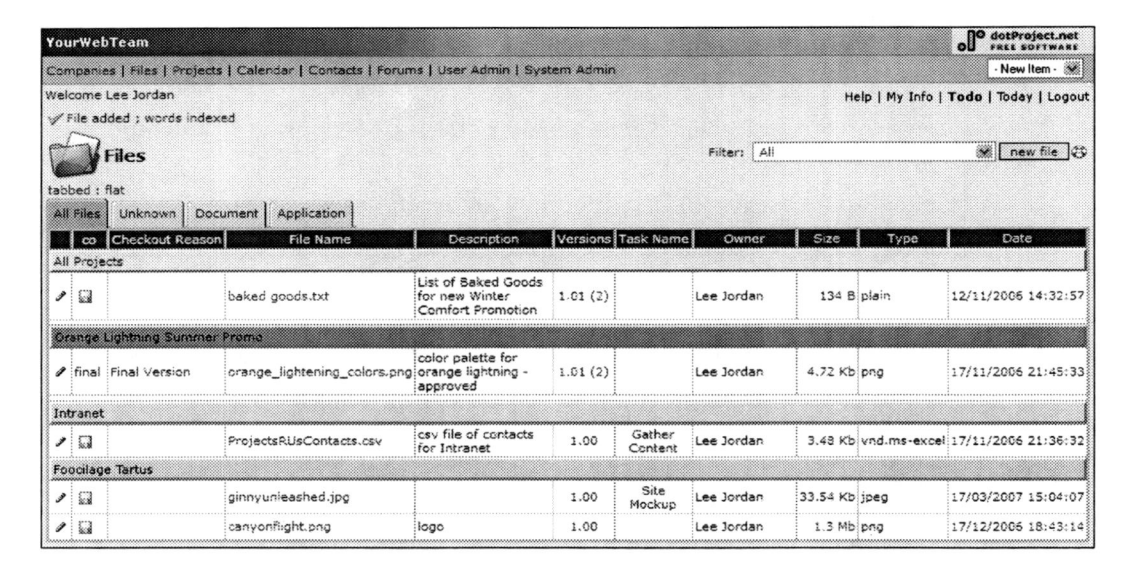

File Repository Terms

The following terms are commonly used when managing files in dotProject:

- **Checkin**: Uploading a revised file to the dotProject file repository.
- **Checkout**: Downloading a file for review or revision.

Chapter 4

There are several places to add files, including the **View Company** screen under the files tab and the **Files** screen. We will add a new image file to the **File** repository so you can get a better idea of how it works. Any user with non-admin permission can add files.

1. Go to the **Files** screen and click on the **new file** button. The **Add File** screen will be displayed.

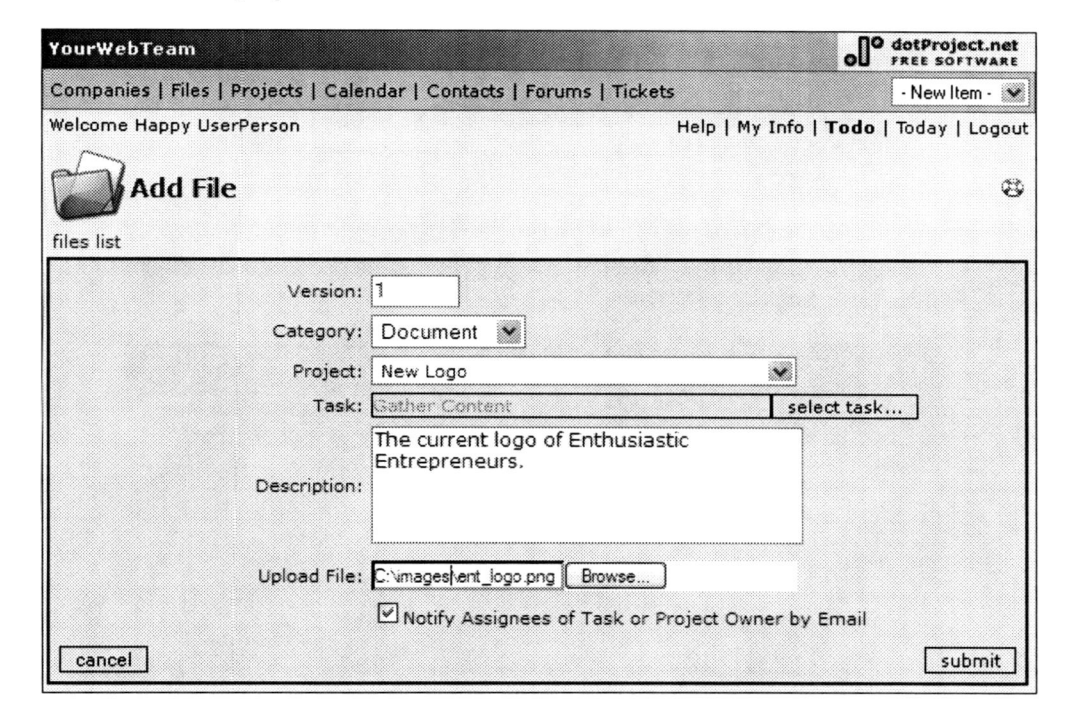

![Add File screen]

2. The default file version is 1. This will dynamically increase each time the file is checked out and back in.
3. **Category**: Select whether the file type is **Unknown, Document,** or **Application**. Most files will be documents. We will select **Document** for the image file.

[79]

Getting Things Done

4. **Project**: **All** is chosen by default. The logo file will be added to the **New Logo** project. A dynamic drop-down menu lists the available projects.

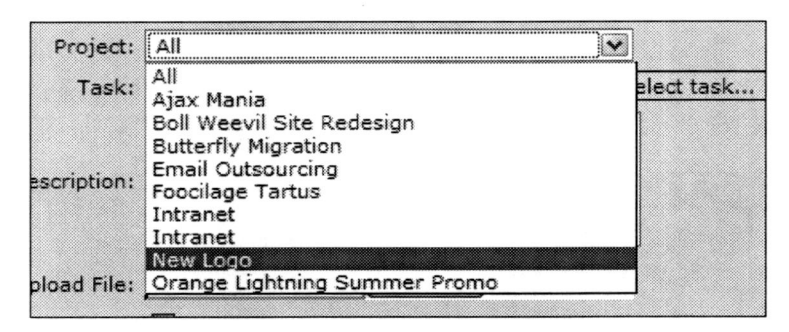

5. **Task**: The task must already have been added to the project selected. A task is not required to upload files. We will choose **Gather Content** from the **Select Task** pop-up window.

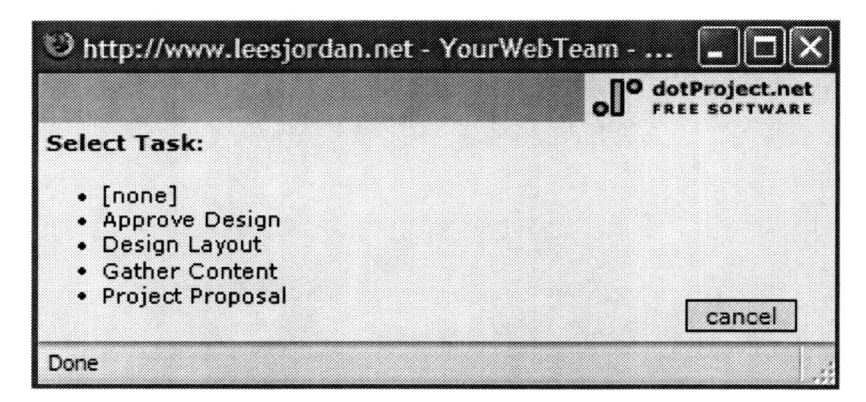

6. **Description**: Type a brief text description of the file.
7. **Upload File**: Click on the **Browse** button to choose the file from the hard drive.
8. **Notify Assignees of Task or Project Owner by Email**: is checked by default. This will notify all users assigned to the task that a file has been added.

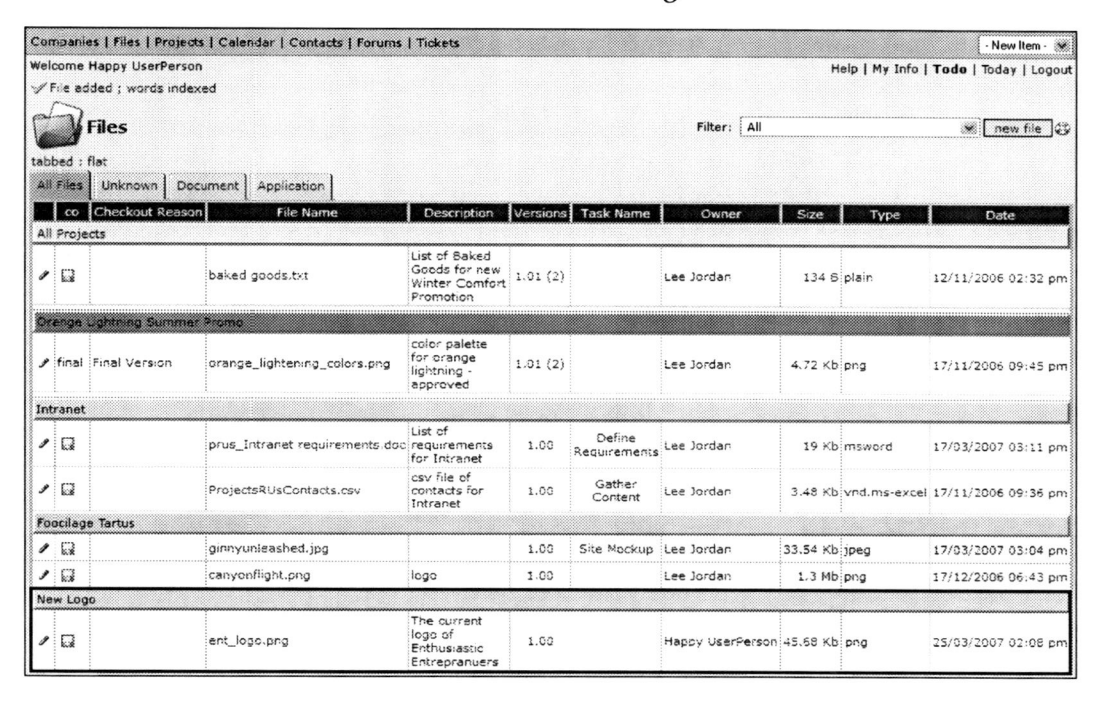

9. Click on the **submit** button to finalize adding the file.

Viewing Files

Project workers and managers may want to view files associated with a project or task as part of their work. Files in the dotProject file repository can be viewed in an Internet browser such as Internet Explorer or Firefox. Users are able to look at the file contents of documents, but not edit them. This is a quick way to preview or examine a file without going through the process of checking out the file. To view a file in your Internet browser, click on the file name. When we click on the `ent_logo.png` file name on the **File** repository list, it opens the file in the browser window as shown in following screenshot:

Here we see the original logo of **Enthusiastic Entrepreneurs**.

Images and text files will display in a browser window, even if they are categorized as unknown.

To download the file on the local system, right-click on the file and choose "Save as...". Spreadsheets and most other documents will give you the choice to open them or save them. This will not check the file out. The best practice is to check the file out using the process described later in *Editing Files*.

Updating Current Files

One thing project managers can count on is change. Project tasks change, people involved in projects change, and project information changes. Project workers and users with non-admin rights can add and update files. If you are not able to update a file, and it is part of your responsibility, contact your administrator to have your permissions updated. Files can be checked out or edited in dotProject.

File Checkout/Checkin

First we will explore the **Checkout/Checkin** process.

1. To update a current file, check it out by clicking on the file checkout symbol.
2. The **Checkout** screen will appear. Make a brief note about why the file is being checked out, then click on the **submit** button.

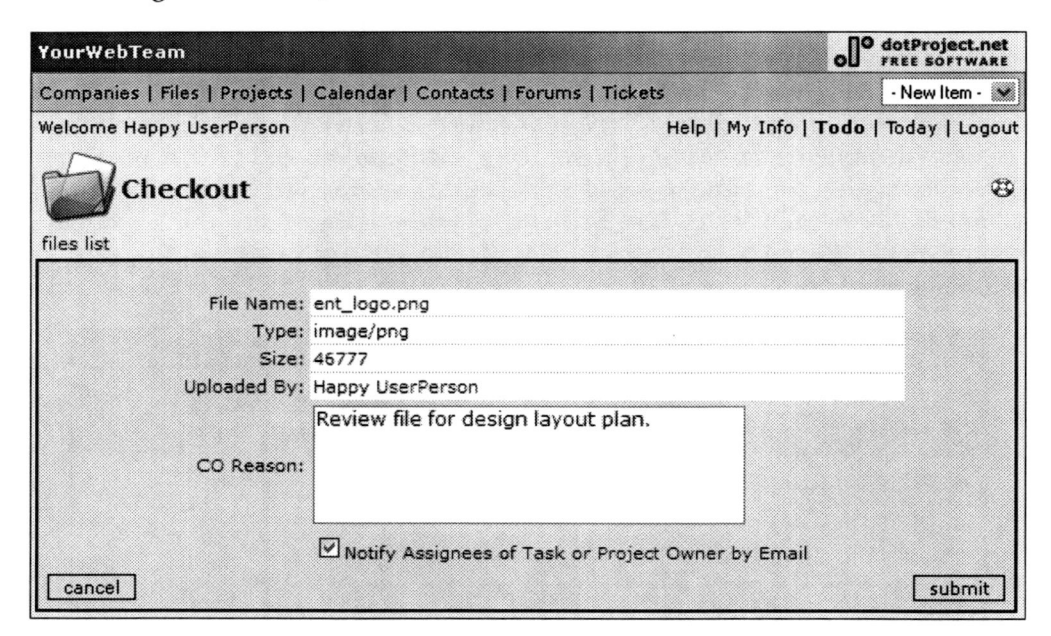

3. The file will be downloaded to your computer.
4. Make any changes needed to the file.
5. Upload the file by clicking on the checked out symbol. It will appear as a square floppy disk with an arrow on top as seen in the following screenshot:

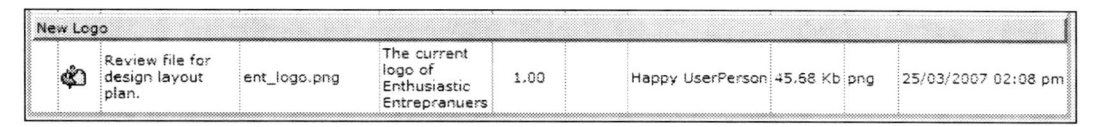

6. When checking the file back in, you must type in a brief text description.
7. Browse for the file on your computer.
8. If this is the final version of the file, check the **Final Version** checkbox. You cannot check the file out again once it is marked as the final version as shown in the following screenshot:

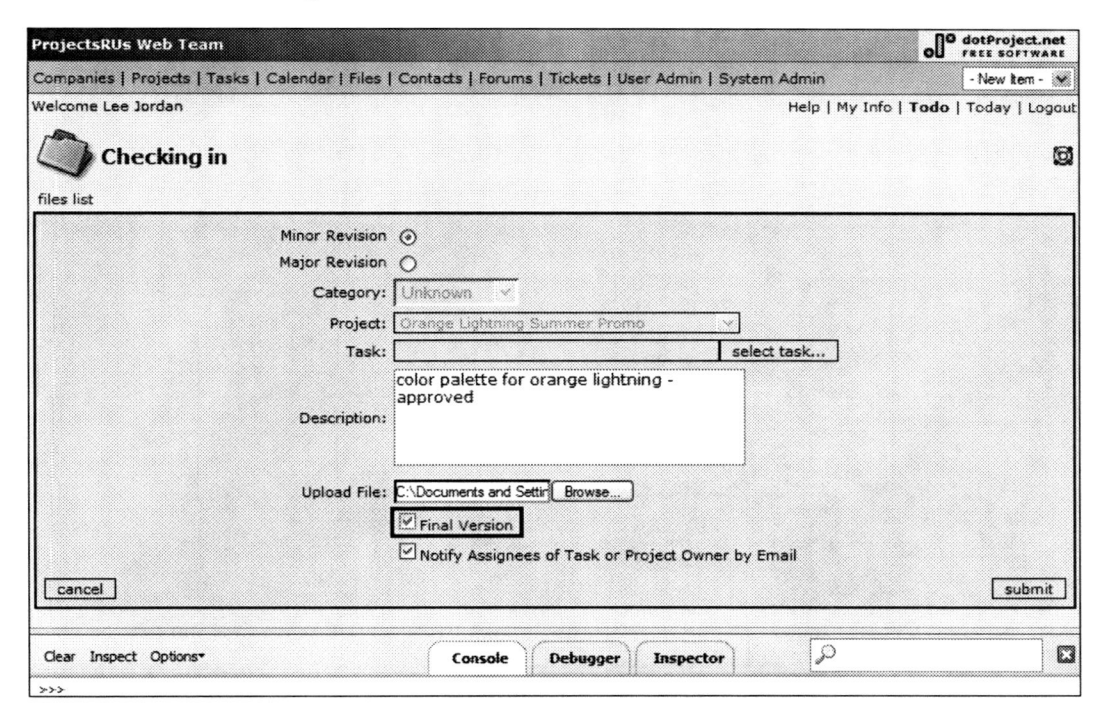

9. Click on the **submit** button to check the file back in. Other users will not be able to view the file until you have done this.

Getting Things Done

> Even if no changes are physically made to the file, you must at least have the **Minor Revision** radio button selected. Be sure to briefly note if no changes were made.

Editing Files

Checking out files is not the same as editing files in dotProject. **Checkout** limits users to editing the file content, updating the version number, changing the category, description, and task. Files cannot be deleted during checkout. Editing files in dotProject gives the user access to change settings related to the file itself. We can perform many different actions on the edit screen, including changing the version number, category, project, task, description, and even deleting the file. The best practice is to limit user's access to the **Edit File** screen using permissions as discussed in Chapter 5.

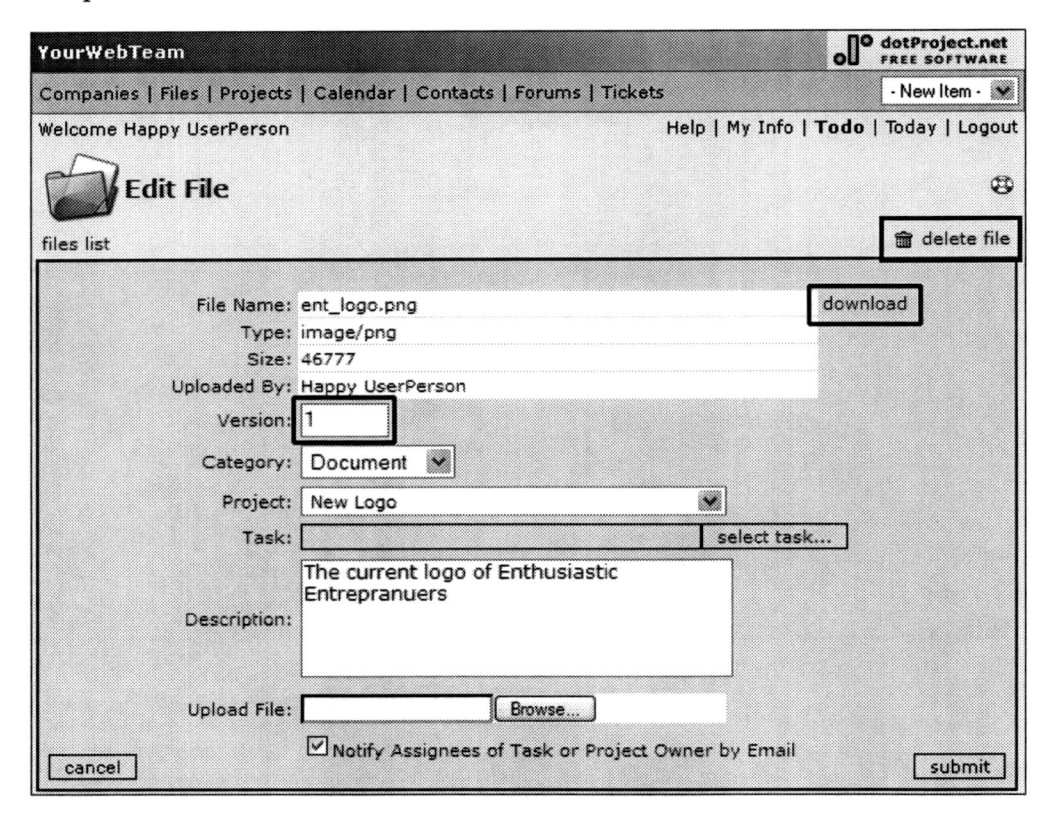

Let's try this out for ourselves. We will change the task and upload a new file to replace the `ent_logo.png` file.

1. Open the edit screen of the file.
2. Click on the **select task** button and choose **Design Layout** from the pop-up window.
3. Change the description to "New Proposed logo".
4. Browse to the new logo on the system.
5. The **Edit File** screen should appear like the following screenshot. Click on the **submit** button to finish editing.

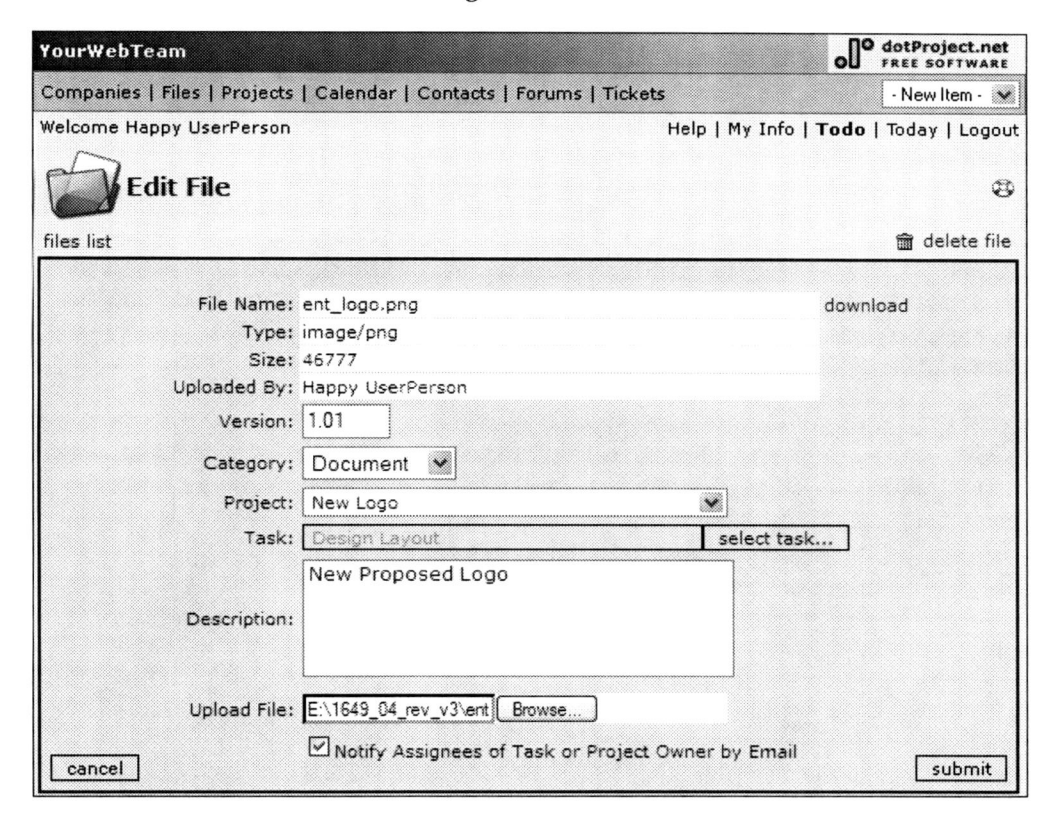

The file listing will show the new file and the information that we altered. Notice the new link to the **Design Layout** task. The time has also changed in the date column.

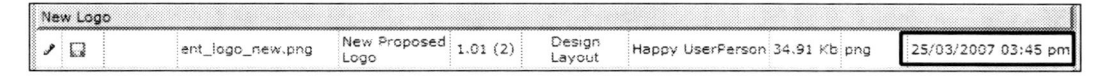

The new file can be viewed by clicking on the download link on the edit screen or by clicking on the name of the file. It will appear in a browser window as shown in the following screenshot:

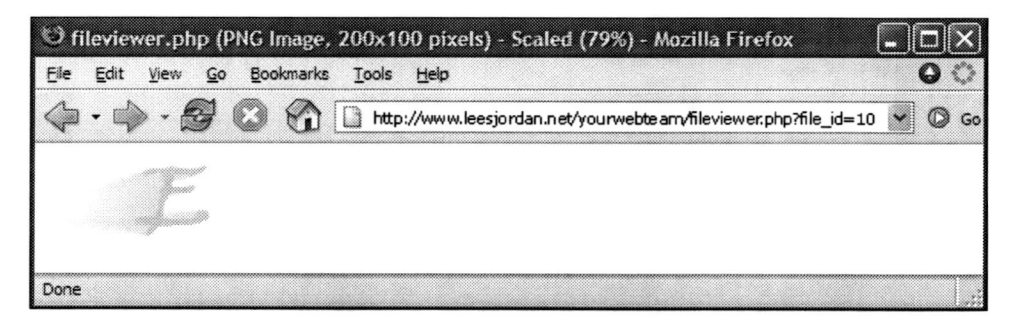

Summary

We learned in this chapter how to really get things done with dotProject. We created, edited, and managed companies, contacts, projects, and files. We learned there are many ways to view dotProject information, including filters, sorting, and searches. We discovered projects can be created from almost any main page within dotProject. Creating a task was the most complicated process, involving multiple sub-screens and careful thinking about the details of the task.

This chapter covered the modules a user is most likely to use daily with dotProject. If you want to find out more about a particular module, Chapter 7 covers each standard module in more detail. In Chapter 5, we will discuss dotProject administration.

Administering dotProject

dotProject uses a highly centralized administration system. Except for the database connection information, all other areas of dotProject are controlled from system administration and user preferences. This grants the administrator greater control over the dotProject environment.

Administrators have granular control over permissions, modules, and the dotProject system as a whole. This flexibility allows administrators to mold dotProject into a project management application that suits their needs.

We will examine all the main areas of system administration within dotProject. The **ProjectsRUs** installation will be modified by using different tools within the system administration interface of dotProject. The actual settings used by administrators will vary depending upon the situation. We will focus on the main uses and issues that users experience when administering dotProject.

This chapter will include:

- System configuration
- LDAP authentication
- User administration
- Setting and managing permissions

System Administration

There are four main areas under System Administration:

- **Language Support**: This contains **Translation Management**, an administrative tool to manage strings and controls which are language specific. For example, system administrators can change the control **Employee** to **Associate** in the English translation.

> In dotProject Strings are phrases of text; Controls are phrases that name or describe actions in dotProject.

- **Preferences** is the main system configuration area. It includes default user preferences, custom fields, and overall system settings.
- **Modules** is an administration panel where module activity is controlled. Modules can be installed, made active, disabled, and managed in other logical ways.
- **Administration**: **User Roles** and **Contacts** can be managed here. There is a special tool in place for the import of contacts from LDAP.

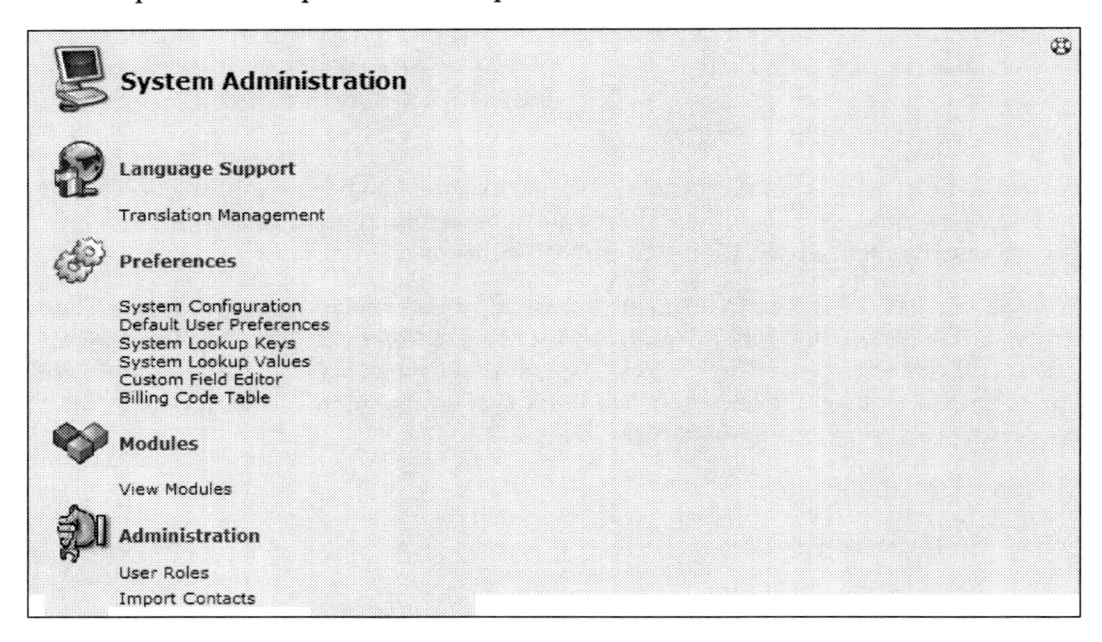

System Administration

Language Support
Translation Management

Preferences
System Configuration
Default User Preferences
System Lookup Keys
System Lookup Values
Custom Field Editor
Billing Code Table

Modules
View Modules

Administration
User Roles
Import Contacts

Language Support

The **Language Support** area of **System Administration** in dotProject contains the **Translation Management** application. **Translation Management** not only allows administrators to customize text phrases for translation purposes, but is also the place to change the labels applied to dotProject modules such as the **Companies** module.

There are many languages that can be used with dotProject. The default installation of dotProject available usually contains only the English language pack. dotProject language packs can be downloaded directly from the dotProject site at: `http://www.dotproject.net/index.php?name=CmodsDownload`.

> dotProject refers to languages and language variations as **Locales**. An example of this is the differences between American English, British English, and Australian English. Each of these languages has its own set of grammar rules and turns of phrase.

Adding a Language to dotProject

dotProject is installed with English as the default language. In a multi-lingual workplace, or in situations where a different language is preferred, an additional language pack needs to be added. Let's download a language pack to get a better idea of how the process works.

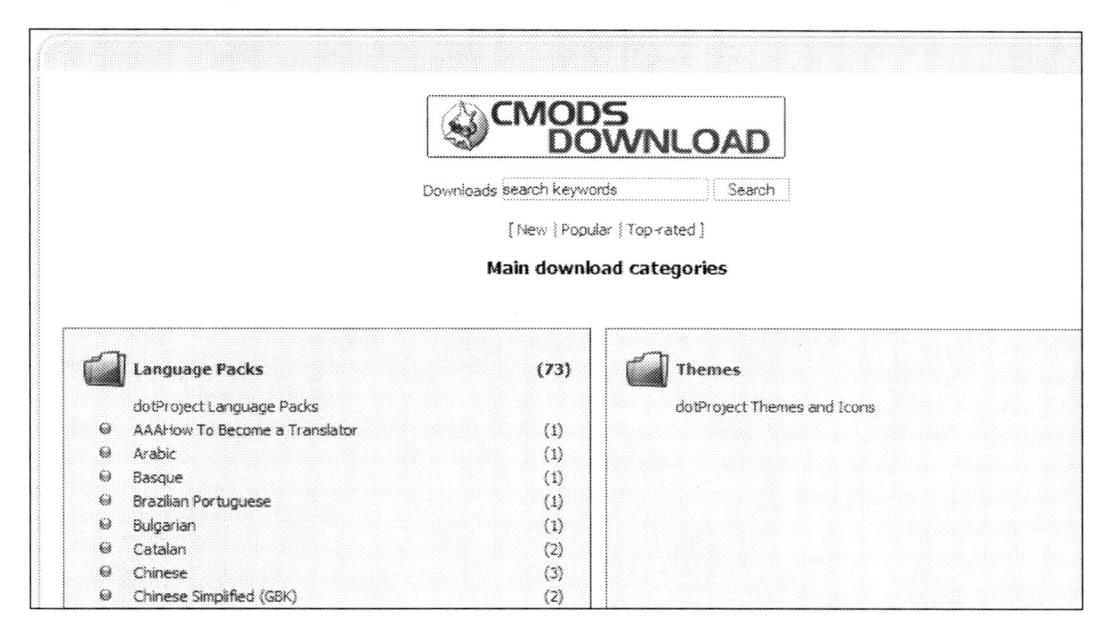

1. From the homepage of the dotProject site click on the **Language Packs** link on the far top right. You will be able to choose from over twenty-five languages. Scroll down until you see **French** listed. Click on the language name to view the download choices.

2. Clicking on **French** will take us to a choice of several different downloads. **French Translation - 2.x compatible** is the first one on the list. Click the title to begin the download.

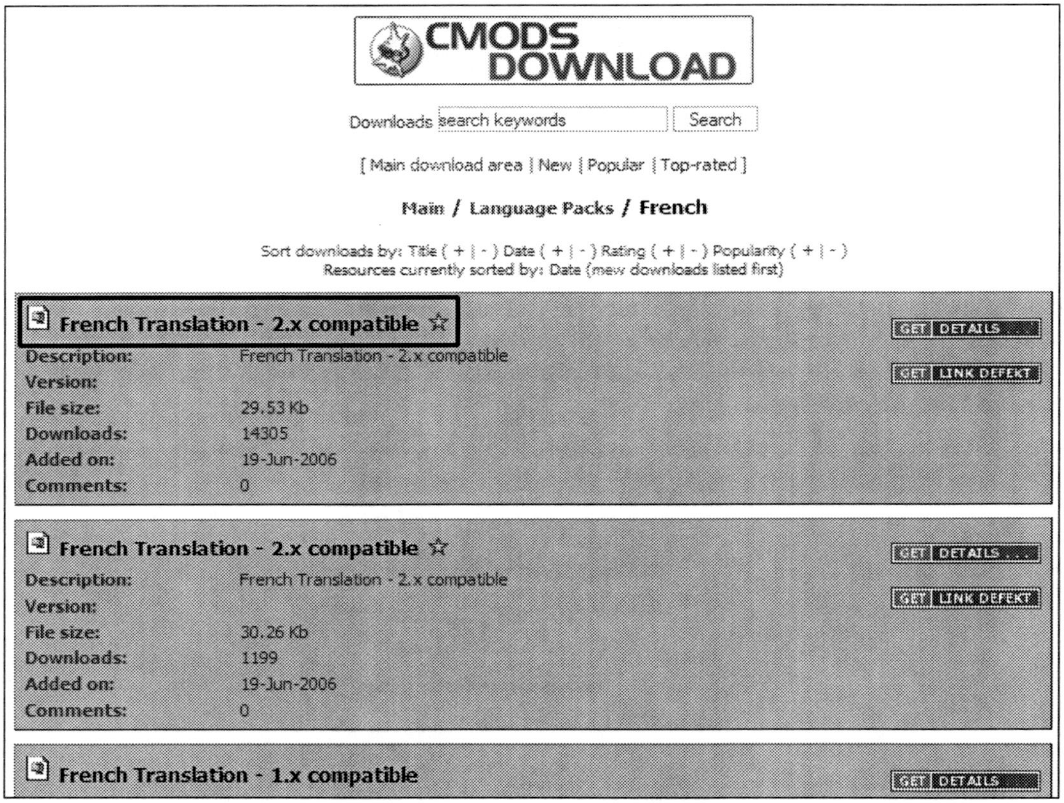

3. Selecting the most recent one will open up a download dialog box that will give an option to save it to the system.
4. The zipped language pack will be downloaded to your computer. Unzip the folder to view the contents. The language pack should include a folder named according to ISO689-2 language standards containing the language files and installation instructions in that language.

> A list of the two-letter language abbreviations that adhere to the ISO689-2 standards can be viewed and downloaded from the United States Library of Congress: `http://www.loc.gov/standards/iso639-2/php/code_list.php`.

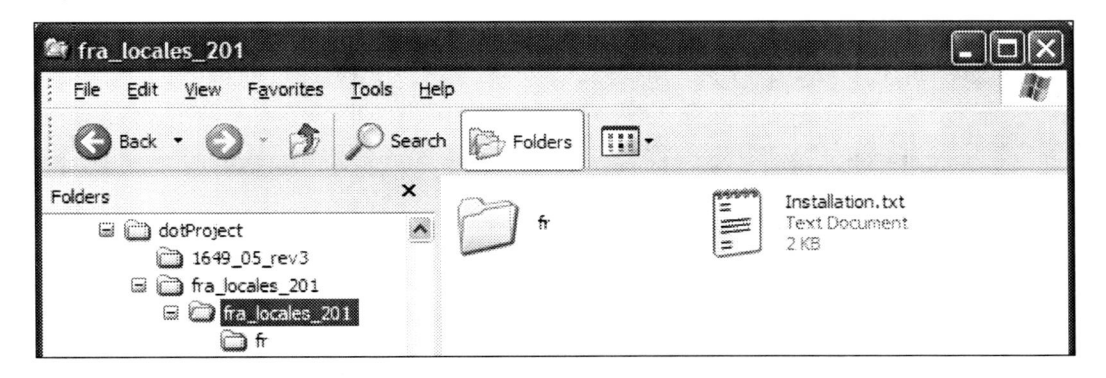

5. If the language pack does not contain a folder using the two-letter language abbreviation, create a new folder under the `locales` directory of your dotProject installation.

   Example: To create a directory for a French language pack I would create a folder named `fr` and upload it to the `locales` directory:

   `yourwebteam/locales/fr/`

6. Upload the contents of the language pack to the `locales` directory of your dotProject installation. If the language folder is already labeled with the two letter ISO689-2 standard abbreviation, upload that folder into the locales folder. Otherwise, upload the contents of the language folder to the properly labeled folder you created in step five. The following screenshot shows the FTP directories:

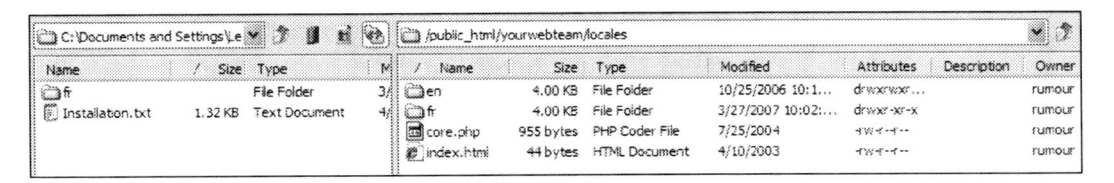

> **Don't upload the language pack folder**
>
> Uploading the language pack folder that contains the language-file folder will prevent the language pack from working properly. Language pack folders usually have descriptive names such as `fra_locales_2001`.

What's in the language folder? Let's take a look. When we open up the `fr` folder in Windows XP, each default module and all popular modules have their own translation files.

The files found in the `fr` folder are displayed as shown in the screenshot below:

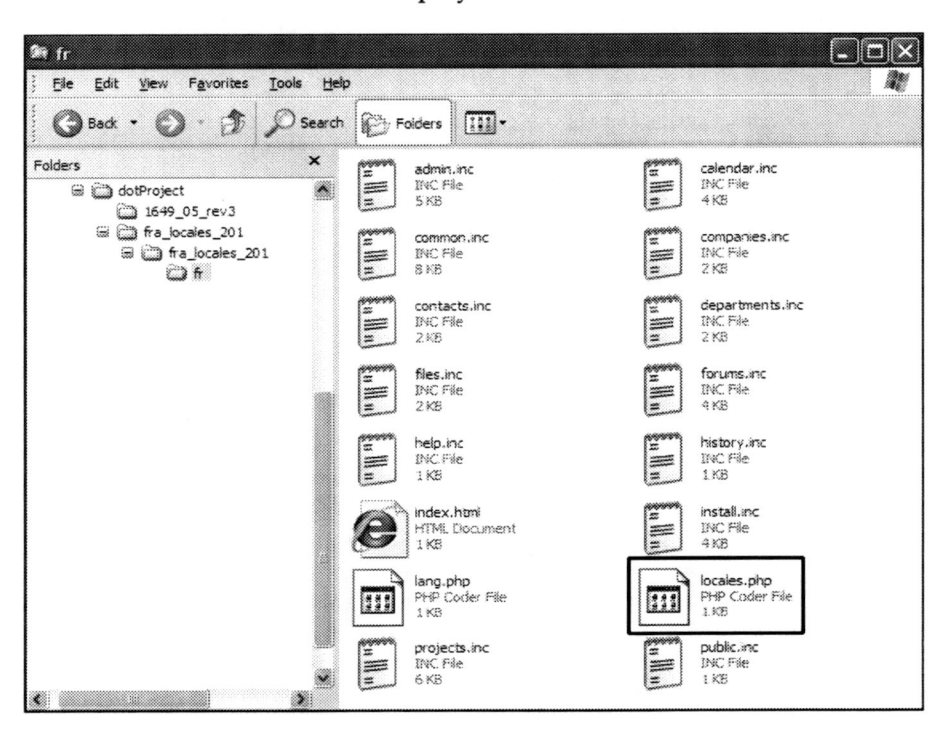

> **Locales and Lang Required**
>
> A `locales.php` file must exist in the uploaded language folder for each language. If your language folder does not contain a `locales.php` file, copy the `locales.php` file from the `/en/` folder. Also a `lang.php` file is required in the folder. If you don't find the `lang.php` file in the `fr` folder then you can copy it from the `/en/` folder and the syntax of the php file would be almost the same except for some minor changes as demonstrated in the following screenshot:
>
> ```
> <?php
> // Entries in the LANGUAGES array are elements that describe the
> // countries and language variants supported by this locale pack.
> // Elements are keyed by the ISO 2 character language code in lowercase
> // followed by an underscore and the 2 character country code in Uppercase.
> // Each array element has 4 parts:
> // 1. Directory name of locale directory
> // 2. English name of language
> // 3. Name of language in that language
> // 4. Microsoft locale code
>
> $dir = basename(dirname(__FILE__));
>
> $LANGUAGES['en_NZ'] = array ( $dir, 'French (FR)', 'French (FR)', 'enf');
> ?>
> ```

Setting Language Preferences

After a language pack folder has been uploaded to the dotProject installation, the language can be chosen by users or administrators in the **Edit User Preferences** screen. The **System Administration** screen for editing user preferences is shown in the following screenshot:

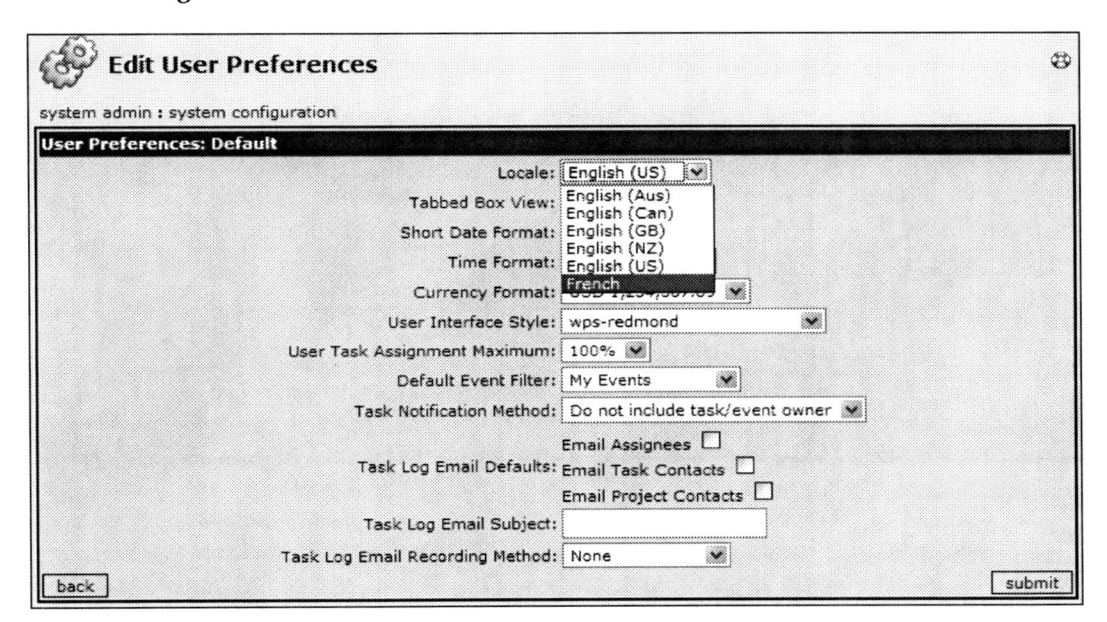

> **Why System-wide or Individual User Preferences for Locales?**
>
> dotProject gives administrators the ability to set a language as default system wide or to let individual users choose their own language. Beware that setting the language at the system level does not guarantee that users will automatically see the new language appear as the default if the users were created before the language was set by the administrator.

Now that the language files have been uploaded to the dotProject installation, the language will need to be set as the default, if it is to be the primary language.

1. Log out of dotProject and log in again as an administrator.
2. Navigate to **Edit User Preferences** under **Preferences** on the **System Administration** screen.
3. Select a language from **Locale** dropdown in **Edit User Preferences**.

Administering dotProject

4. Log out of dotProject then log in—you should see the language already applied to the login screen.

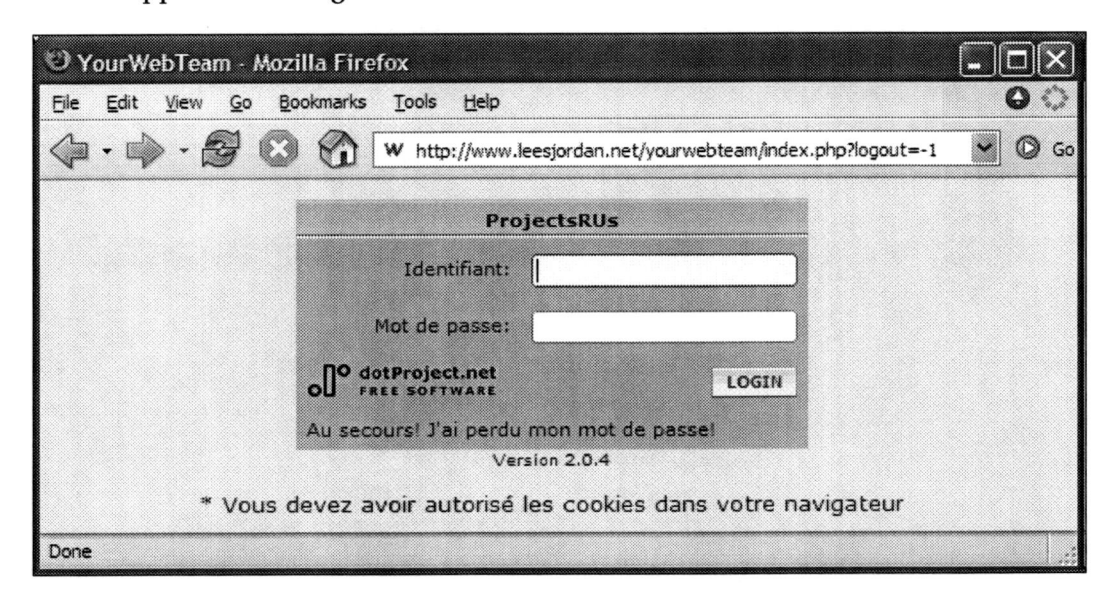

5. Once logged in, if the language does not appear to have been applied to the rest of the installation, the individual user preferences have to be re-set.
6. Click on the **My Info** link at the top right of the dotProject screen to navigate to the **View User** screen.
7. Click the **Edit User Preferences** link.

8. Change the language in the **Locale** dropdown.

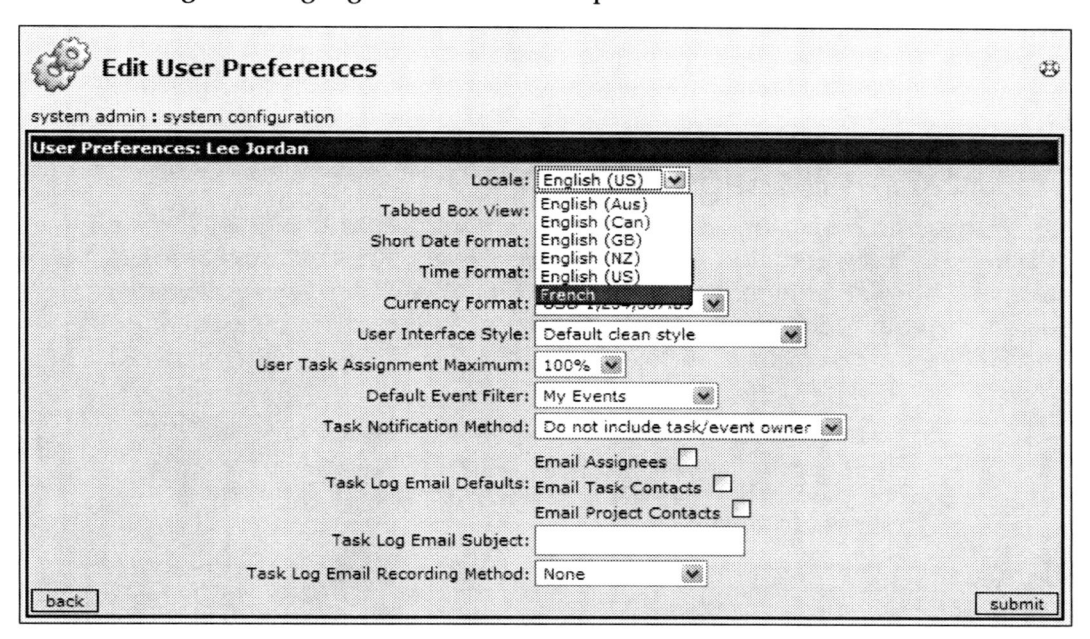

9. Log out of dotProject then log back in.
10. Now changes should be visible as shown in the following screenshot.

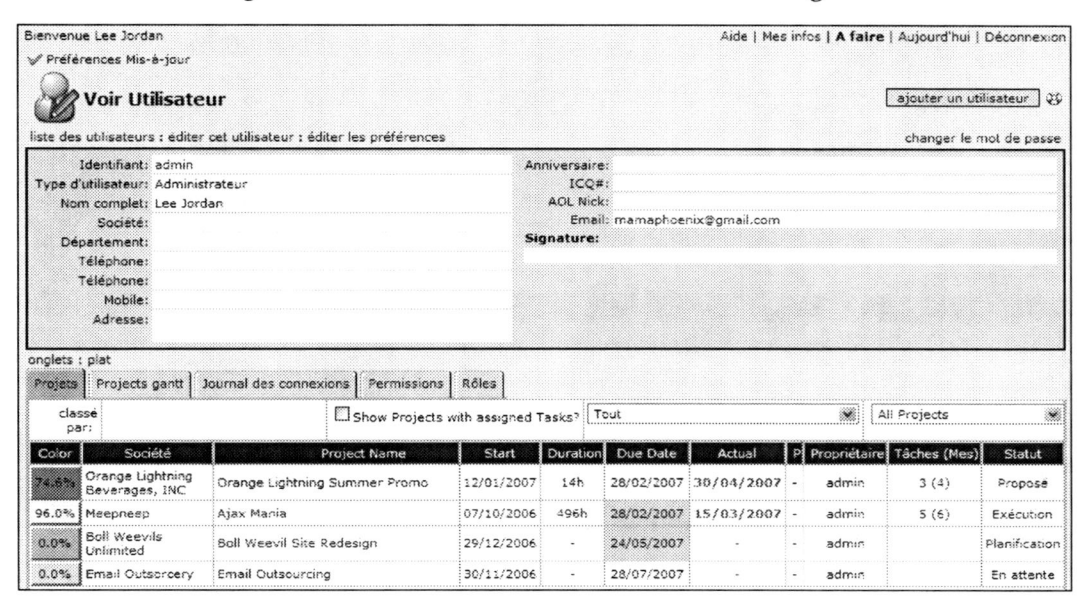

> To set the new language as the system default, change the **Host Locale** variable in the **System Configuration** screen under **System Administration**. This will be covered in the *System Configuration* section.

Translation Management

The **Translation Management** screen allows administrators to edit the text strings of most of the titles and messages found in dotProject. After the language pack files have been uploaded under the **Locales** directory of your dotProject installation, you are ready to begin editing. This is an optional task and is not required for the translations to work within dotProject.

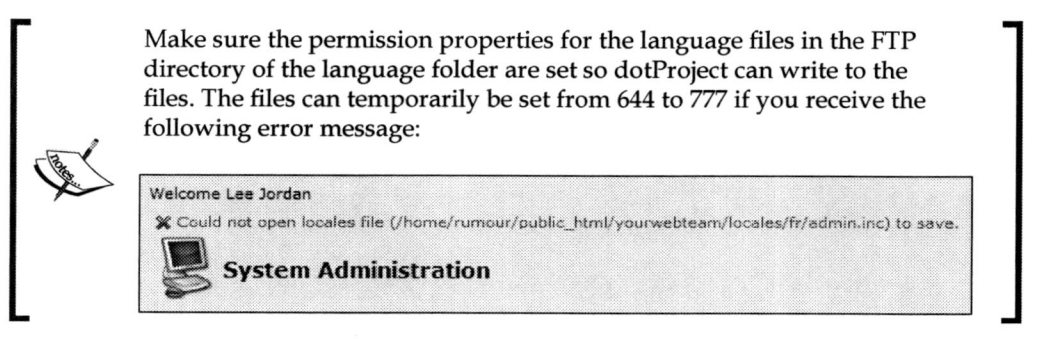

> Make sure the permission properties for the language files in the FTP directory of the language folder are set so dotProject can write to the files. The files can temporarily be set from 644 to 777 if you receive the following error message:
>
> Welcome Lee Jordan
> ✗ Could not open locales file (/home/rumour/public_html/yourwebteam/locales/fr/admin.inc) to save.
> **System Administration**

1. Click on the **Translation Management** link under the **Language Support** section of the **System Configuration** screen. The **Translation Management** screen will appear. The administrative module information is listed by default.

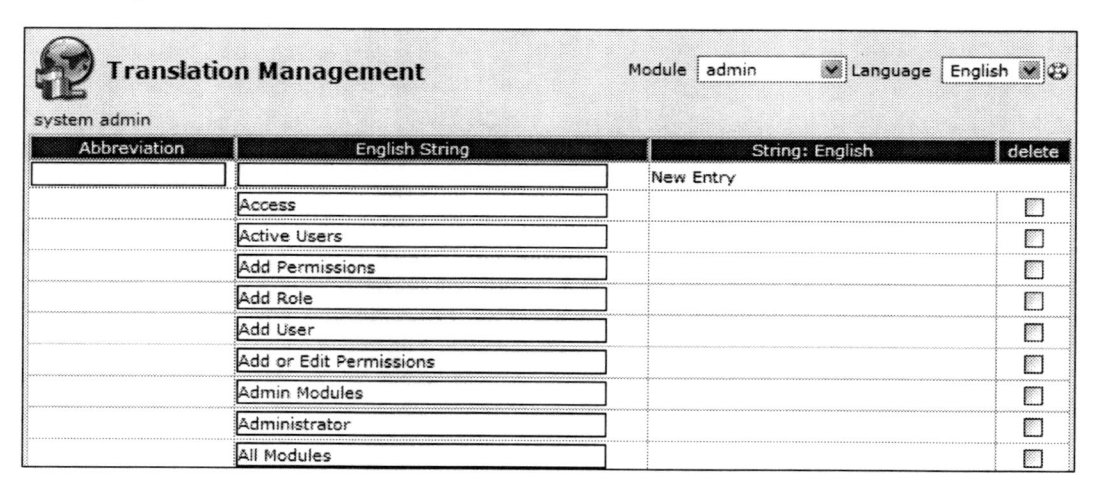

Abbreviation	English String	String: English	delete
		New Entry	
	Access		☐
	Active Users		☐
	Add Permissions		☐
	Add Role		☐
	Add User		☐
	Add or Edit Permissions		☐
	Admin Modules		☐
	Administrator		☐
	All Modules		☐

Module: admin   Language: English

system admin

2. To select a different language, use the dropdown on the upper right. When **French** is selected from the **Language** dropdown, as shown in the previous screenshot, the **Translation Management** screen will refresh with an updated **String** column containing the French language strings.

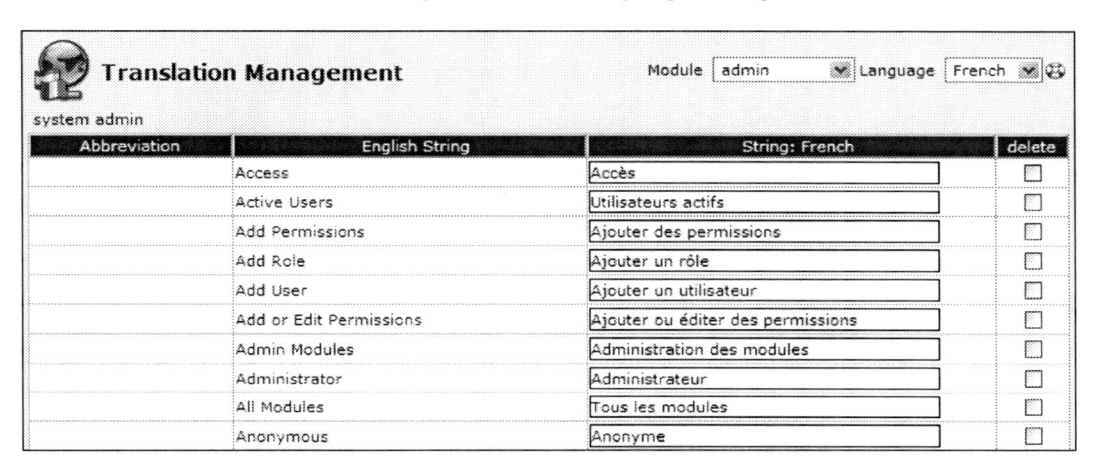

Abbreviation	English String	String: French	delete
	Access	Accès	☐
	Active Users	Utilisateurs actifs	☐
	Add Permissions	Ajouter des permissions	☐
	Add Role	Ajouter un rôle	☐
	Add User	Ajouter un utilisateur	☐
	Add or Edit Permissions	Ajouter ou éditer des permissions	☐
	Admin Modules	Administration des modules	☐
	Administrator	Administrateur	☐
	All Modules	Tous les modules	☐
	Anonymous	Anonyme	☐

3. Click the **submit** button to save the French translation.

Editing Module Text Strings in Translation Management

The text strings for different languages may not be precise translations, or they may not fit your company's current terminology. The text strings for individual modules can be edited for more consistency and customization.

1. Choose the module you wish to edit using the **Module** filter dropdown on the right side of the screen.
2. The screen will refresh and show just the information for that module.
3. Make any edits as needed. Click the **submit** button when the **String** phrases of a module have been edited.

> **User Preferences** determines which language is displayed to a user by default. If you are receiving errors and have properly loaded the php include files for the language under the locales directory of your dotProject installation, check the dotProject support forum for additional information about bugs or other issues.

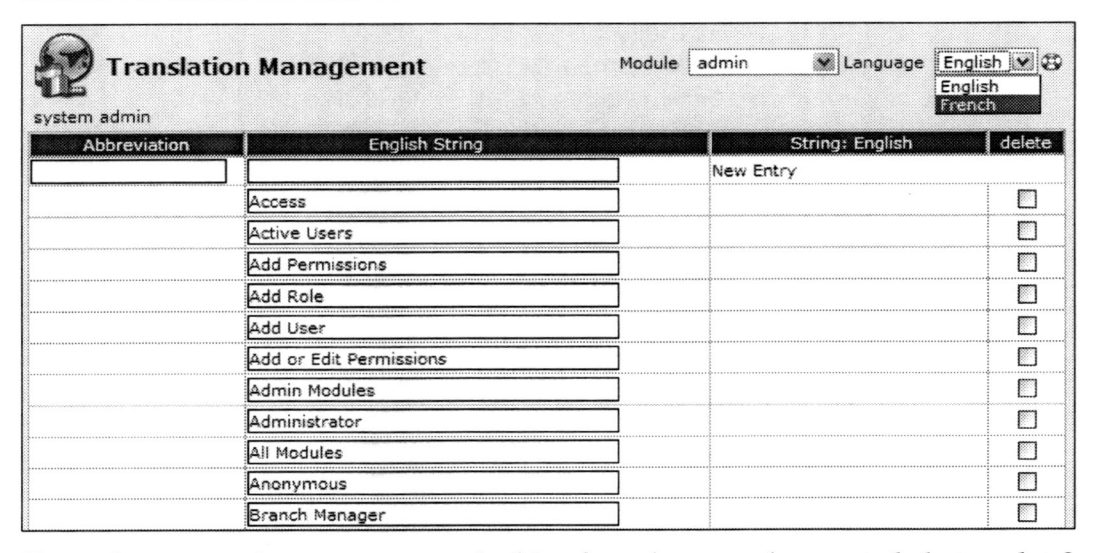

Abbreviation	English String	String: English	delete
		New Entry	
	Access		☐
	Active Users		☐
	Add Permissions		☐
	Add Role		☐
	Add User		☐
	Add or Edit Permissions		☐
	Admin Modules		☐
	Administrator		☐
	All Modules		☐
	Anonymous		☐
	Branch Manager		☐

If you do not see a language you are looking for, why not volunteer to help translate? The language packs are translated by volunteers. You can also help improve the language packs by reporting any translation errors you find in dotProject. Additional language packs are also available for download from sourceforge.net at http://sf.net/projects/dotproject/ and http://sf.net/projects/dotmods/.

Preferences

The **Preferences** section of the **System Administration** screen contains choices that configure the core technical features of dotProject. Changing certain values or configurations in this part of the environment can be very risky. Be sure to take a back up before altering any critical configuration settings.

> Backing Up: The dotProject database and the installation folders should be saved before any critical or major changes are made. Detailed instructions on back-up procedures are in Appendix A of this book.

System Configuration

The **System Configuration** screen is where the core settings of dotProject can be altered. In most cases administrators need not change these settings. Before making any changes, review the variable options and have a backup plan in case of any problems. You will notice that the developers of dotProject take up a full paragraph of the screen explaining the danger of altering values carelessly.

There are quite a few items on the screen to discuss. We will examine each one and discuss best practices for system configuration of dotProject. The following screenshot shows the system configuration variables that are viewable without scrolling. Notice that each variable field has a question mark link in parenthesis to the right. The (?) links to a help pop-up menu that describes what each field is for.

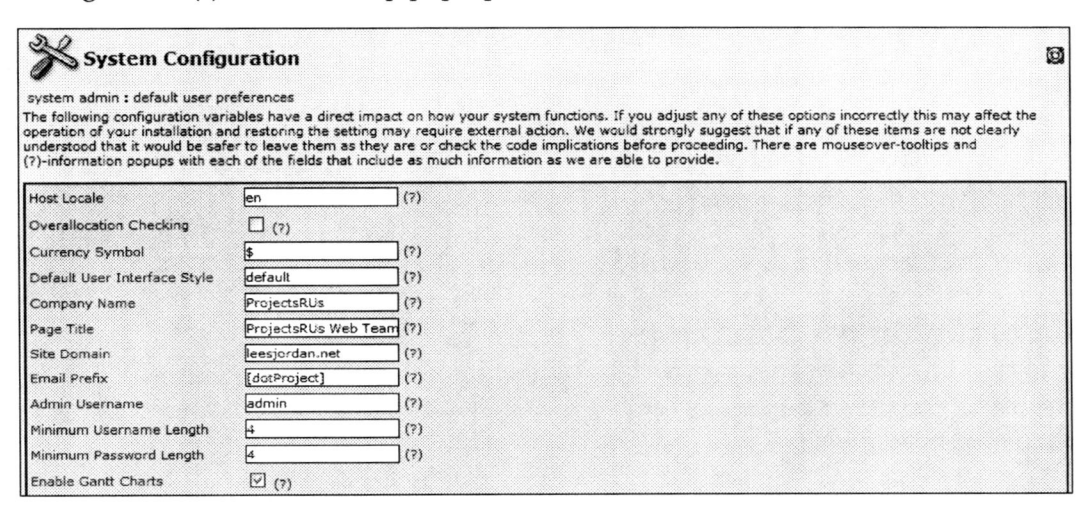

General Settings

The general settings for system configuration are as follows.

Host Locale

The default host locale is English, shown as variable **en** in the variable field. This sets the default locale in **User Preferences** and resets the default language for all new users added after it is set. Instead of administrators or users having to select the preferred default language by scrolling the drop-down list, it will appear at the top of the **Locales** drop-down list and already be set for all new users without administrators having to specify the language in **User Preferences**.

The ISO 689-2 standard for two letter language identification standards must be used for any variable entered. Even though you can type other words into the field such as "French", they will not work properly. The variable must be the same language identification code as the locale/language installed under the locales directory in your dotProject installation; in this case it would be fr for French.

To change the default locale, delete the current variable and replace it with a value from the drop-down list. To view changes we need to log in to dotProject again. The changes can be viewed in **Edit User Preference** screen under the **Preferences** section in **System Administration**.

The new selection made will be the default language. Users created before the locale was changed will have the previous language (in this case English) as their default.

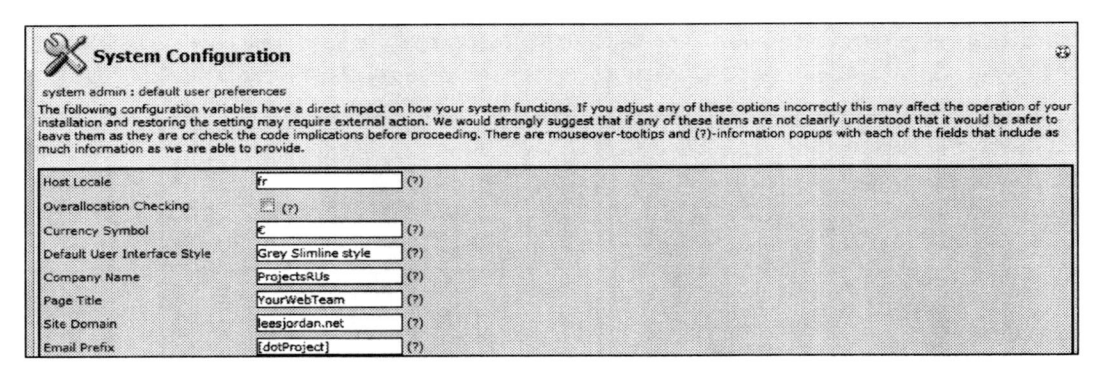

![System Configuration screenshot showing fields: Host Locale (fr), Overallocation Checking, Currency Symbol (€), Default User Interface Style (Grey Slimline style), Company Name (ProjectsRUs), Page Title (YourWebTeam), Site Domain (leesjordan.net), Email Prefix ([dotProject])]

Overallocation Checking

The **Overallocation Checking** checkbox will allow administrators to control the maximum percentage a worker can be assigned to a project. This function is currently incomplete.

Currency Symbol

If currency is not displaying properly even after localization has been applied (displaying British Pounds symbol instead of American Dollars for example), the currency symbol can be set system wide by entering the appropriate variable.

> HTML entities are a series of special characters that if used properly and consistently display symbols commonly used in the presentation of mathematics, languages, and other specialized information.

A currency symbol must be entered to represent different forms of currency. The suggestion next to the **Currency Symbol** field in the help pop-up will not work. At this time currency symbols cannot be represented in the **Currency Symbol** text field using HTML entities. For example, to display the Euro currency symbol, copy and paste it into the **Currency Symbol** text field and click on the **submit** button.

> **dotProject HTML issue**
>
> The Euro symbol (€) will not display correctly if we enter its HTML code (€). Instead, dotProject will attempt to display the information as it is typed into the text box. It does not convert it from HTML code into a useful symbol.

Default User Interface Style

The **Default User Interface Style** sets the look of dotProject system wide. What we usually think of as website templates or themes are referred to in dotProject as **User Interface Styles**. This setting works the same as the **Host Locale** settings. Users who are already created in dotProject will not be affected by the change.

Unfortunately, instead of a drop-down menu of available themes, the administrator must type the **User Interface Style** into the text field. Once again, changing the name of the **User Interface Style** here will not result in a visual change for current users. The style will show up as the default choice on all **User Preferences** screens.

If you want to change the **User Interface Style** shown, navigate to the **Edit User Preferences** screen, copy the name of the style exactly, and then paste it into the text field. Click on the **submit** button to finalize the change. We will cover the application of this setting in more detail in Chapter 6, when we customize the look of dotProject.

Company Name

The **Company Name** field sets the name that appears on the login screen when users log in to dotProject. Any short phrase can be entered here and then applied instantly system wide by clicking the **submit** button.

Page Title

The text that appears at the top of the browser window and in the header area of the dotProject installation is edited here. The text entered in the **Page Title** text field will appear in the dotProject header just below the main navigation area and the site title at the top of the browser window will immediately change.

Site Domain

The value in the **Site Domain** text field is set to the dotProject installation by default. Its purpose is to form a correct email address if a user's email address was incomplete.

Email Prefix

The characters in the **Email Prefix** field will be sent as the first phrase in the subject of any email sent out through dotProject.

Admin Username

The **Admin Username** preference is not used to change the primary dotProject administrator. Instead, it is used to propose a dotProject user as an administrator of dotProject. I tried to see how this would be used and even after research and experimentation it is not clear what purpose this really serves.

Minimum Username Length

This preference sets the minimum length for usernames in dotProject. It is a best practice to create usernames that contain at least four characters.

Minimum Password Length

The minimum password length field controls the minimum length required for user passwords. It is also a best practice to create passwords that contain at least four characters.

Enable Gantt Charts

Gantt charts can be enabled or disabled system wide by selecting or not selecting the checkbox and clicking the **submit** button.

JpGraph Locale

The **JpGraph Locale** should be left blank. It is not necessary to specify the path to the locale.

Log Changes

The **Log Changes** checkbox should be selected if the administrator wants changes automatically added to the **History** log. This may take up extra database and system resources. The choice of whether to do this depends upon the needs and any business requirements related to the collection of such information. Most organizations should be able to keep this box unchecked by default.

Check Task Dates

When the **Check Task Dates** checkbox is selected, users must always enter a start and end date for tasks when they are created.

Translation Warning

Selecting the **Translation Warning** checkbox will cause warnings to appear if a phrase in the dotProject installation has not been automatically translated. I recommend setting this only on test or development installations, not in production environments. It should be used for testing and debugging purposes only.

Translation Alert String

Sets the default warning text for **Translation** errors. This string can be a single character or a short phrase. It will be added to any text that has not been properly converted during the automatic translation process.

Daily Working Hours

The average number of hours in a working day for project management purposes can be set in the **Daily Working Hours** text field. It should be formatted as a decimal, such as 8.0 or 9.5.

Show Debug Messages

The **Show Debug Messages** setting should only be selected in testing or development environments. It should not be turned on if the **Debug Level** described below is set to higher than one.

As we scroll down the **System Configuration** screen, we see many other items to configure. The following screenshot shows the configuration items we will discuss next:

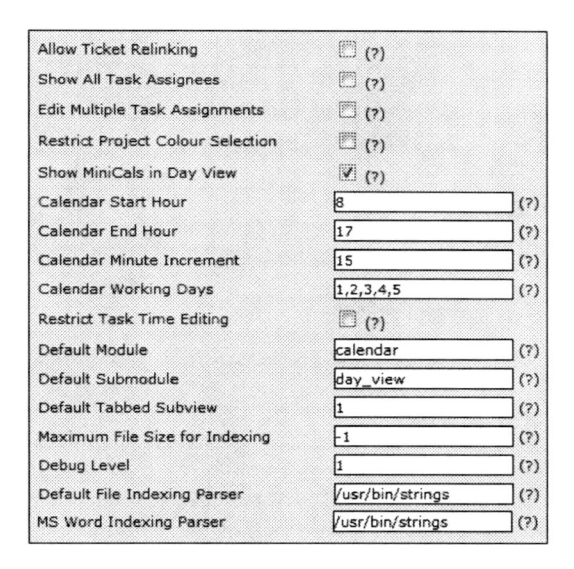

Allow Ticket Relinking

This setting is used only if the TicketSmith module is activated. It allows tickets in TicketSmith to be re-linked to a parent ticket.

Show All Task Assignees

Set this option on if you wish to show all assignee names in the project task list or switch it off, if you would prefer to see just the main assignee name and a count in brackets of the number of other assignees.

Edit Multiple Task Assignments

Turning this option on will allow you to edit task assignments and other options (per task block) in the main Task Module view.

Restrict Project Colour Selection

The **Restrict Project Colour Selection** checkbox is used to limit project workers to selecting only the preset colors for their projects. This is ideal for when users are not adhering to guidelines for project colors. When users create or edit a project, they will be unable to select from the full color palette.

Show MiniCals in Day View

Three month miniature calendars will always appear on the right side of the **Day View** screen, if this option is checked. It is selected by default.

Calendar Start Hour

Similar to the **Daily Working Hours**, the **Calendar Start Hour** field requires a positive integer such as 6 or 22 to set the start time for each calendar day.

Calendar End Hour

The **Calendar End Hour** should be a positive integer between 0 and 23.

Calendar Minute Increment

The amount of time in minutes to show as blocks of time on the calendar.

Calendar Working Days

Lists the number of weekdays that are considered working days. Lists the required working days in a comma separated list where 0 is Sunday. The default is 1, 2, 3, 4, 5. Users who have a longer or shorter weekday schedule can modify it by typing the correct sequence of numbers in the text field.

Restrict Task Time Editing

Check this box to prevent project workers who are not project or task owners from changing the task time.

Default Module

The **Calendar** module is the default module that displays when users log in to dotProject. To change the module that users first see when they log in, type the exact name of the module, all in lower case. Most modules do not have a default sub-module that can be used. Leave the **Default Submodule** field blank in those cases.

After making the changes click the **submit** button and log out. The new default module will be in effect the next time a user logs in.

Default Submodule

The **Default Submodule** is the day view submodule of the calendar view. If a submodule is not available for a module, this field should be left blank.

Default Tabbed Subview

This setting is supposed to enable a personalized start page. I can't find any documentation and have uncovered no practical application of this in my research. The best practice is to keep this value set to **1**.

Maximum File Size for Indexing

This variable is set to **-1** by default, which will allow all files of all sizes to be indexed. Unless there is a situation where file size is a concern, I recommend leaving this value at its default setting.

Debug Level

The debug level can be set to an integer value of 0 to 10. It can be very helpful in testing. Setting the value to 0 will display no debug messages. The complete range of messages will be available if the debug level is set to 10, but this can cause severe performance issues. The recommended level for normal use is 1.

Default File Indexing Parser, MS Word Indexing Parser, HTML File Indexing Parser

Each of the above items usually have their variable path set to the same location of `usr/bin/strings`. This path variable tells the dotProject code where to look to process the files.

PDF Indexing Parser

The PDF indexing parser variable also is a path to the location of a parser. dotProject looks in the specified path for information on converting PDF documents to text for indexing.

Preserve File Settings on CI

This setting is selected by default. It provides an extra measure of security by preventing users from changing the file name, project, and file type an uploaded file has on check in.

Allow Editing of Previous Versions

This variable is also related to the **Files** module. It restricts users from editing previous versions of files if it is checked.

Memory Limit for Gantt

The memory limit is set to "8M" (8 Megabytes) by default. If there are problems displaying the Gantt charts, set this to a higher value such as "64M" or "128M". The Gantt charts should then appear properly.

User Authentication Settings

User Authentication Settings consists of the user authentication method and PostNuke standard login, which are explained next.

User Authentication Method

There are different ways to authenticate users in dotProject. The three choices available without adding additional integration modules are Standard dotProject, PostNuke, and LDAP.

PostNuke Login Also Allows Standard Login

Administrators who also use the PostNuke content management system can select this checkbox to allow users to log in to dotProject separately from PostNuke.

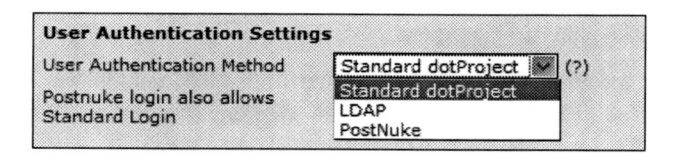

PostNuke Authentication

dotProject can be set up to authenticate against the PostNuke databases, which is very handy for those who are already using PostNuke. A special module, dplink, will need to be installed. The **dplink** module is available from within the `[dotproject installation root]/misc/postnuke/` subfolder. It is also available from a developer Cas Nuy's site: `http://www.nuy.info/downloads/index.php?dir=Developments%20by%20CMS/DotProject/Postnuke/`.

It allows administrators to control dotProject authentication in the PostNuke environment. It is for versions of dotProject 2.0 and above. A side benefit of the module is administrators can leverage an HTTP authentication system as well.

You must be an administrator of PostNuke in order to fully set up the dPLink module. Those of you who are very comfortable with adding new modules to PostNuke can go ahead and transfer a copy of dPLink to your modules directory in PostNuke and install it normally. The rest of us will need to take it one step at a time.

1. Copy the `dplink` folder from the `/misc/postnuke/` subfolder in your dotProject installation. The files are included in dotProject versions 2.0.1 and above. There should also be a `readme` file included in the PostNuke folder. It contains instructions from the creator of the module.

2. Upload the `dplink` folder to the `modules` folder of your PostNuke installation.

3. Log in to dotProject as an administrator and navigate to the **System Configuration** settings from within the **System Admin** module. Select **PostNuke** as the **User Authentication Method**.

4. Log in to **PostNuke** as the administrator. Go to **Modules** administration and click the **regenerate** link. Scroll down to the `dplink` listing and choose **initialize**, then activate.

Modules

[View | Regenerate | Modify configuration]

View

[A | B | C | D | E | F | G | H | I | J | K | L | M | N | O | P | Q | R | S | T | U | V | W | X | Y | Z]   Uninitialized

Module name	Display name	Description	Directory	Version	State	Actions
Autolinks	Autolinks	Automatically link key words	Autolinks	1.0	Uninitialized	[Initialize | Remove | Edit]
AvantGo	AvantGo	AvantGo Mobile News Module	AvantGo	1.4	Uninitialized	[Initialize | Remove | Edit]
Banners	Banners Admin	Administer Banners on your site	Banners	1.0	Uninitialized	[Initialize | Remove | Edit]
dplink	dplink	Postnuke to dotProject login manager	dplink	1.11	Uninitialized	[Initialize | Remove | Edit]

Administering dotProject

5. Go back to the main **PostNuke** administration screen. The dPLink icon should be there. Click on the link and go to the admin area of dPLink.

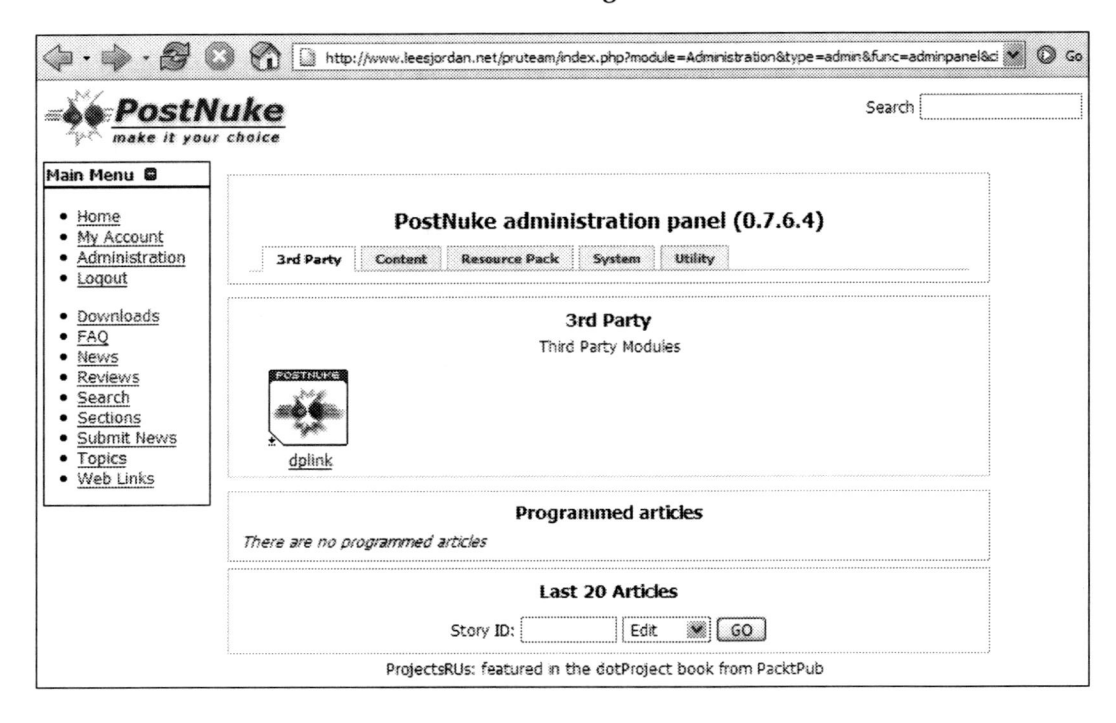

6. Type the full URL of the dotProject installation. Using `http://` will ensure that PostNuke will not choose attempt to use a relative link instead.

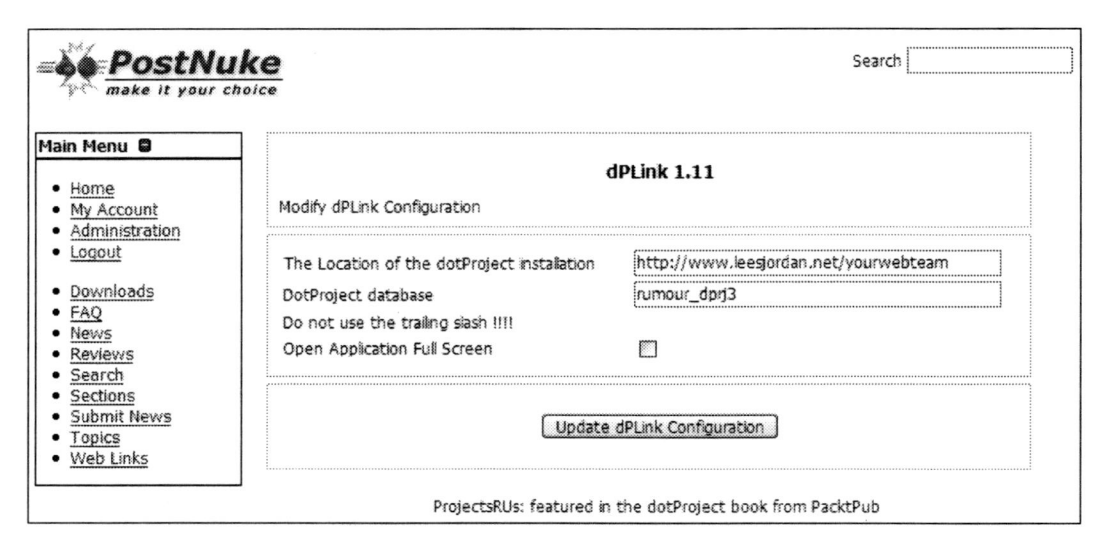

7. Go to **Blocks** under the **Administration** menu of PostNuke. Select edit by the menu block. Add a menu link with the exact URL of **{dplink}**. The bracketed text is a way **PostNuke** links to modules internally. The {dplink} will be parsed by PostNuke and the actual link will be automatically created for you. It is important at this point to determine how you want users to continue to log in to dotProject. If you want them to still be able to log in to dotProject outside of PostNuke, go to the **System Configuration** screen and check the box by **Postnuke login also allows Standard Login**.

8. Log in to dotProject as an administrator and navigate to the **System Configuration** settings from within the **System Admin** module. Select **postnuke** as the `login_authenication` method.

LDAP Settings

> **LDAP Authentication**
> Versions of dotProject 2.0 and greater allow administrators to set up LDAP authentication instead of using the default SQL database authentication.

Html File Indexing Parser	/usr/bin/strings (?)
PDF Indexing Parser	/usr/bin/pdftotext (?)
Preserve File Settings on CI	☑ (?)
Allow Editing of Previous Versions	☐ (?)
Memory Limit for Gantt	8M (?)
User Authentication Settings	
User Authentication Method	Standard dotProject (?)
Postnuke login also allows Standard Login	☑ (?)
LDAP Settings	
LDAP Host	localhost (?)
LDAP Port	389 (?)
LDAP Version	3 (?)
LDAP Base DN	dc=saki,dc=com,dc=au (?)
LDAP User Filter	(uid=%USERNAME%) (?)
LDAP Search User	Manager (?)
LDAP Search User Password	****** (?)
LDAP also allows standard login	☑ (?)

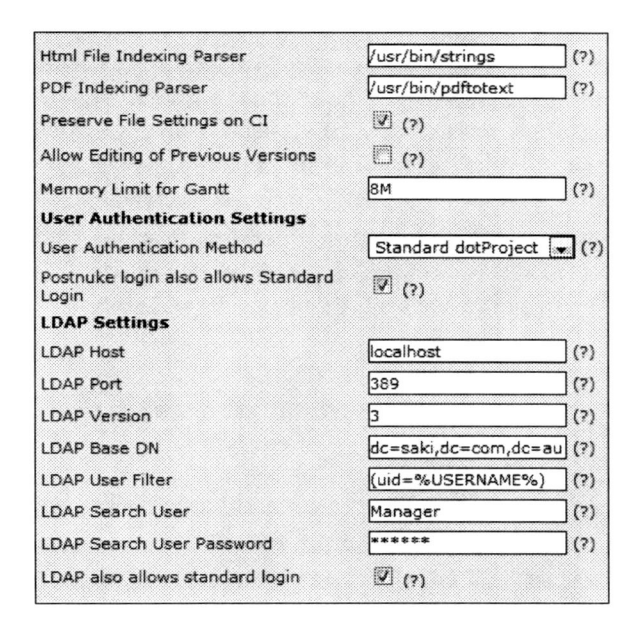

Special variables in the **System Configuration** screen as shown in the previous screenshot several pages back, must be set in order for LDAP authentication to work properly with dotProject.

A list of each variable followed by brief description is below:

- `auth_method` — Must be set to **ldap** on the LDAP server in order for dotProject users to be authenticated.
- `ldap_host` — Should be set to the hostname or IP address of the LDAP Server to be contacted for authentication of users. The default setting is localhost.
- `ldap_port` — The port number of the LDAP service. The default (port 389) is appropriate for most configurations where there is no concern about possible security breaches related to using the default port.
- `ldap_version` — The version of LDAP being used should be set here. The correct version will depend upon which directory system is being used. LDAP Version 3 is the default support version for OpenLDAP. The version might have to be changed to integrate properly with the directory system being used. If you receive a protocol error, change the version number. The default is 3, which should work in most cases.
- `ldap_base_dn` — This setting will be different for different LDAP installations. It searches for users of dotProject. The LDAP bind authentication process also uses this variable.
- `ldap_user_filter` — LDAP entries are found by using this filter. Like many of the other variables the actual setting relies upon which LDAP installation is being used. The default filter works under the assumption that each user will have a posixAccount object class from the NIS schema (default is `(uid=NaV)`). The string `NaV` should be used to indicate where the username parameter should be applied. In some cases when the default string does not work, the string `(uid=%USERNAME%)` may work instead.
- `ldap_search_user` — This variable represents the Full DN of the user the administrator wants to bind as for searching purposes. Make sure the user chosen has permission to search the users directory.

> DN is the acronym for Distinguished Name.

- `ldap_search_pass` — The search user password is represented here.
- `ldap_allow_login` (Allow standard logins) — It is recommended that this setting be used so that SQL users as well as those in the LDAP system can log in.

LDAP users will be able to log in to dotProject after the system configuration variables are properly set. Users are given the default role of "Anonymous" by the system. Administrators will need to alter permissions for users in the **User Admin** module. **Roles** or customized access can be set.

To learn more about LDAP, consult the documentation of your current installation or visit http://www.openldap.org/doc/admin23/quickstart.html for more information about how LDAP works.

The following email configuration settings depend upon whether the administrator wants to use the default PHP mail settings or an SMTP server. **SMTP** stands for **Simple Mail Transfer Protocol.** Check with your email administrator or Internet service provider if you are not sure which settings to use.

Email Settings

The email settings for dotProject consists of email transport and SMTP settings.

Email Transport

Select PHP Default or SMTP, depending on whether there is an SMTP server available to transport and process the email.

SMTP Host

When using PHP Default this should be set to **localhost**. It should contain the host name of the SMTP server if using SMTP.

SMTP Port

The standard port used for SMTP is 25. This is the default setting and will usually work fine unless a different port has been reserved by the email administrator.

Host Requires Login

If your email host requires authentication, this box will need to be selected.

SMTP Username, SMTP Password

If host authentication is selected, enter the username and password in their respective text fields. These fields are usually left blank.

Queue Email for Later Sending

Mail can be sent later instead of immediately upon creation. The best practice is to keep this option unselected. Selecting the option will require setting the **Scan Event Queue** option in **Session Handling**.

SMTP Server Timeout

The variable in the **SMTP Server Timeout** text field shows the time in seconds dotProject will wait before declaring a time-out and stating failure to contact the SMTP server.

Session Handling Settings

This extends the session handling of PHP to beyond browser-based sessions and stores the session information in the database. This allows for prolonged sessions with lower overheads.

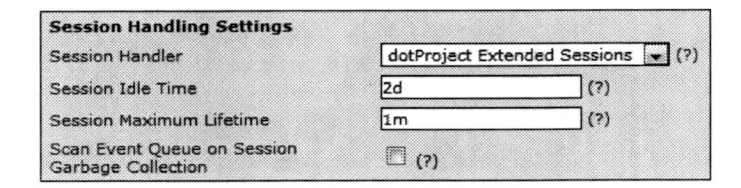

Session Handler

Administrators can choose from **PHP Default** or **dotProject Extended Sessions** for their session handling. **dotProject Extended Sessions** is active by default. It allows dotProject to use the database when handling sessions. The best practice is to use dotProject Extended Session handling.

Session Idle Time

Sessions have a maximum idle time in dotProject. For security purposes, it is a good practice to restrict session idle time to no more than 10 hours or the average period of time a user is expected to be logged in. Idle time is the amount of time before the session is considered to be inactive. Values for this text field are set in seconds but can be appended with letters. Only one character can be included in a string. This means that while the maximum number of days can be set, the maximum number of days and hours cannot. 1d2h is an invalid entry. 26h is a valid entry for the text field.

The characters used to indicate days, hours, months, and years are as follows:

- h = hours
- d = days
- m = months
- y = years

Session Maximum Lifetime

The maximum amount of time before a session is ended by the dotProject application, no matter what time is set in the **Session Idle Time** field. The lower the number, the better it is. The default is one month. It is a best practice to limit this to no longer than one week (7d).

Scan Event Queue on Session Garbage Collection

This checkbox should be selected if the administrator needs to queue email for later sending.

Task Reminder Settings

These are email reminders set for a task.

Send Task Reminders

Users will be reminded every day that a task is due until the task is completed. This is unchecked by default.

Number of Days Warning for Due Tasks

The value in this field will determine how many days beforehand a user will be reminded of a due task. The default value is 1.

Maximum Number of Reminders to Send

The total number of reminders to be sent about a task can be set here. 100 is a large number. I recommend setting this value no higher than 25.

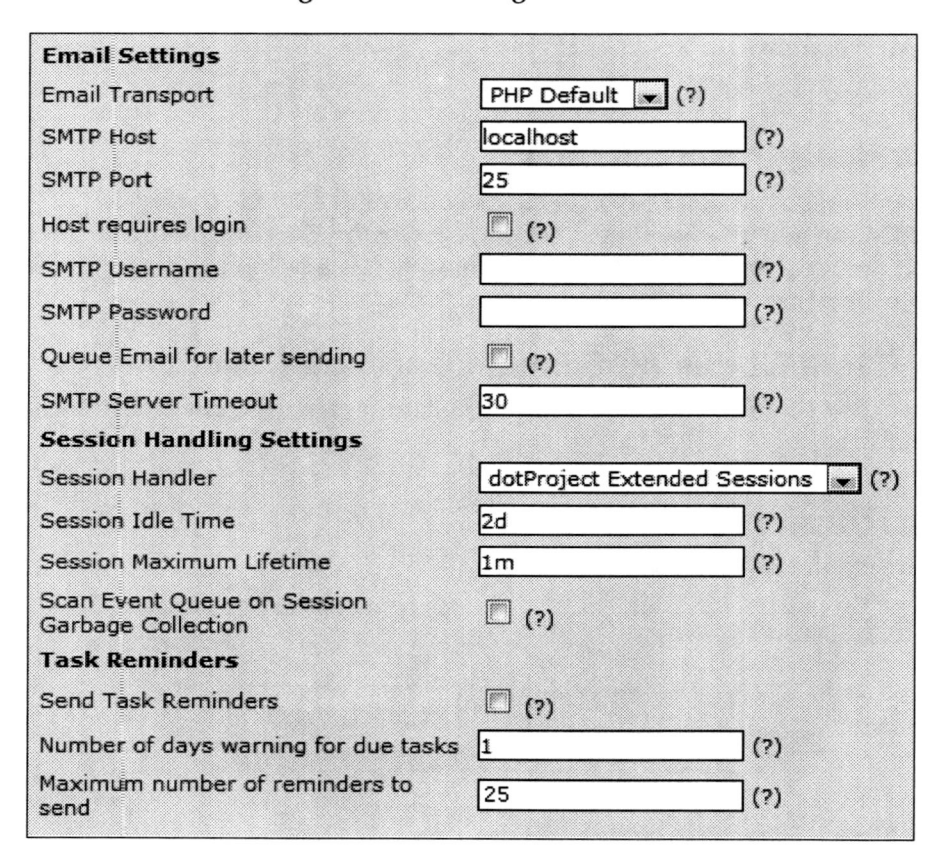

Email Settings	
Email Transport	PHP Default (?)
SMTP Host	localhost (?)
SMTP Port	25 (?)
Host requires login	☐ (?)
SMTP Username	(?)
SMTP Password	(?)
Queue Email for later sending	☐ (?)
SMTP Server Timeout	30 (?)
Session Handling Settings	
Session Handler	dotProject Extended Sessions (?)
Session Idle Time	2d (?)
Session Maximum Lifetime	1m (?)
Scan Event Queue on Session Garbage Collection	☐ (?)
Task Reminders	
Send Task Reminders	☐ (?)
Number of days warning for due tasks	1 (?)
Maximum number of reminders to send	25 (?)

Click the **Save** button to finish editing the System Preferences.

Default User Preferences

The **Edit User Preferences** screen allows administrators to set global preferences for users. Think of it as how the user will experience dotProject. You can change the **User Interface**, select a different locale, alter the date and time formats, and more. The changes are all fairly intuitive. I will mention again that if a new language pack has been added, and you want to now use it as the default, it should be chosen as the **Locale** on the **Edit User Preferences** screen.

We will discuss the **User Preference** items in detail. However, certain tabs like date, time, and currency have been exempted as these are self-explanatory:

- **Locale**: The default language setting for dotProject installations is English with a locale of English (Aus). The requisite changes can be made by selecting a language from the drop-down list.
- **Tabbed Box View** controls whether all users see tabs, flat links, or either in all areas of dotProject that display links as tabs. The **Projects** list and Task submenu below the main content area are examples of modules in dotProject that display links with tabs, plain links, or display tabs by default and give the user a link to switch to flat list view.
- **User Task Assignment Maximum** sets the maximum percentage of a task a user can be assigned to. This can be set for all users here. If users have been created after this value is set, they can override it if they have edit access to their personal user preferences.

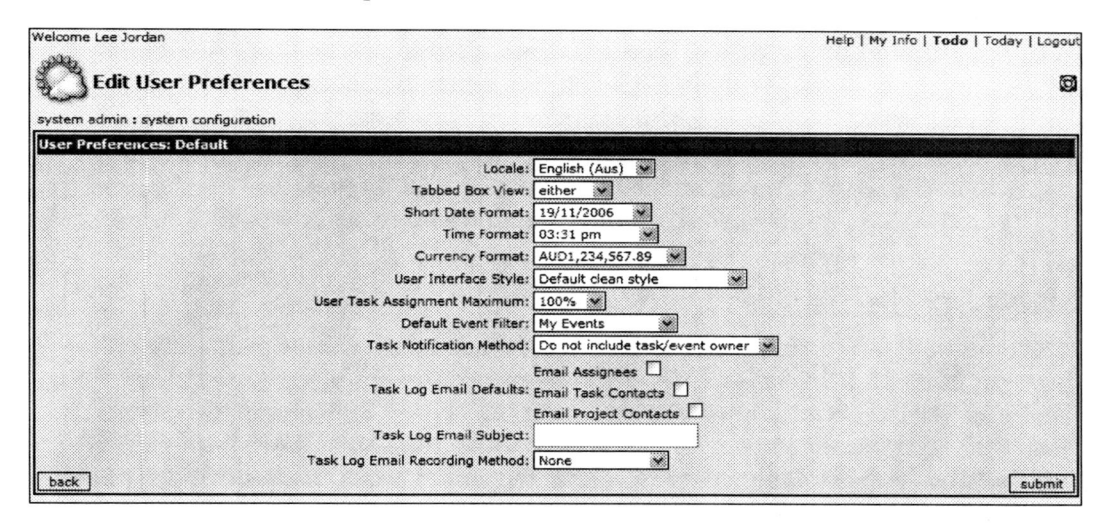

The **User Task Assignment Maximum** setting controls what percentage of a task any user can be assigned. It is useful to change this setting if most project workers will not be responsible for 100% of a task. For smaller teams, keeping the setting at the default 100% will work just fine.

- **Default Event Filter**: The event filter has a default setting of **My Events** on installation. Administrators can change the setting to **Events created** or **All Events** as well. Which filter setting to choose depends upon which makes sense for users in the organization.

- **Task Notification Method**: The **Task Notification Method** gives the administrator the option to have the task/event owner notified along with all other task assignees. The default setting is to not include the owner.
- **Task Log Preferences**: The **Task Log Preferences** are a series of settings that control different features of the **Task Log**. They may be left as is or leveraged to keep a more detailed record of email records related to tasks.
- **Task Log Email Defaults**: The **Task Log Email Defaults** is a series of three checkboxes. They are all unchecked by default. Checking any of the boxes causes an email to be sent automatically. Users who do not want an email sent when a task is managed will need to uncheck the notify box on the individual task.
    - **Email Assignees**
    - **Email Task Contacts**
    - **Email Project Contacts**
- **Task Log Email Subject**: You can include an email subject for task logs by typing it into the text field provided. This subject will be included in every task email sent out, so it should be generic enough to be appropriate for all tasks.
- **Task Log Email Recording Method**: There are two choices for recording email task logs: **None**, which is the default, and **Append to Log**. **Append to Log** will make a record of who the email was sent to for a particular task.

Lookup Values

Have you been wondering where to change the names in various drop-down lists throughout the dotProject application? **System Lookup Values** is the place to change values for select lists and other system lookup key types. The information listed on tabs in the **Companies** screen (**Client**, **Guest**, **Supplier**, **Consultant**, **Government**, and **Internal**) is controlled here. Notice that the values contain a number separated from a text phrase. The number values tell the dotProject code the size and order of the list the items are put into. Programmers will recognize these as key-value pairs.

Before any changes are made, the administrator should make sure that the database and installation of dotProject have been backed up. Appendix A contains details on backing up your dotProject installation.

Important information about **System Lookup Values**:

- Any changes made could possibly be overwritten by an upgrade to dotProject, or by installation of add-on modules.
- Changes to any titles must be made also in the PHP code of dotProject. This will be done through a find/replace of the code.

Modifying the values must follow a specific 'number|value name' format as seen in the following screenshot:

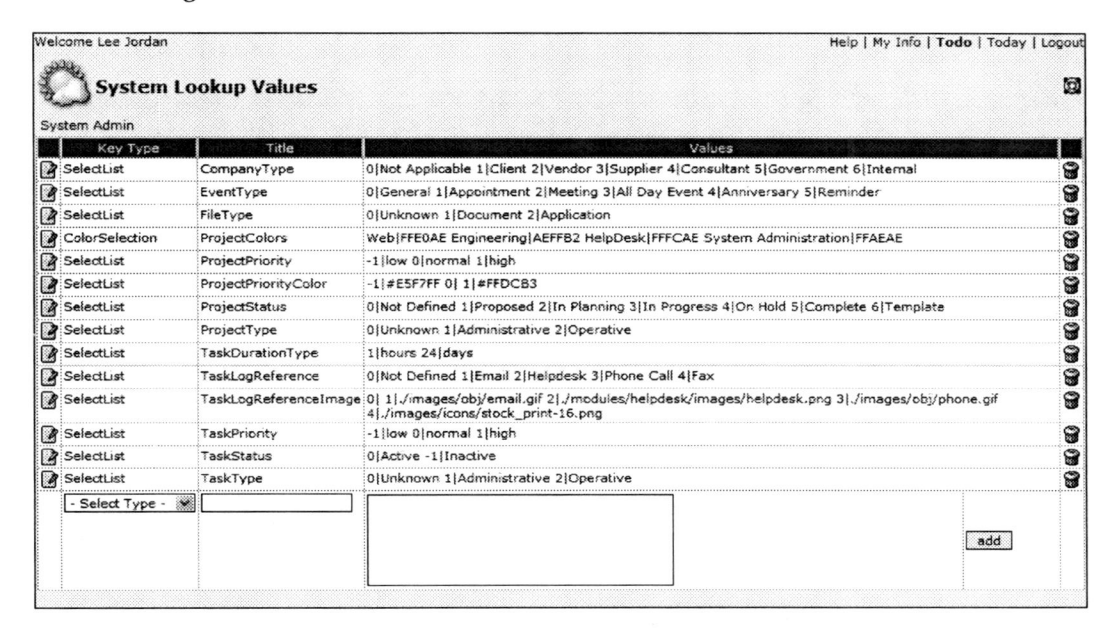

- The syntax is n|somevaluename. It can also be reversed as shown in the following example.

    In **ColorSelection** the **Lookup Value** controls preset color values for the **Project** colors. They can be changed to fit the organizational structure and color preferences. The default values are:

    Web|FFE0AE
    Engineering|AEFFB2
    HelpDesk|FFFCAE
    System Administration|FFAEAE

    They can be changed by clicking on the pencil icon to the left of the field row.

    Typing in the following exactly as shown in the value column will alter the preset color values:

    Creative|F0F0FF
    Engineering|AEFFB2
    Marketing|003366
    System Administration|FFAEAE
    Project Management|66FF99

Click the **edit** button when the changes are complete.

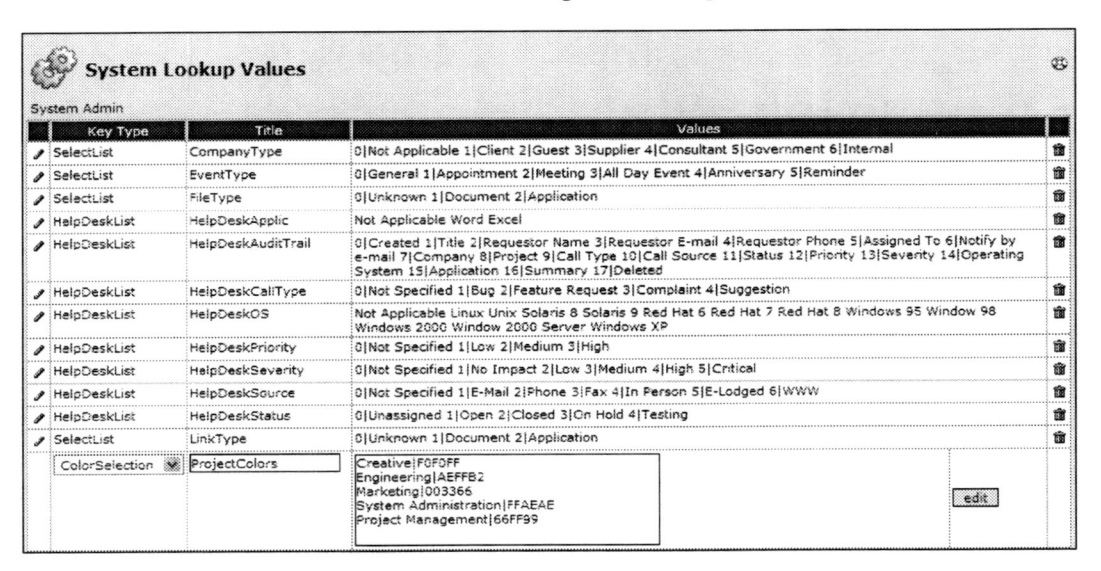

Key Type	Title	Values
SelectList	CompanyType	0|Not Applicable 1|Client 2|Guest 3|Supplier 4|Consultant 5|Government 6|Internal
SelectList	EventType	0|General 1|Appointment 2|Meeting 3|All Day Event 4|Anniversary 5|Reminder
SelectList	FileType	0|Unknown 1|Document 2|Application
HelpDeskList	HelpDeskApplic	Not Applicable Word Excel
HelpDeskList	HelpDeskAuditTrail	0|Created 1|Title 2|Requestor Name 3|Requestor E-mail 4|Requestor Phone 5|Assigned To 6|Notify by e-mail 7|Company 8|Project 9|Call Type 10|Call Source 11|Status 12|Priority 13|Severity 14|Operating System 15|Application 16|Summary 17|Deleted
HelpDeskList	HelpDeskCallType	0|Not Specified 1|Bug 2|Feature Request 3|Complaint 4|Suggestion
HelpDeskList	HelpDeskOS	Not Applicable Linux Unix Solaris 8 Solaris 9 Red Hat 6 Red Hat 7 Red Hat 8 Windows 95 Window 98 Windows 2000 Window 2000 Server Windows XP
HelpDeskList	HelpDeskPriority	0|Not Specified 1|Low 2|Medium 3|High
HelpDeskList	HelpDeskSeverity	0|Not Specified 1|No Impact 2|Low 3|Medium 4|High 5|Critical
HelpDeskList	HelpDeskSource	0|Not Specified 1|E-Mail 2|Phone 3|Fax 4|In Person 5|E-Lodged 6|WWW
HelpDeskList	HelpDeskStatus	0|Unassigned 1|Open 2|Closed 3|On Hold 4|Testing
SelectList	LinkType	0|Unknown 1|Document 2|Application
ColorSelection	ProjectColors	Creative|F0F0FF Engineering|AEFFB2 Marketing|003366 System Administration|FFAEAE Project Management|66FF99

Since the changes may not be permanent, it is usually not worth it to change the values or titles unless doing so has a definite benefit for the users.

Custom Fields

Need to store company information different from what is provided by default in dotProject? Do your projects, tasks, or calendar events require that specialized information be collected or shared? Custom Fields give administrators a way to add additional form fields to specific areas of dotProject.

Custom Fields can be added to:

- **Companies**
- **Projects**
- **Tasks**
- **Calendar Events**

Adding a custom field is a simple, six-step process. After the information surrounding the purpose of the field has been gathered and approved, the administrator goes to the **System Administration** screen and clicks on the **Custom field editor** link.

Let's add a custom field to the **Projects** module. Currently, there is no way to know if a client has approved overtime, paid for a rush job, or made other special requests unless that information has been added to the files or the description. We'll add a special form field to notify project workers when special circumstances apply to a project.

1. The first step to adding a new field is to navigate to the **Custom Field Editor** from the **System Administration** screen. When the **Custom Field Editor** screen appears you will see multiple choices for custom fields divided into sections by module. Click on the **Add a new Custom field to this Module** under the **Projects** section.

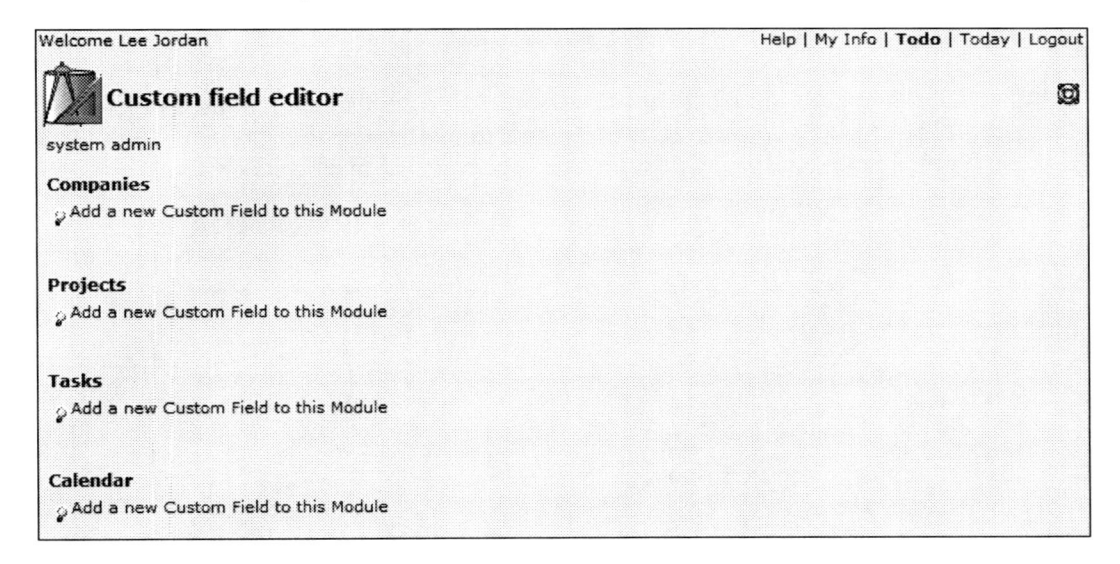

```
Welcome Lee Jordan                                    Help | My Info | Todo | Today | Logout

    Custom field editor
system admin

Companies
  Add a new Custom Field to this Module


Projects
  Add a new Custom Field to this Module


Tasks
  Add a new Custom Field to this Module


Calendar
  Add a new Custom Field to this Module
```

2. In the **Custom Fields** screen, type in a unique field name in the **New Custom Field** in **Projects** module. It is important that the name still be descriptive enough to identify the new field. The name should be short and use only alphanumeric characters. Any spaces or punctuation used will be removed by the editor. This field will be hidden from the user. Let's give it the descriptive code name **CustomScripting**.

3. Next, type in the **Field Description**. This text will appear next to the form field as a label. We will label this field **Custom Scripting**.

Administering dotProject

4. Choose a field display type. Here we are selecting the type of input box we want. The process for all but the select list is the same. Select lists will have a separate entry field for each item in the drop-down list. We are creating a checkbox, so no special item entry field will appear.

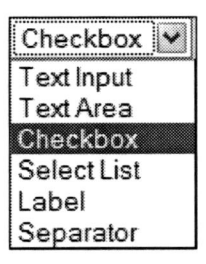

5. The HTML tag options section is meant to add additional styling using HTML. I have found through experimentation that it does not work reliably. A better practice is to add tags to the description box or use CSS tags and add them to the style sheet in the dotProject installation.

6. Click the **submit** button.

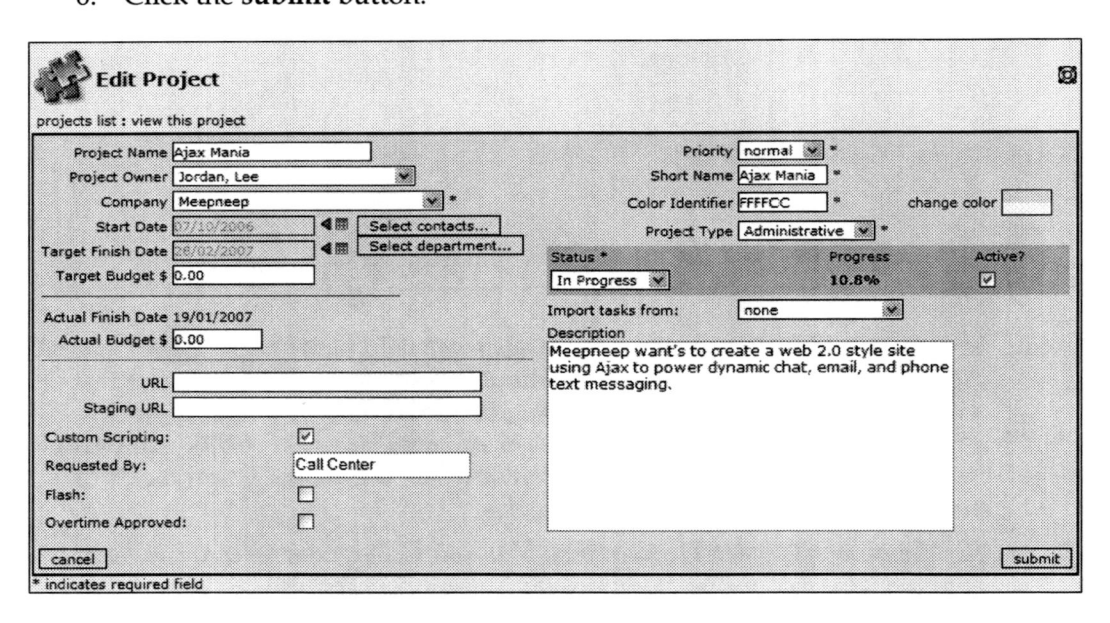

The custom field has now been added to the **Project** module. The custom field checkbox **Custom Scripting** will be available on both add and edit forms of each project as shown in the following screenshot:

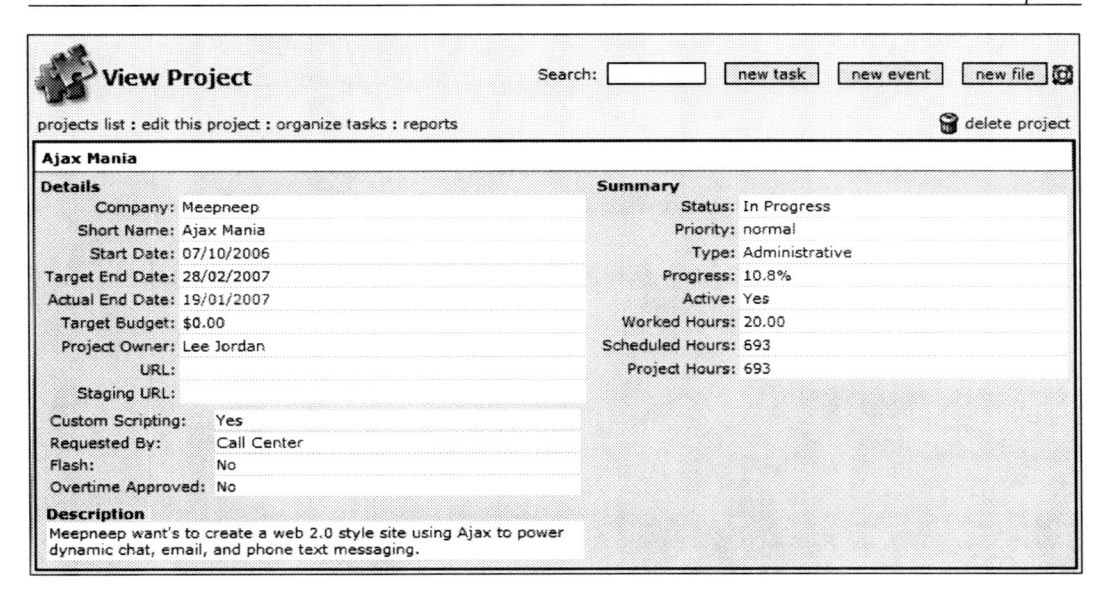

Custom Field Notes

- The new custom field will appear on all **Company**, **Project**, and **Task** screens created before the custom field was added.
- The custom field will appear in the general section of the **Company**, **Project**, **Tasks**, or **Event** screen.
- As of version 2.0.4, there is not a way to control the location where the custom field appears within a module.
- It is also not possible to create a required field using the **Custom Field** form.
- All form widgets created as a custom field will appear on the module edit screen or add screens. The actual data will appear as text information under the general section of a module's view page.

Billing Code Table

The **Billing Code Table** is located under **Preferences** on the **System Administration** screen. **Billing Codes** are customized flags used to control how project time is budgeted. There can be separate billing codes for departments, and types of work (administrative, operative, and consulting). The most common method to use is to define the codes by department for budgeting purposes. Billing codes are an optional feature of dotProject. There is no requirement to use them for projects.

Administering dotProject

To access the **Edit Billing Codes** screen, click on the **Billing Code Table** link under **Preferences**. You will see a company dropdown, and several text fields. The column for each field is described:

- **Billing Code**: Alphanumeric phrase that briefly describes the code.
- **Value**: The amount charged for the service described. This is usually an hourly amount.
- **Description**: A full descriptive phrase can be entered here to explain the purpose of the billing code.

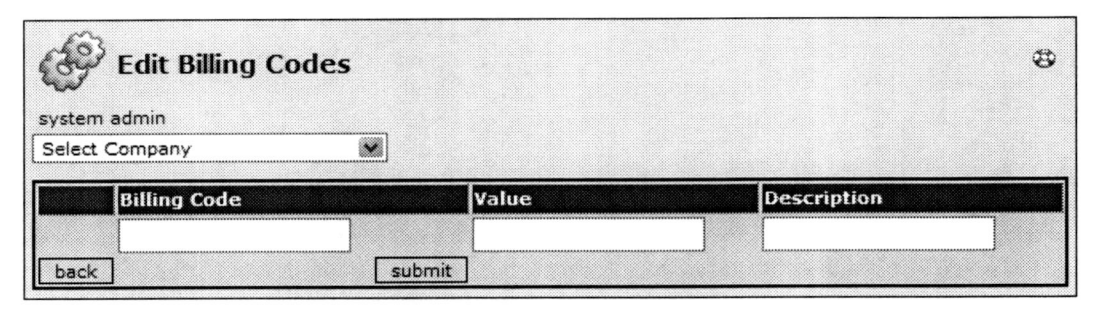

Billing codes can be specific to companies. If a company-specific billing code is required, first select the company from the drop-down list.

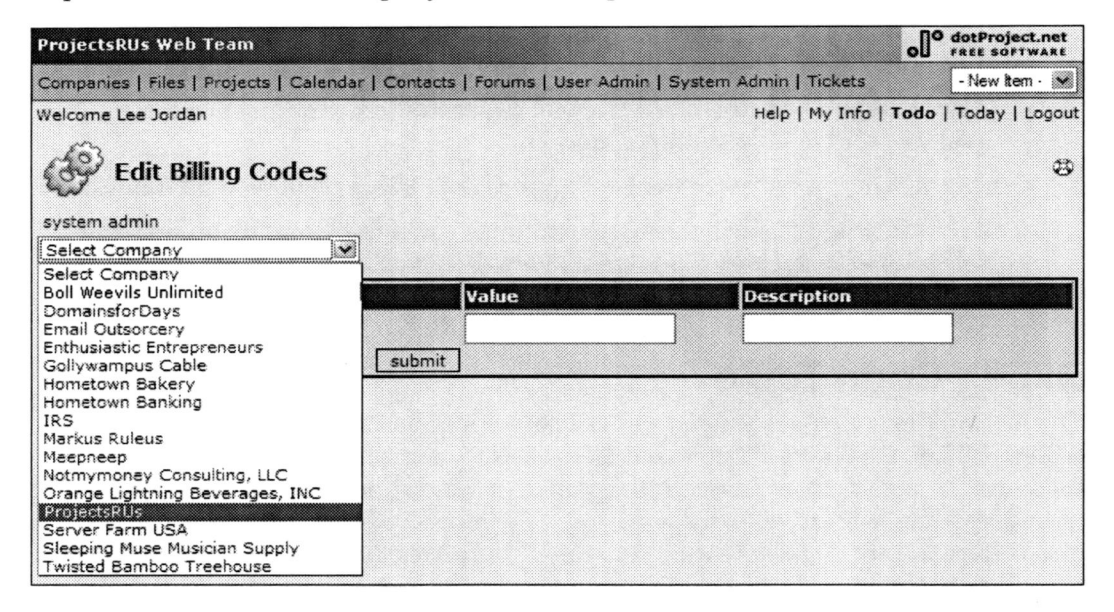

In this example the **ProjectsRUs** company has been selected. This already has a billing code for web content.

We want to add an additional billing code for our administrative staff. Notice a numerical code is now being used instead of a text string for the **Billing Code**. The value is a positive integer, 25, and the description shows what department the billing code applies to.

Once the billing code has been successfully entered by clicking the **submit** button, the screen refreshes to display the new billing code.

Module Management

Modules are very easy to administer in dotProject. If you have used a content management system such as PostNuke before, the process will be very familiar. dotProject installations have most standard modules turned on by default. Administrators can turn off unnecessary modules, activate disabled modules, and install other modules from one interface. Administrators can also determine module order from the same screen.

Installing Modules

dotProject has a group of modules listed in the **Modules** section of **System Administration** that are not installed by default. This is similar to PostNuke's method of handling **Modules**. **Modules** that are present in the system, but not yet initialized or activated are considered to be in an uninstalled state. We will install the **Smart Search** module to practice module installation.

1. To begin installation, go to the **Modules** screen under **System Administration**.
2. Click the **install** link to the right of the module.
3. The **SmartSearch** module now has a blinking yellow bubble icon with a disabled link to the right. Notice that the module can also be removed.

Administering dotProject

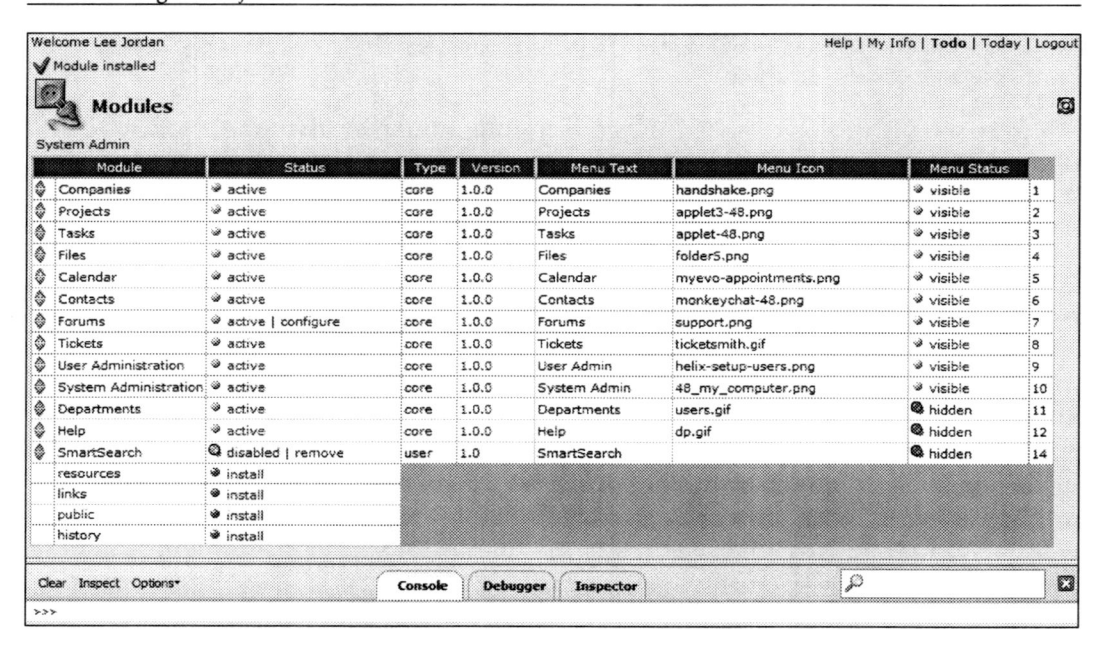

Module	Status	Type	Version	Menu Text	Menu Icon	Menu Status	
Companies	active	core	1.0.0	Companies	handshake.png	visible	1
Projects	active	core	1.0.0	Projects	applet3-48.png	visible	2
Tasks	active	core	1.0.0	Tasks	applet-48.png	visible	3
Files	active	core	1.0.0	Files	folder5.png	visible	4
Calendar	active	core	1.0.0	Calendar	myevo-appointments.png	visible	5
Contacts	active	core	1.0.0	Contacts	monkeychat-48.png	visible	6
Forums	active | configure	core	1.0.0	Forums	support.png	visible	7
Tickets	active	core	1.0.0	Tickets	ticketsmith.gif	visible	8
User Administration	active	core	1.0.0	User Admin	helix-setup-users.png	visible	9
System Administration	active	core	1.0.0	System Admin	48_my_computer.png	visible	10
Departments	active	core	1.0.0	Departments	users.gif	hidden	11
Help	active	core	1.0.0	Help	dp.gif	hidden	12
SmartSearch	disabled | remove	user	1.0	SmartSearch		hidden	14
resources	install						
links	install						
public	install						
history	install						

If you want to install a module that is not on the list, you will need to upload the file to the dotProject installation. There is no method to directly upload module files from within the dotProject application itself.

Activating Modules

Activating modules is a simple process:

1. The module is set to active by clicking on the disabled link. The link in the **Status** column will change from **disabled** to **active** and the circle will change from orange to green. Notice that the module is still hidden. Setting the module's status to **active** makes it available for users in the dotProject installation.

Chapter 5

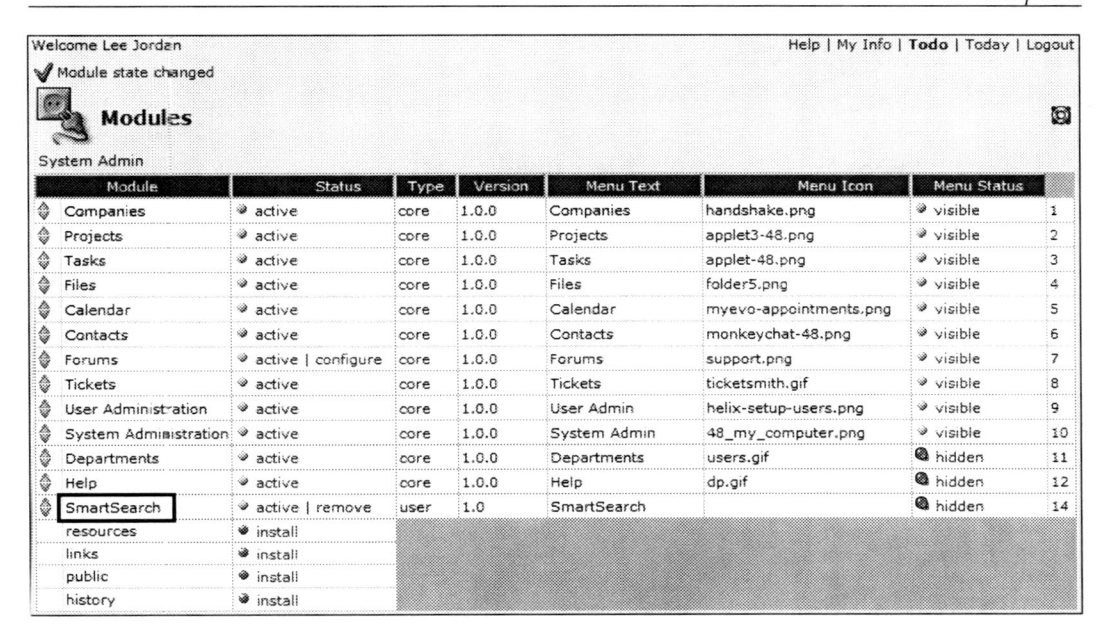

Module	Status	Type	Version	Menu Text	Menu Icon	Menu Status	
Companies	active	core	1.0.0	Companies	handshake.png	visible	1
Projects	active	core	1.0.0	Projects	applet3-48.png	visible	2
Tasks	active	core	1.0.0	Tasks	applet-48.png	visible	3
Files	active	core	1.0.0	Files	folder5.png	visible	4
Calendar	active	core	1.0.0	Calendar	myevo-appointments.png	visible	5
Contacts	active	core	1.0.0	Contacts	monkeychat-48.png	visible	6
Forums	active	configure	core	1.0.0	Forums	support.png	visible	7
Tickets	active	core	1.0.0	Tickets	ticketsmith.gif	visible	8
User Administration	active	core	1.0.0	User Admin	helix-setup-users.png	visible	9
System Administration	active	core	1.0.0	System Admin	48_my_computer.png	visible	10
Departments	active	core	1.0.0	Departments	users.gif	hidden	11
Help	active	core	1.0.0	Help	dp.gif	hidden	12
SmartSearch	active	remove	user	1.0	SmartSearch		hidden	14
resources	install						
links	install						
public	install						
history	install						

2. The **Menu Status** column indicates whether a module is visible on the main navigation menu. A green circle and the word **visible** means a link to the module is listed on the menu. If you see a red circle and the word **hidden** then the module is not shown on the menu. Click on the **hidden** link under **Menu Status** to make the module visible. It should now appear in the main navigation menu as seen in the following screenshot:

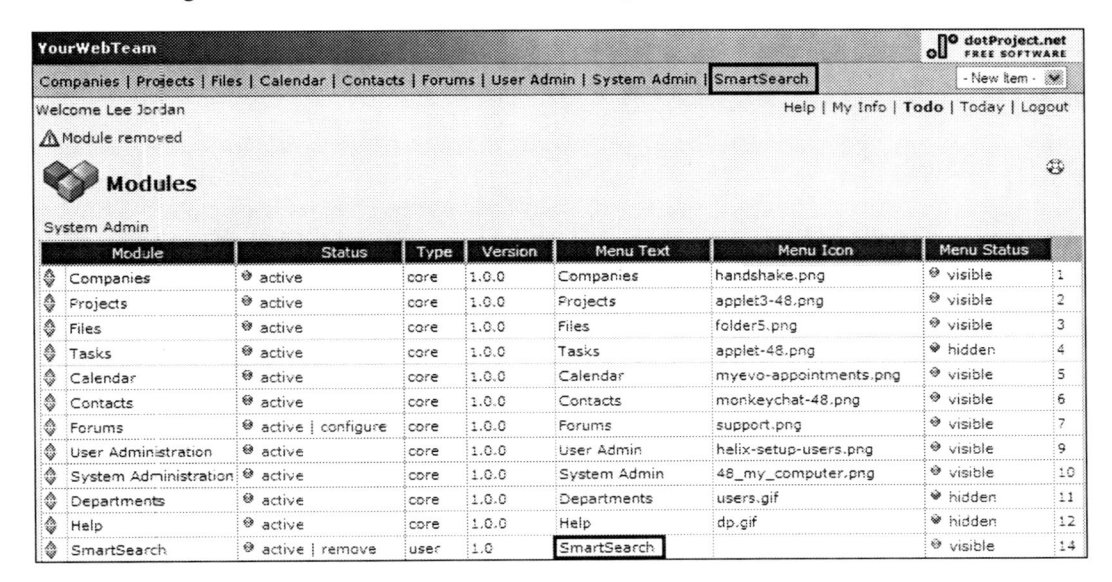

Module	Status	Type	Version	Menu Text	Menu Icon	Menu Status	
Companies	active	core	1.0.0	Companies	handshake.png	visible	1
Projects	active	core	1.0.0	Projects	applet3-48.png	visible	2
Files	active	core	1.0.0	Files	folder5.png	visible	3
Tasks	active	core	1.0.0	Tasks	applet-48.png	hidden	4
Calendar	active	core	1.0.0	Calendar	myevo-appointments.png	visible	5
Contacts	active	core	1.0.0	Contacts	monkeychat-48.png	visible	6
Forums	active	configure	core	1.0.0	Forums	support.png	visible	7
User Administration	active	core	1.0.0	User Admin	helix-setup-users.png	visible	9
System Administration	active	core	1.0.0	System Admin	48_my_computer.png	visible	10
Departments	active	core	1.0.0	Departments	users.gif	hidden	11
Help	active	core	1.0.0	Help	dp.gif	hidden	12
SmartSearch	active	remove	user	1.0	SmartSearch		visible	14

Re-Ordering Modules

Re-ordering modules in dotProject is as easy as clicking an arrow. Click on the up or down arrows to the left of a module name to move it. The module name will show up in a different location on the main navigation menu.

1. We want to move the **Files** module to a new location underneath the **Companies** module. Click the up arrow next to the **Files** module.
2. Click the arrow one more time. The **Files** module will now be located directly beneath the **Companies** module.

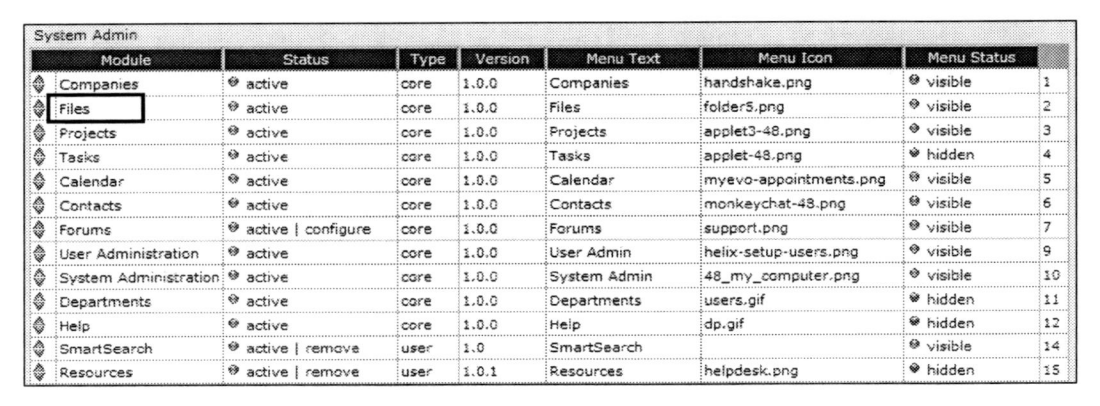

Module	Status	Type	Version	Menu Text	Menu Icon	Menu Status	
Companies	active	core	1.0.0	Companies	handshake.png	visible	1
Files	active	core	1.0.0	Files	folder5.png	visible	2
Projects	active	core	1.0.0	Projects	applet3-48.png	visible	3
Tasks	active	core	1.0.0	Tasks	applet-48.png	hidden	4
Calendar	active	core	1.0.0	Calendar	myevo-appointments.png	visible	5
Contacts	active	core	1.0.0	Contacts	monkeychat-48.png	visible	6
Forums	active	configure	core	1.0.0	Forums	support.png	visible	7
User Administration	active	core	1.0.0	User Admin	helix-setup-users.png	visible	9
System Administration	active	core	1.0.0	System Admin	48_my_computer.png	visible	10
Departments	active	core	1.0.0	Departments	users.gif	hidden	11
Help	active	core	1.0.0	Help	dp.gif	hidden	12
SmartSearch	active	remove	user	1.0	SmartSearch		visible	14
Resources	active	remove	user	1.0.1	Resources	helpdesk.png	hidden	15

The **Modules** can be ordered in any way needed, by use, alphabetically, etc. All the standard modules that are active upon dotProject installation will be listed first, then disabled modules, and then modules waiting for installation.

Administering Users

Users are administered in the **User Management** area within dotProject. The **User Management** screen can be reached by clicking on the **User Admin** link in the main navigation screen. The current users will then be displayed as well as information about their activity with dotProject.

There are several different ways for an administrator to pull up information about a user or group of users:

- Search for users by typing in a name or value into the **search** box.
- Click the **All** link next to **Show:** to display all users.
- Click one of the alphabetical links to view all users whose first name, last name, or user name begins with a particular letter of the alphabet.

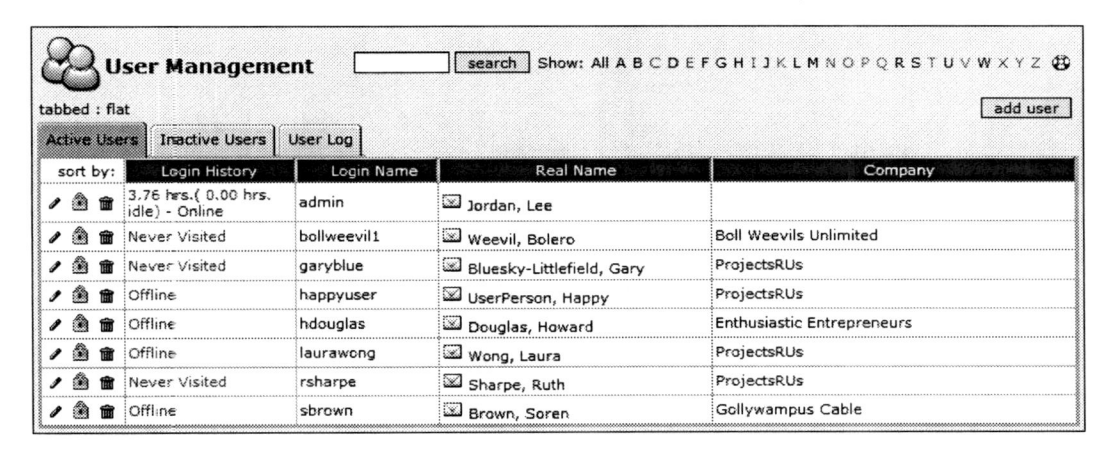

![User Management screen showing Active Users tab with list of users]

The tabbed content area allows administrators to view **Active Users**, **Inactive Users**, and **User Log**. The user log is organized by date. The default date range is the current date. Click the **submit** button to view activity under the current date, or follow these steps to specify a date range:

1. Click on the **User Log** tab.

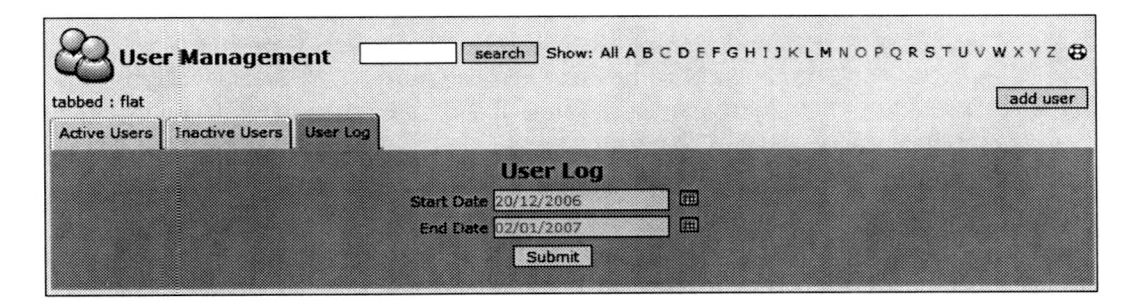

![User Management screen showing User Log tab with Start Date and End Date fields]

2. Click on the small calendar icon next to the **Start Date** to specify a different date to begin the user activity log results. The calendar will appear.
3. After a date is selected, the administrator will be returned to the **User Log** screen.
4. Follow the same process to alter the **End Date** as necessary.

5. Click the **Submit** button to view the results.

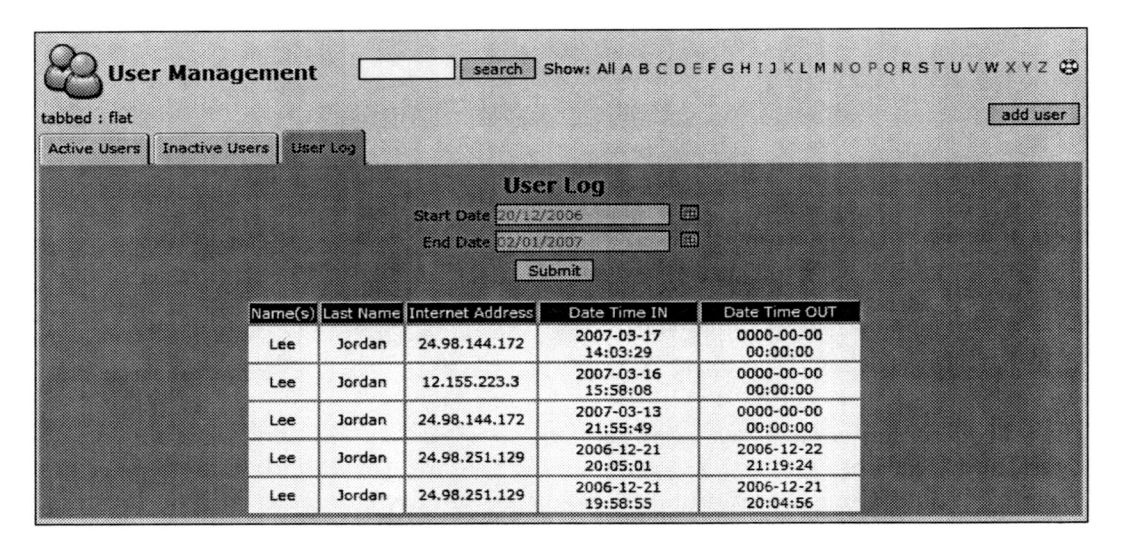

Viewing Users

The tabbed content area displays users who can then be sorted by **Login History**, **Login Name**, **Real Name**, and **Company**. The individual user information can also be viewed by clicking on the yellow lock icon in the same row as the user listing. The **View User** screen will then appear. Individual user log can then be viewed, as well as the permissions and roles for that user.

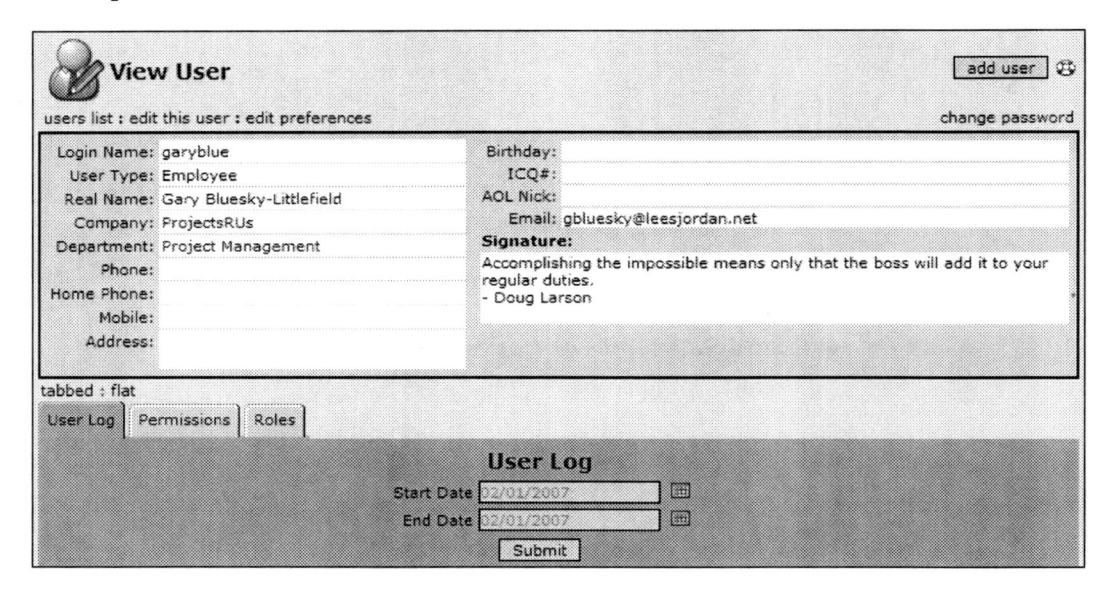

Chapter 5

Adding Users

Adding users in dotProject requires simply filling out a short form. There are additional portions of the user information that will need to be added later to the contact portion of the site.

1. To begin, click on the **Add User** button in the top right portion of the **User Management** screen. The **Add User** screen will appear.
2. All fields except the **Department** and **Email Signature** fields are required.
3. Click the **edit contact info** link if you want to go ahead and alter the contact information for the user as well.
4. Click the **submit** button when you are done.

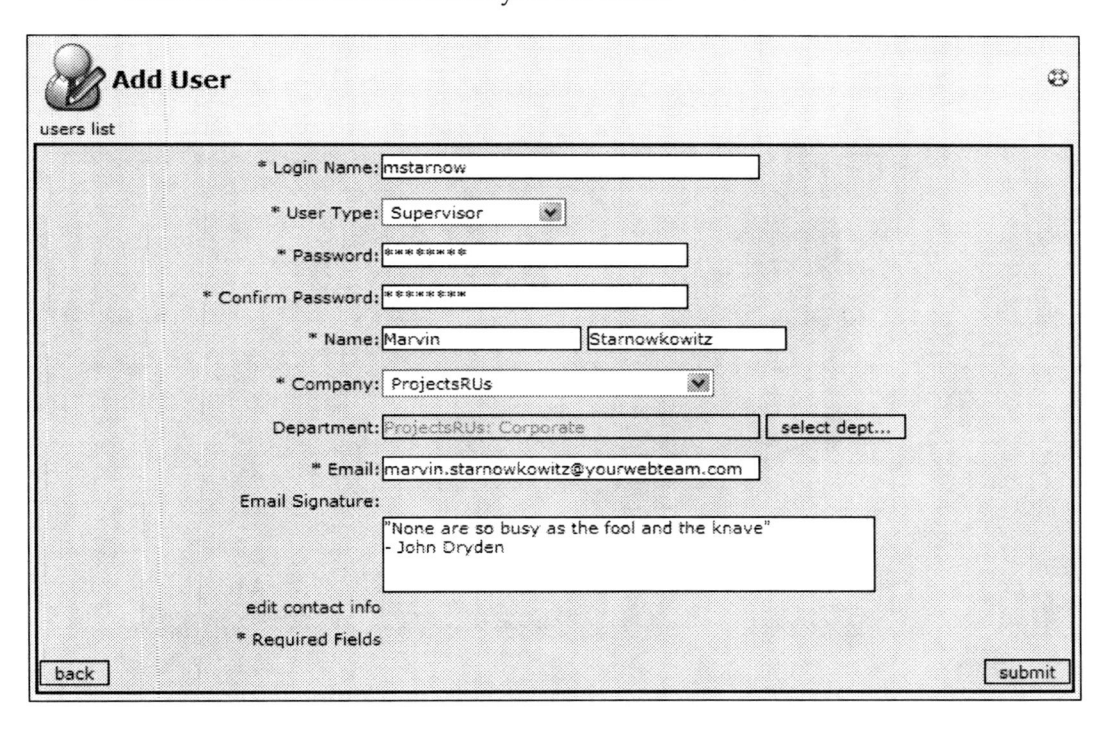

The **View User** screen will appear once the user has been added. A reminder to add permissions and roles for the user is at the top of the screen.

Editing Users

dotProject users can be edited by clicking on the notepad and pencil icon on the left side of the user listing in the **User Management** window. The **Edit User** screen is almost exactly like the **Add User** screen. Notice that the user password now is in an encrypted format. The password can still be changed. Type the password in the **Password** field, and then again in the **Confirm Password** field. Just as on the **Add User** screen, the **Department** and **Email Signature** fields are the only ones not required. **User Preferences** can be edited by clicking on the **edit preferences** link underneath the **Edit User** page title. You can also view the user by clicking on the **view this user** link in the same location.

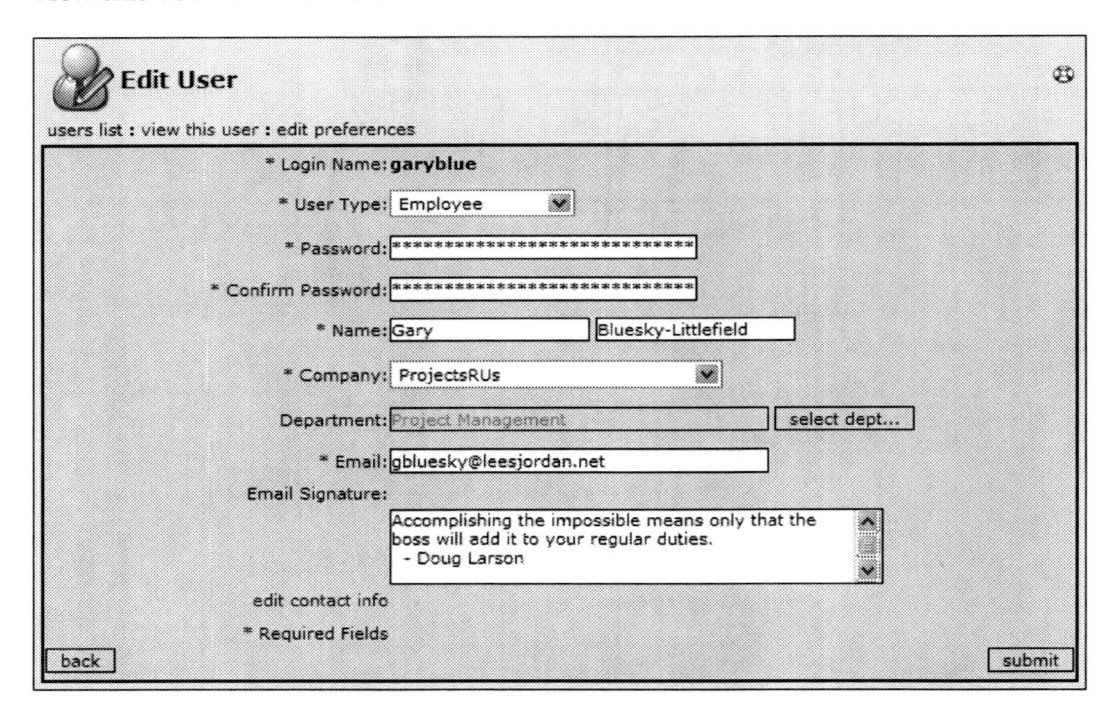

Deleting Users

It is very simple to delete users in dotProject, perhaps too simple. Once they are deleted, they are gone. dotProject will automatically reflect this change as soon as the administrator confirms the deletion. All projects the user was owner on will be assigned automatically to another user within the company. The user will be deleted from any tasks he or she was assigned to. This can cause confusion and disorganization for users. There is not a way to assign a user as a replacement for projects and tasks when the other user is deleted. You will also not be prompted to assign another user in their place.

> **An Alternative to Deleting Users**
> There is currently no option to disable a user. If you are trying to restrict or disallow user access, the best practice is limiting their permissions and altering their role. Remember that without a role assigned, a user cannot log in to dotProject.

We are going to delete a user from the **YourWebTeam** dotProject installation. Marvin Starnowkowitz has left the company, so we no longer need to keep his user listing in dotProject.

1. The trash can icon to the left of the **User** name will begin the deletion process. Click on the trash can icon to the left of Martin's listing on the **User Management** screen.
2. A pop-up window will appear asking you if you want to delete the user.
3. Click the **OK** button to confirm that the user should be deleted.

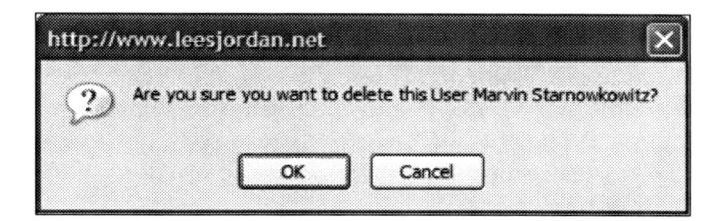

4. The **User Management** screen will reload with a special red triangle and the message **User Deleted** at the top of the screen. The user will no longer be listed under **User Management**, in any of their former projects, or as a contact.

Setting Permissions

Before getting started with permissions in dotProject, it is important to have a clear plan for managing access to dotProject. It is important to consider who will be accessing dotProject and what they will need to be able to do. The best practice when planning permissions is to set up a chart or grid containing representative users' roles, and modules. We will work through several different examples of permissions using realistic access situations.

The good news is dotProject comes with several default permission sets for users requiring different access levels. It may be that you can get away with using the default roles and not have to create any new ones. Understanding how permissions work in dotProject will give administrators the freedom to customize the environment to match their own needs.

dotProject uses a permissions system based on the open-source package phpGACL. The "php" stands for the programming language used. The **GACL** is an acronym for **Generic Access Control List**.

Roles

A user must be assigned a role as well as any other permission. Without a role, a user will not be able to log in. dotProject requires the use of roles as part of the permissions system. The roles should be determined before most users are added. Creating a chart with representative users or groups will help an administrator decide what roles need to be created and which default roles from dotProject will be used. Administrators may want to use an organization chart or have users sorted into functional groups.

Users

Every user in dotProject must be assigned a role. The user will be inactive until a role is assigned. Roles contain default permission sets. Customized permissions can be granted to individual users. These should be the exception, not the rule for ease of maintenance. Users must first be created in the **User Administration** section. As you will recall, when a user is created dotProject will automatically redirect the creator to the **View User** screen. This is the best time to go ahead and assign roles and add any other additional permissions.

Here we see that Ruth Sharpe has been assigned the role of project worker. To assign the role the following steps were taken:

1. Click on the security lock icon next to the user name under the **inactive user** tab in the **User Management** screen.
2. Click on the **Roles** tab on the **View User** screen.
3. Select a role from the drop-down list under **Add Role**.
4. Click the **add** button.
5. The role will appear on the right.
6. The user will now be able to log in to dotProject.

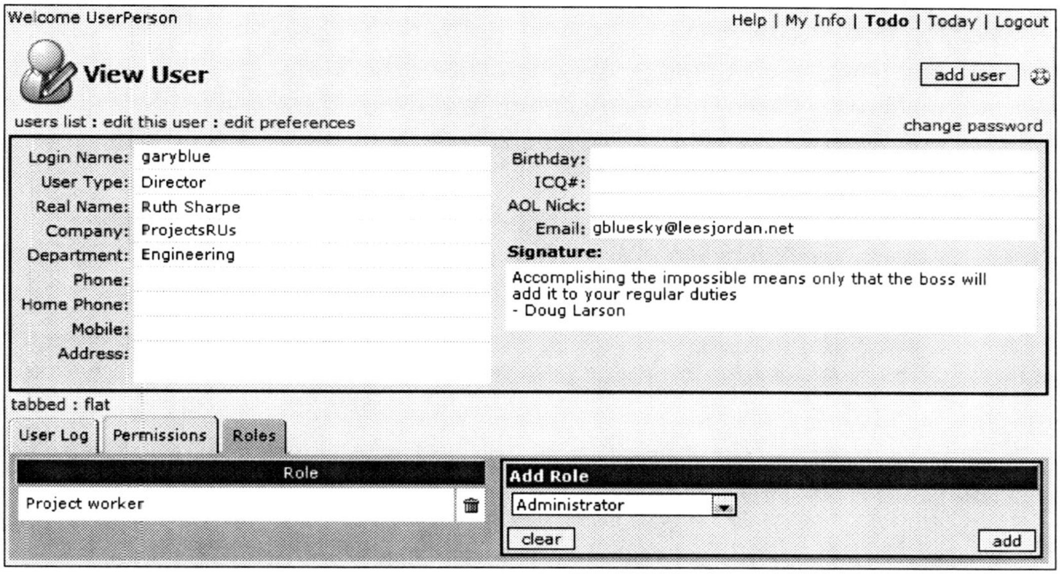

Roles are the easiest way to set up user permissions. dotProject comes with four roles by default:

- **Administrator**—Has access to all administrative and non-admin modules.
- **Anonymous**—Can view the navigation menu and various screens, cannot see any information such as projects, files, etc.
- **Guest**—Can view non-admin modules that match their company.
- **Project Worker**—Can view non-admin modules of any company, can add new projects and edit projects.

Users can have multiple roles assigned to them. Administrators can also expand the **Permissions** set by the roles. Adding permissions to specific items on the **Permissions** list will grant or deny access. **Permissions** can be set by individual module, all modules, or sets of modules.

We can get very detailed and make this a very complicated topic; using common sense and having a plan in mind when creating and assigning roles and permissions will help prevent it from being overwhelming. Thinking about what individual users need to do will keep it all in focus. We will explore other examples of roles and permissions later in the chapter under *Common Permission Setups*.

Administering dotProject

Adding New Roles

Administrators who feel limited by the default dotProject **Roles** can alter them or add their own roles. I recommend not altering the default roles unless they clash with the security standards of your organization. Instead, create new roles to customize access to your requirements.

To add a role, navigate to the **System Administration** area and choose the **User Roles** link under the **Administration** section. The **Roles** screen will display with options to **edit, view, delete,** and **add** roles.

When you are charting out permissions access, if several users require the same type of access, a custom role should probably be created for them.

To create a role:

1. Type in a role ID to represent the role. Let's use "developer" since that is the position of the users who will be using this role in the company.
2. Type in a **Description** of the role. This will also be the title of the role. We are going to use **Developer** for our new role description text.
3. Click the **add** button to add the role to the **Roles** screen.

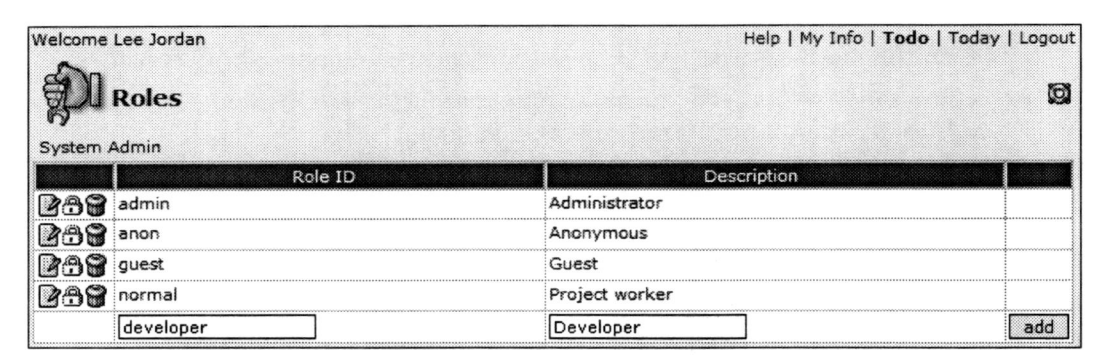

Role ID	Description	
admin	Administrator	
anon	Anonymous	
guest	Guest	
normal	Project worker	
developer	Developer	add

The role has been added, but no custom permissions have been assigned. It is as if we have created the pastry crust for a pie and not yet added the filling. It may seem strange that we do not set up the access levels when the role is created, but that is how it has been designed. It does give us a chance to reflect on what permissions we will be setting for a role.

The icons on the **Roles** screen operate a little differently than on other screens. Clicking on the notepad icon will take the administrator to a screen to edit the role ID and role description. To edit a role, administrators need to click on the security lock icon. The deletion is done by clicking on the universal trash can icon.

So we've created a role and have nothing but a new name to show for it. Let's add permissions to the role so it is ready to use. We are creating a new role called **Developer** for our dotProject installation. The developer mainly does coding and other development work. They need to be able to **view**, **add**, and **edit** the **Projects**, **Tasks**, **Files**, and the **Calendar**. They will not need the right to delete any modules.

A chart mapping out the modules, access type, and status required has been created prior to setting any permission. This is a good way to keep track of specific sets of permissions when documenting processes.

Developer Role
role id: developer description: Developer

Module	Type	Status
Projects	Access View Add Edit	Allow
Files	Access View Add Edit	Allow
Tasks	Access View Add Edit	Allow
Task Log	Access View Add Edit	Allow
Calendar	Access View Add Edit	Allow

1. Click on the security lock icon to bring up the **View Role** screen.
2. First we will add permissions to the **Projects** module. Select **Projects** from the module dropdown.
3. Set the **Access** dropdown to **Allow**. Check the **Access**, **View**, **Add**, and **Edit** checkboxes. Click the **add** button.

Administering dotProject

4. The **Projects** permission set will appear on the left side of the screen.

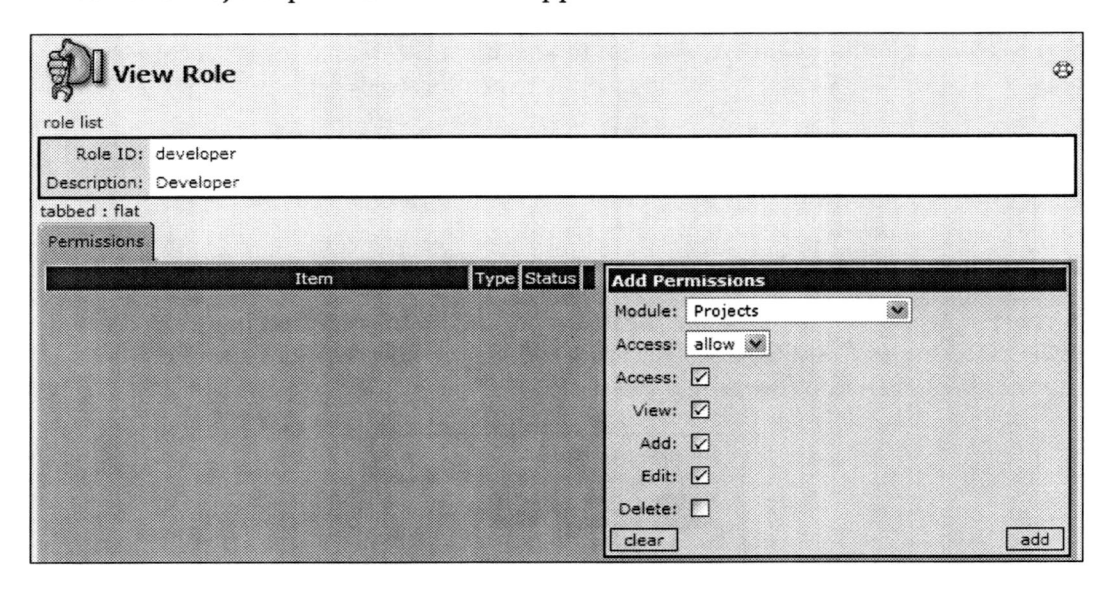

5. Repeat the process for the **Files**, **Tasks**, **Task Log**, and **Calendar** modules.

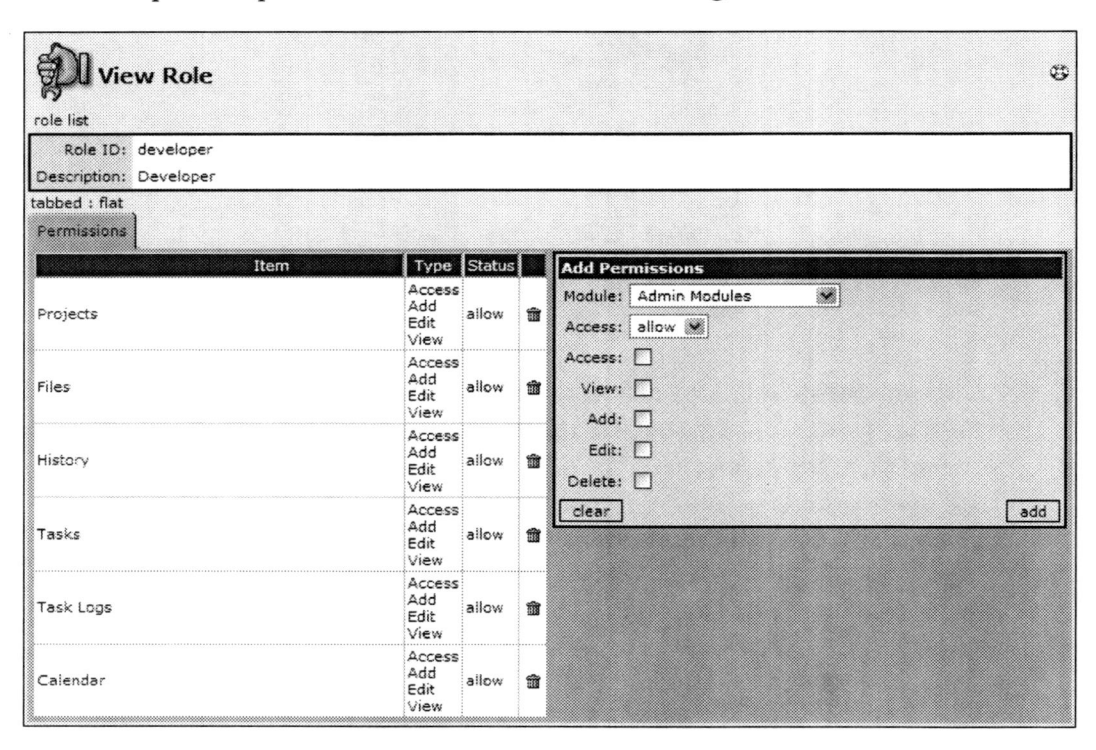

[136]

The **Developer Role** is now ready to be used for any programmers, or other users, whose roles are largely technical without administrative access.

Common Permissions Setups

Here we will explore permission setups that most administrators will need to consider when using permissions in dotProject. Don't forget that unless access to a module is specified, it is denied by default. dotProject permissions are designed with a focus on granting rights instead of taking them away in order to set permissions. The only situations where administrators should need to deny access is when they are customizing a role at the user level.

Basic permissions situations include:

- Full access to all modules
- Access to administrative modules only
- Access to non-administrative modules only
- User administration access
- Restricted file viewing
- Specialized project worker access

We already worked through an example of a restricted project worker role when we created a new role called **Developer** earlier in the roles section of this chapter. Now we will take a look at examples of the basic situations most administrators encounter when setting up permissions in dotProject. These can be applied at the **User Access** level as permissions or created as specialized roles and then applied. If you know that you will use the same set of permissions repeatedly, it will save time to create a role for that permissions set.

Full Access to All Modules

ProjectsRUs has hired a new IT manager Ruth Sharpe who wants full access to dotProject. We will set up a full access role for her.

Administering dotProject

Click on the view user icon (golden lock) next to Ruth Sharpe's listing in **User Management**. The **View User** screen will appear in the same window.

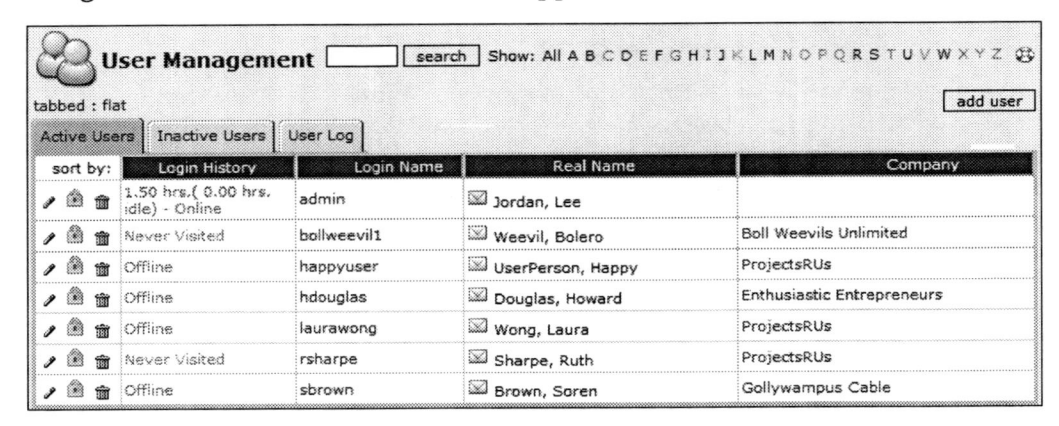

The **Permissions** tab is located below the main user listing. Click on the **Permissions** tab to begin adding permissions to Ruth's user account. Select **All Modules** on the **Module** dropdown. Leave the **Access** dropdown set to allow.

Check all boxes: **Access, Add, View, Edit,** and **Delete**. Click the **add** button to add the new permissions set to Ruth Sharpe's user listing.

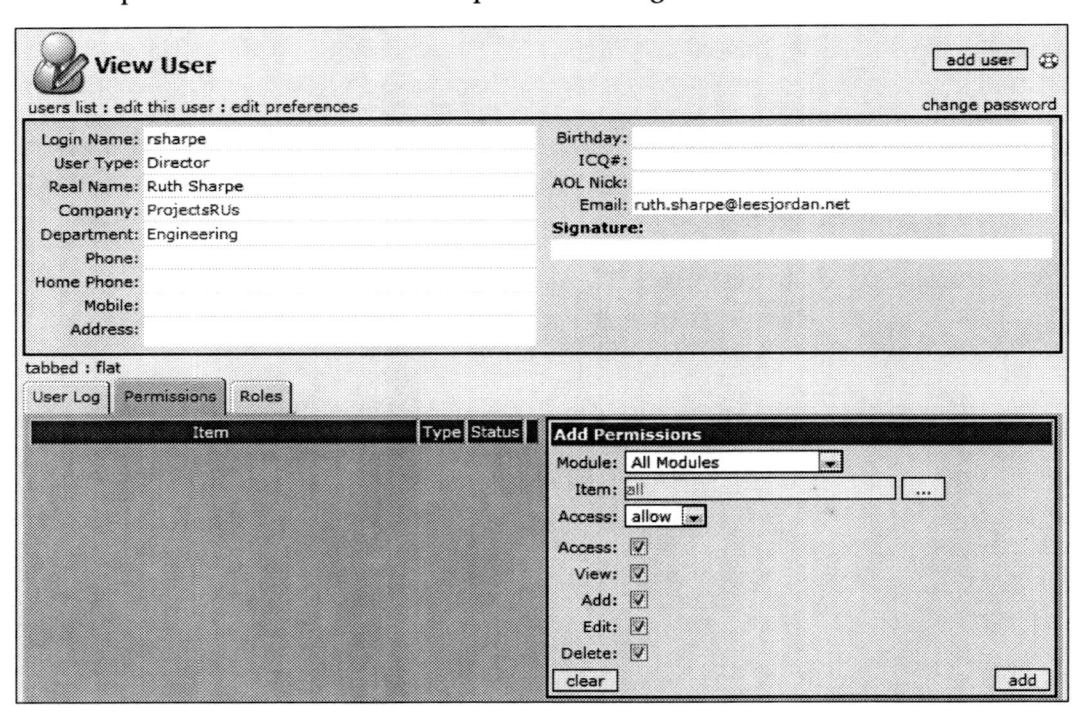

Click the **add** button to add the new permissions set to Ruth Sharpe's user listing. The new set of permissions will appear on the left side of the screen directly under the **Permissions** tab. Ruth will now have full administrative access to all modules.

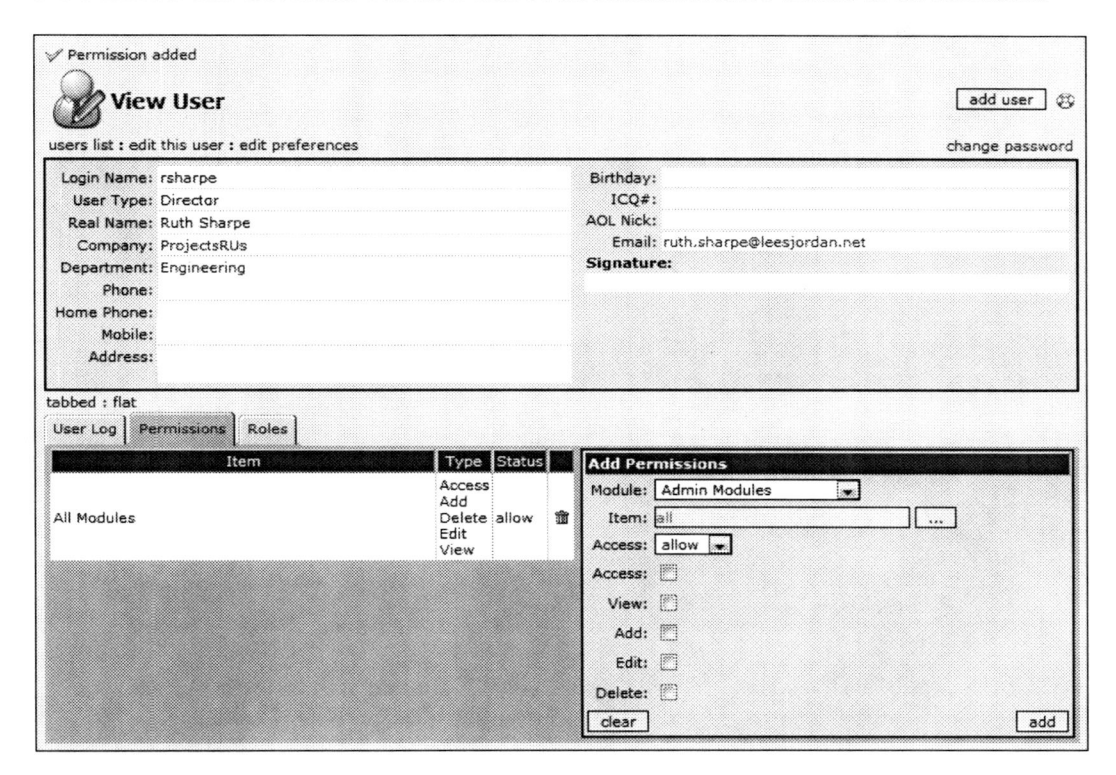

Administrative Roles

Sometimes there are users who only need access to the administrative portions of dotProject. Email administrators, IT managers, and administrators whose role is to maintain and back up the dotProject installation. They do not need to work with the projects themselves. We will create a role that will streamline user permission setup of administrative users.

Administering dotProject

Click on **User Roles** under the **Administration** section of **System Administration**.

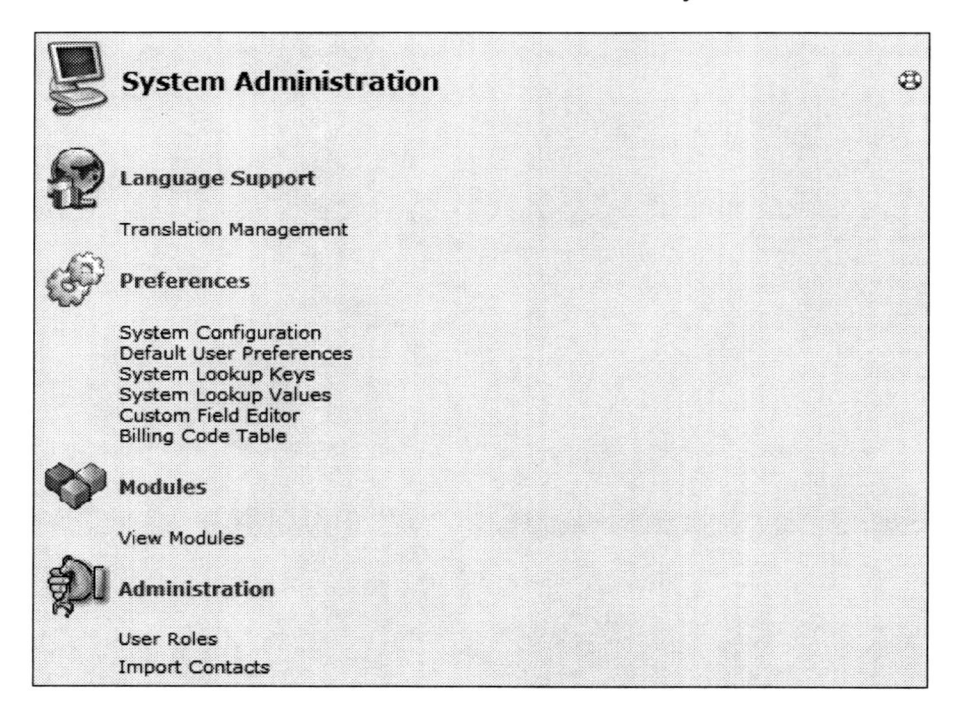

System Administration

Language Support
Translation Management

Preferences
System Configuration
Default User Preferences
System Lookup Keys
System Lookup Values
Custom Field Editor
Billing Code Table

Modules
View Modules

Administration
User Roles
Import Contacts

The **Roles** screen will appear. To add a new **User Role**, we will enter text into the form fields at the bottom of the screen. Type in a unique role ID such as **adminmodonly** in the text field contained in the **Role ID** column. Type **Admin Module Worker** in the text field at the bottom of the **Description** column. Click the **add** button to finish adding the new user role.

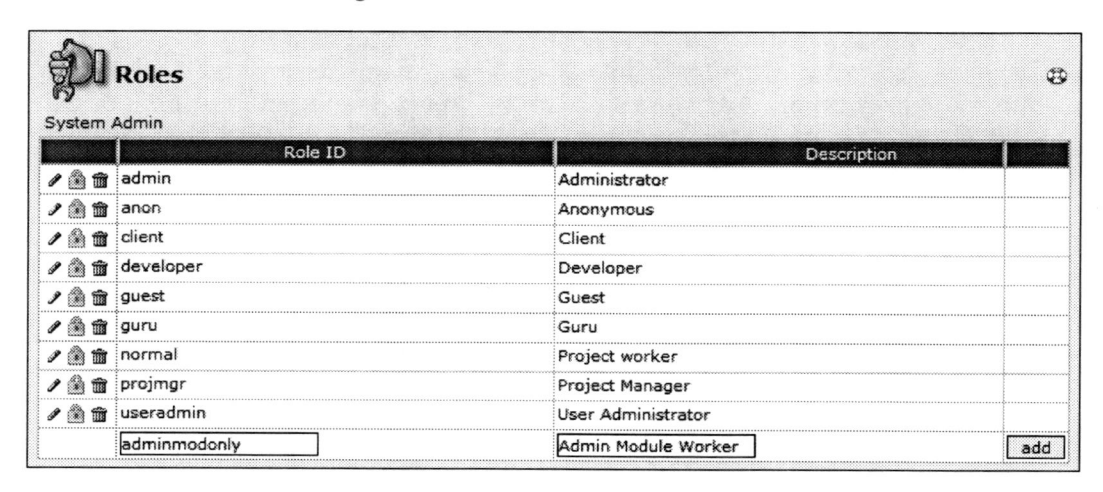

Roles

System Admin

	Role ID	Description	
	admin	Administrator	
	anon	Anonymous	
	client	Client	
	developer	Developer	
	guest	Guest	
	guru	Guru	
	normal	Project worker	
	projmgr	Project Manager	
	useradmin	User Administrator	
	adminmodonly	Admin Module Worker	add

After the **Role** screen refreshes, click on the view role icon (golden lock) to the left of the new user role to set the permissions for the **Admin Module Worker** role.

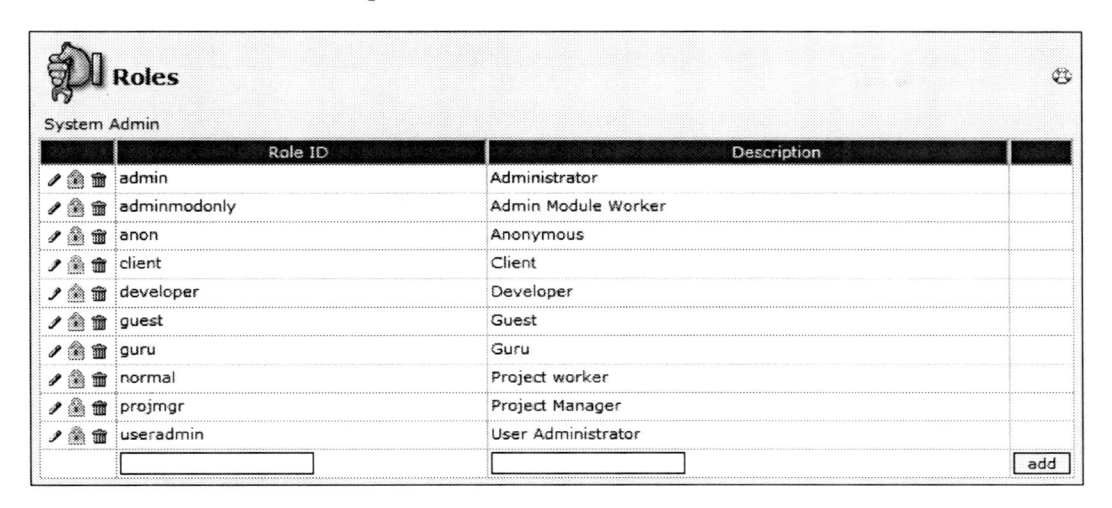

Role ID	Description
admin	Administrator
adminmodonly	Admin Module Worker
anon	Anonymous
client	Client
developer	Developer
guest	Guest
guru	Guru
normal	Project worker
projmgr	Project Manager
useradmin	User Administrator

Select **Admin Modules** from the **Module** dropdown. Leave **allow** selected on the **Access** dropdown. Check all boxes: **Access**, **Add**, **View**, **Edit**, and **Delete**. Save the changes by clicking the **add** button.

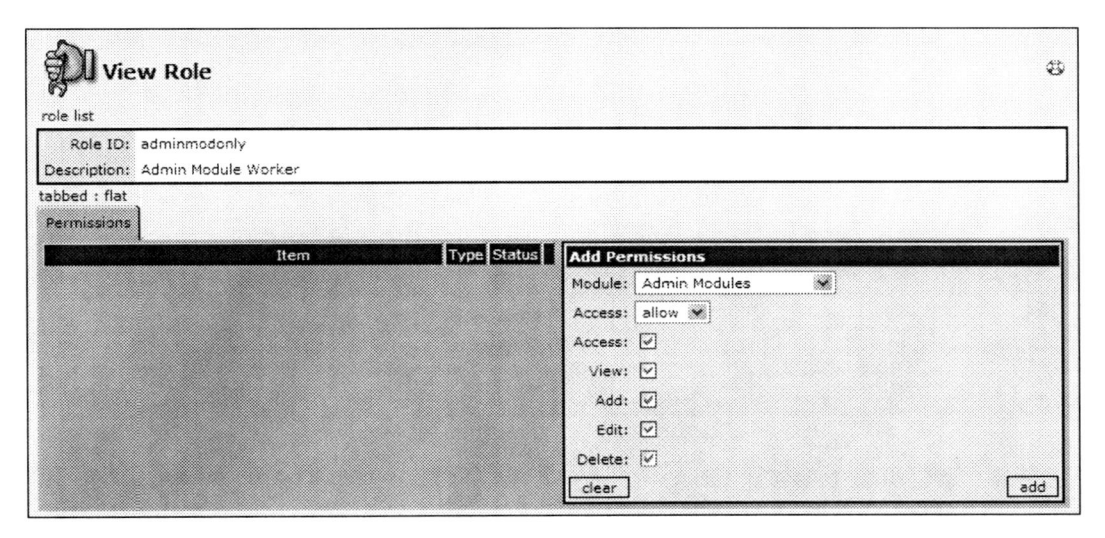

View Role

role list

Role ID: adminmodonly
Description: Admin Module Worker

tabbed : flat
Permissions

Add Permissions
- Module: Admin Modules
- Access: allow
- Access: ✓
- View: ✓
- Add: ✓
- Edit: ✓
- Delete: ✓

The **Permissions** will appear to the left of the **Add Permissions** box directly under the **Permissions** tab as shown in the following screenshot.

Administering dotProject

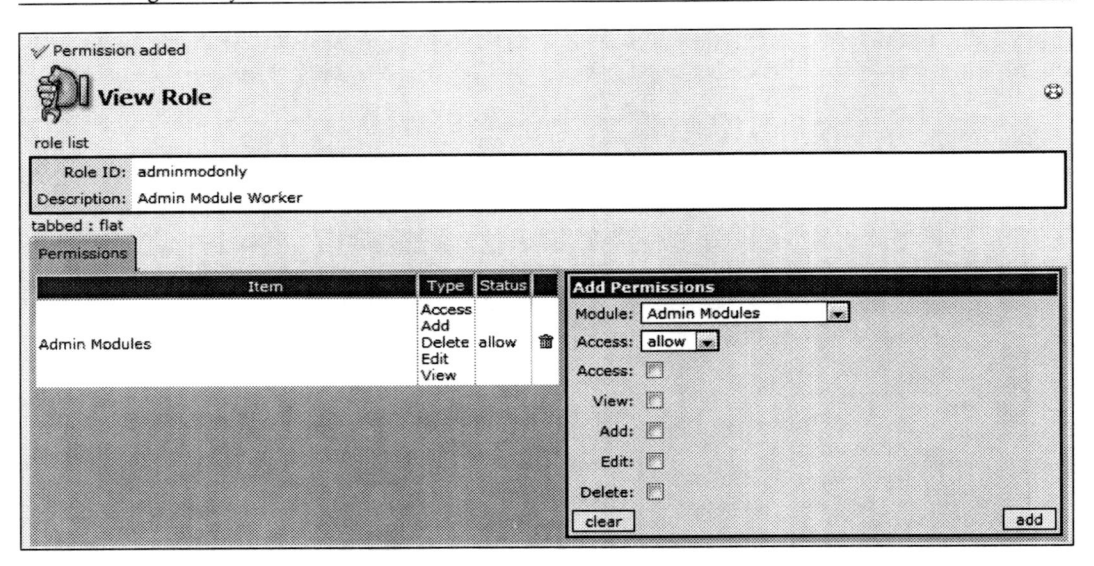

> ✓ Permission added
>
> **View Role**
>
> role list
>
> | Role ID: | adminmodonly |
> | Description: | Admin Module Worker |
>
> tabbed : flat
>
> **Permissions**
>
> | Item | Type | Status | | Add Permissions | |
> |---|---|---|---|---|---|
> | Admin Modules | Access
Add
Delete
Edit
View | allow | 🗑 | Module: Admin Modules
Access: allow
Access: ☐
View: ☐
Add: ☐
Edit: ☐
Delete: ☐ | |
> | | | | | clear | add |

Restricted Administrator: Users Only

Administrators may be further separated by function. Examples of this are the administrator who specializes in user administration, administrators who only work on **System Configuration**, or those who work with modules exclusively. The following steps show how to set up a restricted administrator in dotProject. We will set up a User Administration role.

1. Click on **User Roles** under the **Administration** section of the **System Administration** screen as illustrated above under **Administrative Roles**.

2. Type in a unique role ID. We'll use **useradmin** this time. Type **User Administrator** in the **Description** field. Click the **add** button.

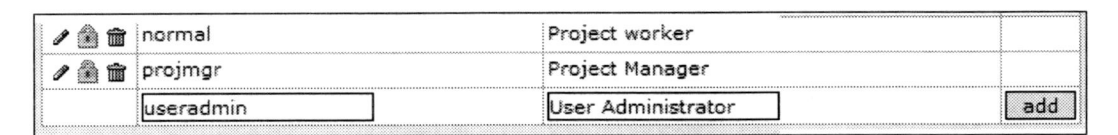

🖉 🔒 🗑	normal	Project worker	
🖉 🔒 🗑	projmgr	Project Manager	
	useradmin	User Administrator	add

3. After the **Role** screen refreshes, click on the view role icon to set the permissions for the **User Administrator** role.

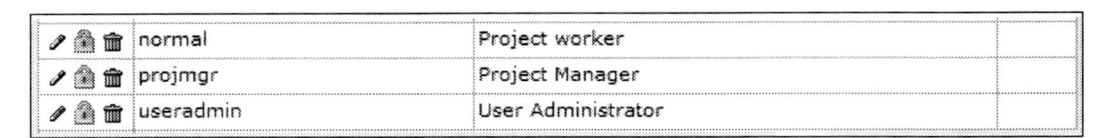

🖉 🔒 🗑	normal	Project worker	
🖉 🔒 🗑	projmgr	Project Manager	
🖉 🔒 🗑	useradmin	User Administrator	

4. Select **User Administration** from the **Module** dropdown. Leave **allow** selected on the **Access** dropdown. Check all boxes: **Access**, **Add**, **View**, **Edit**, and **Delete**. Save the changes. The new permissions will appear on the left side of the screen.

5. Select **User Table** from the **Module** dropdown. Leave **allow** selected on the **Access** dropdown. Check all boxes: **Access**, **Add**, **View**, **Edit**, and **Delete**. Save the changes.

    The new permissions will appear on the left side of the screen as seen in the following screenshot. We have now created a layered permissions filter for a **Role**.

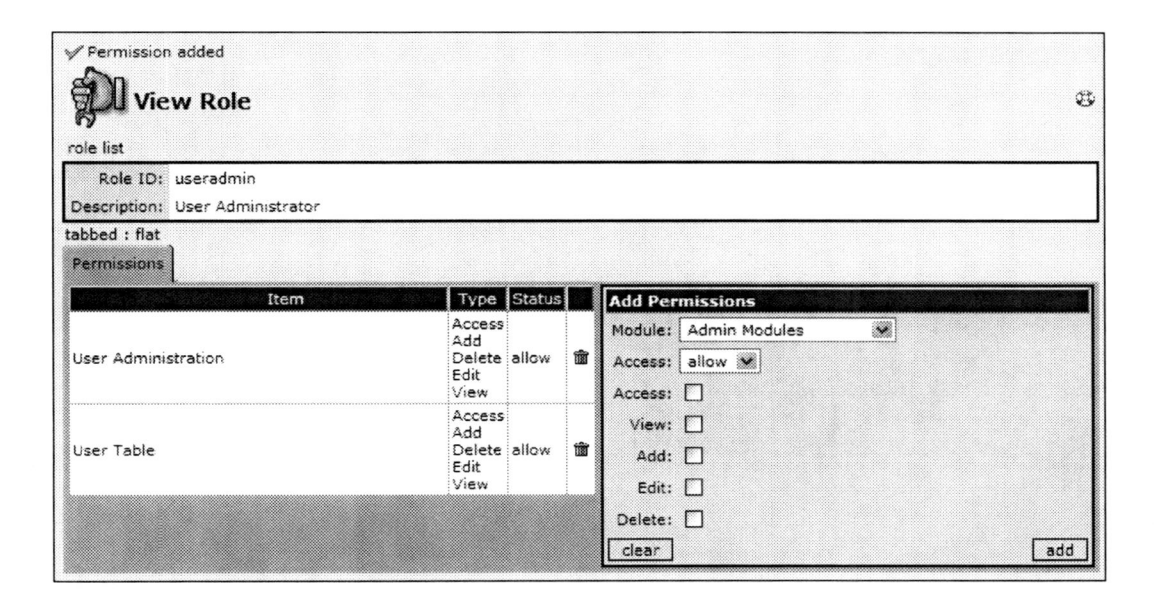

Administering dotProject

Restricted File Access

It is not always a good idea to allow all users in a company to view files stored in the file repository. To restrict file access to users assigned to a particular project, the following specialized access can be set up. It does require additional permissions masking at the individual user level, so it should be used only when necessary.

1. Click on **User Roles** under the **Administration** section of **System Administration**.
2. Type the unique role ID **projectfileobserver**. Type **Project File Observer** in the **Description** field. Click the **add** button.

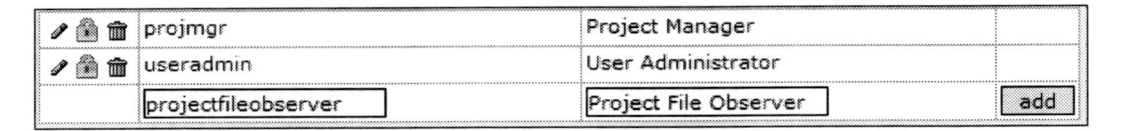

projmgr	Project Manager	
useradmin	User Administrator	
projectfileobserver	Project File Observer	add

3. After the **Role** screen refreshes, click on the **view role** icon to set the permissions for the **Project File Observer** role.

    Select **Projects** from the **Module** dropdown. Leave **allow** selected on the **Access** dropdown. Check only the **Access** box. Save the change.

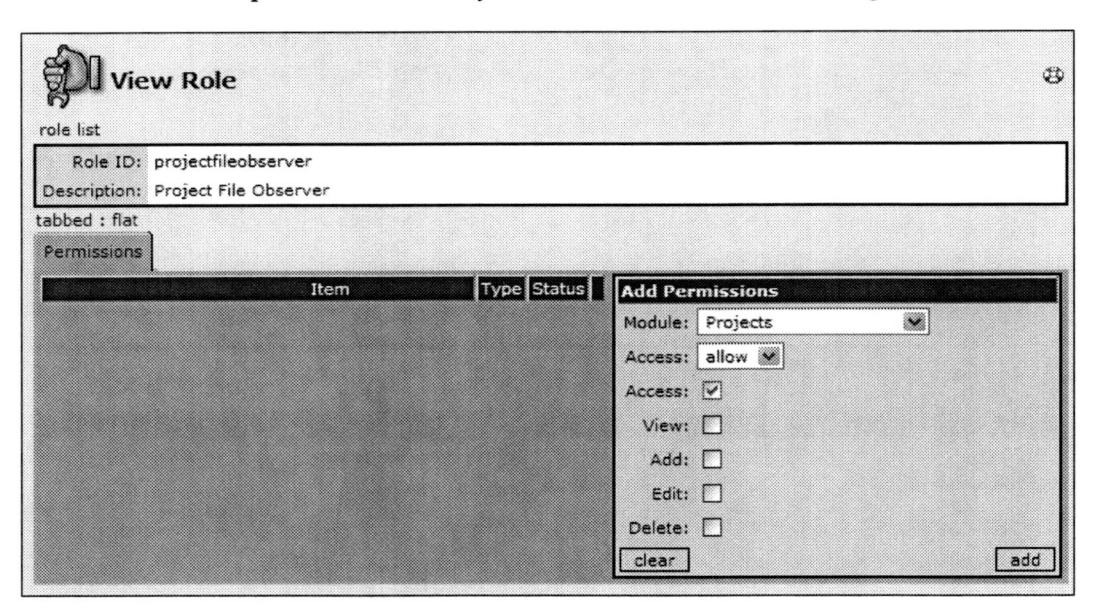

View Role

role list

Role ID: projectfileobserver
Description: Project File Observer

tabbed : flat

Permissions

Item	Type	Status

Add Permissions

Module: Projects
Access: allow
Access: ☑
View: ☐
Add: ☐
Edit: ☐
Delete: ☐

clear   add

Select **Tasks** from the **Module** dropdown. Check only the **View** box. Save the change.

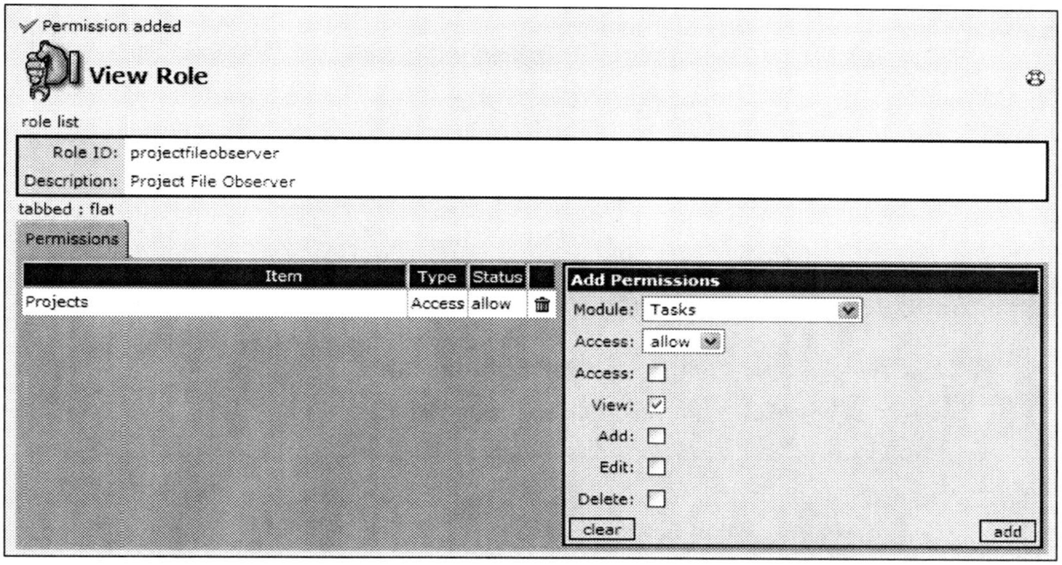
Permission added
View Role
role list
Role ID: projectfileobserver
Description: Project File Observer
tabbed : flat
Permissions
Item
Type
Status
Projects
Access
allow
Add Permissions
Module: Tasks
Access: allow
Access:
View:
Add:
Edit:
Delete:
clear
add

4. Select **Files** from the **Module** dropdown. Check the **Access** and **View** boxes. Save the changes. Check only the **View** box.

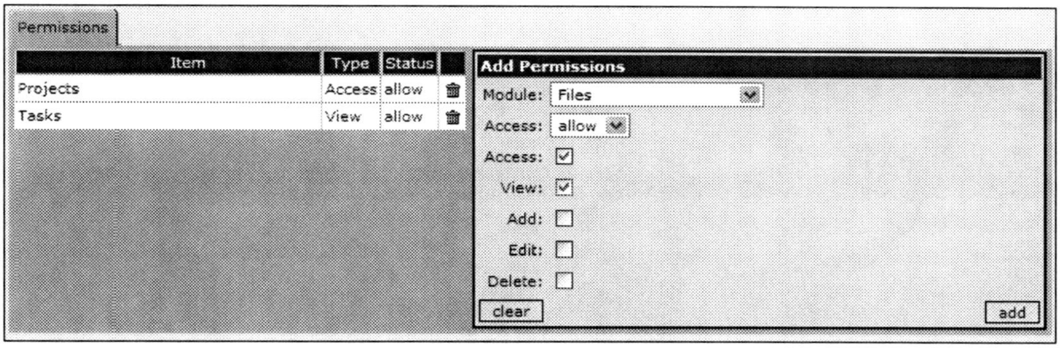
Permissions
Item
Type
Status
Projects
Access
allow
Tasks
View
allow
Add Permissions
Module: Files
Access: allow
Access:
View:
Add:
Edit:
Delete:
clear
add

Go to **User Administration** and select a user who needs file access restricted. We will use ProjectsRUs employee Ken Vandiver, who is an intern who already has his permissions restricted to **Non-Admin** modules. He will be a good example of a user who might need limited access to **Files**.

Administering dotProject

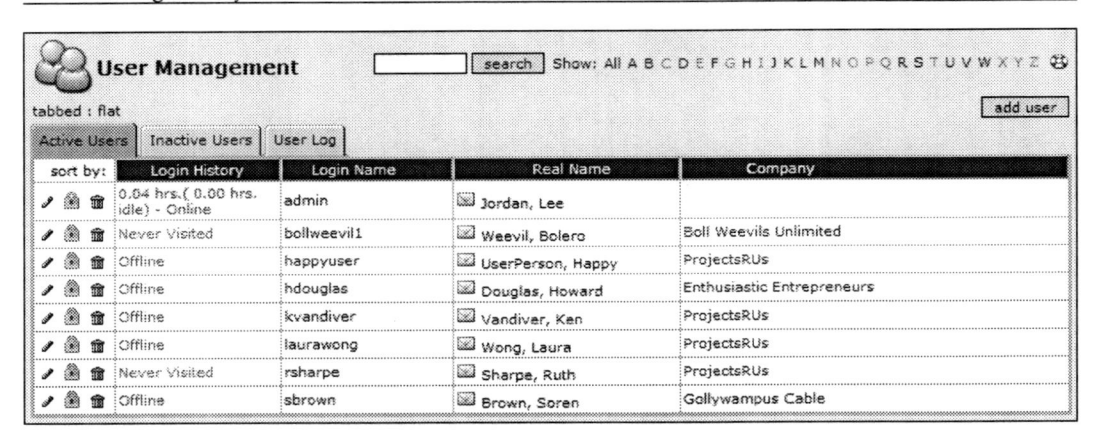

5. View the user and click on the **Permissions** tab.
6. Select **Companies** from the **Module** dropdown.

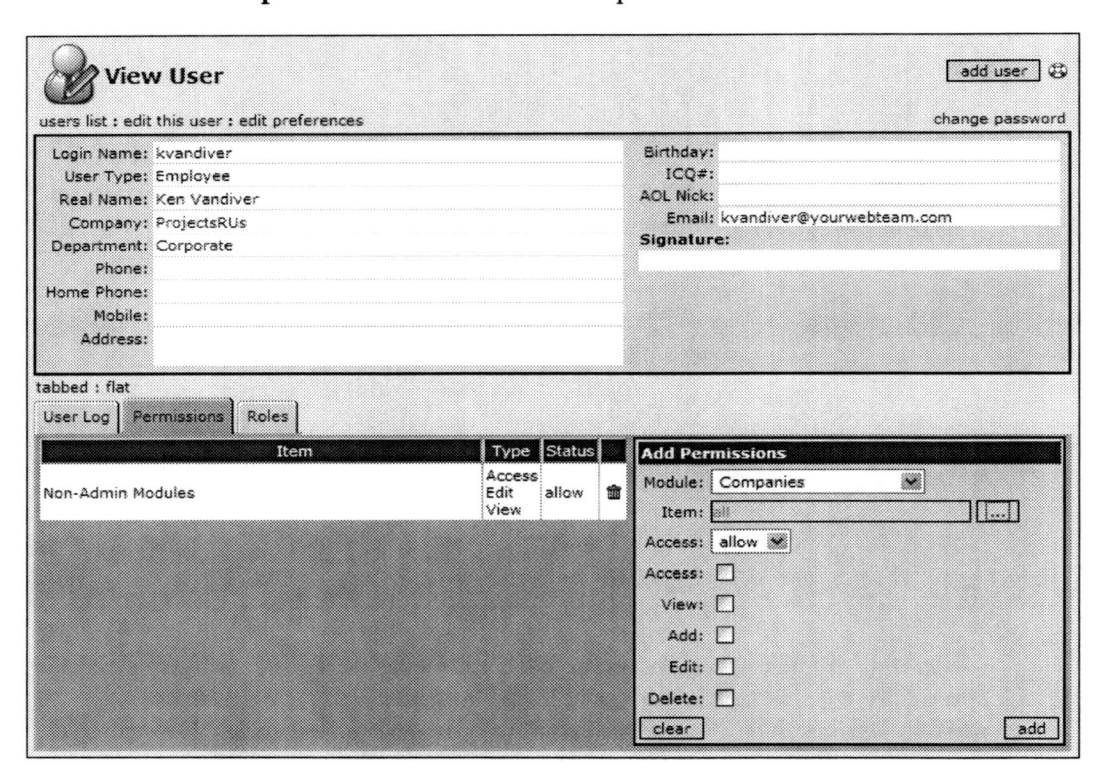

[146]

Click the **[...]** button next to the **Item** selector. Choose the company to restrict access to. We will select **ProjectsRUs** for this example. Once we have selected a company by clicking on the company name, you will be returned to the **User permissions** screen.

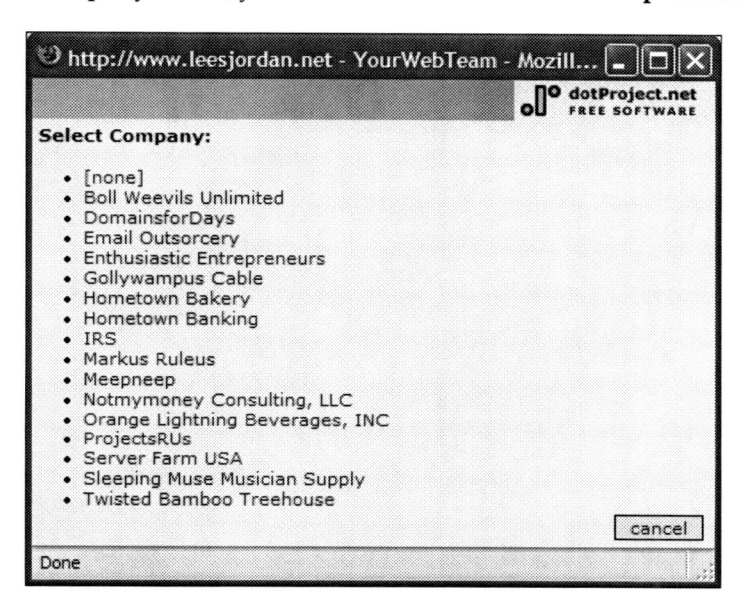

7. Check the **Access** and **View** boxes. Save the changes.

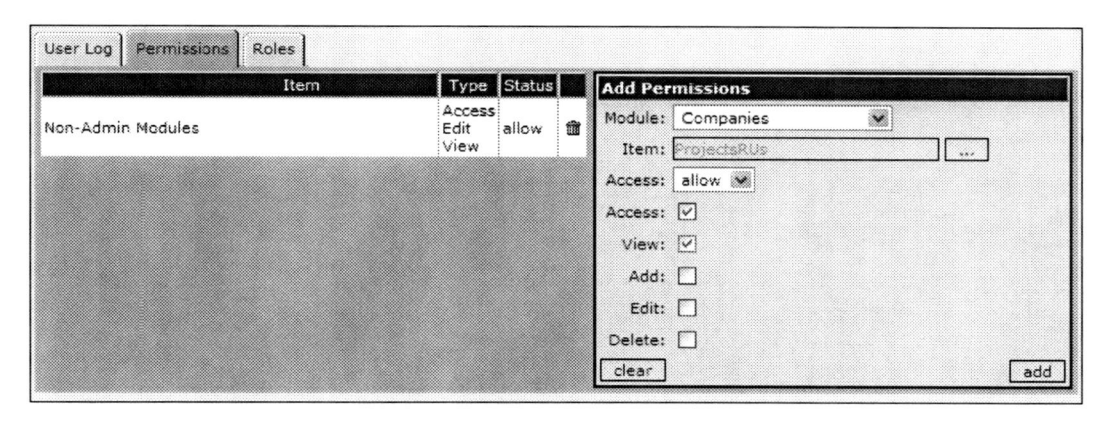

8. Before we set the user's access to a specific project, we must deny him access to other projects. Click on **Projects** in the **Module** drop-down list, leave **Item** set to **All**, set **Access** to "deny", and select the **View, Add, Edit,** and **Delete** checkboxes.

Administering dotProject

Select **Projects** from the **Module** dropdown. Click the **[...]** button next to the **Item** selector. Choose the project to restrict file access to. We will choose **Orange Summer Lightning Promo** from the project list.

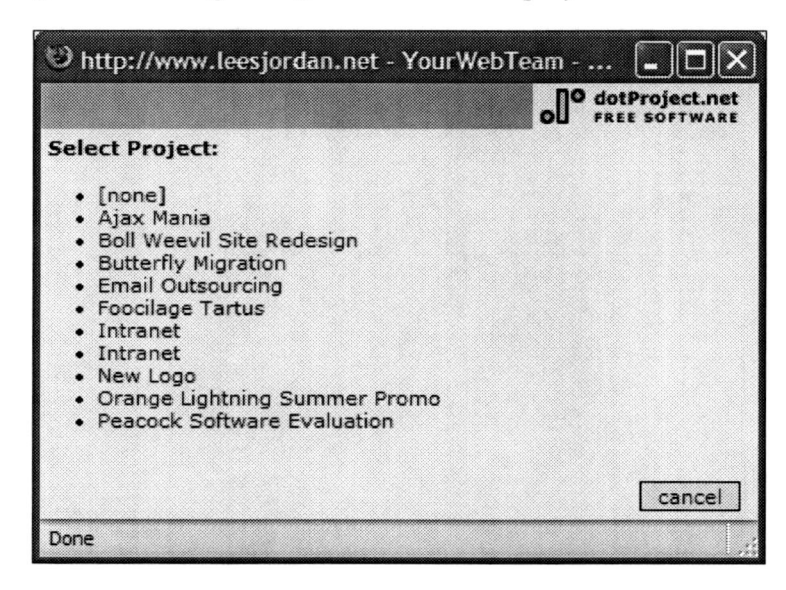

9. Check the **View** checkbox. The following screenshot shows our choices under the **Add Permissions** area so far.

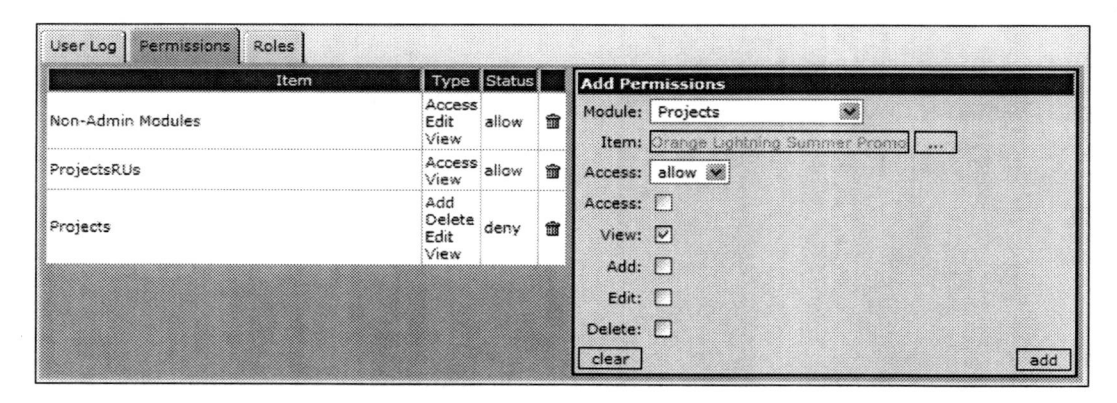

10. Save the changes. The permissions will appear to the left under the **Permissions** tab.

[148]

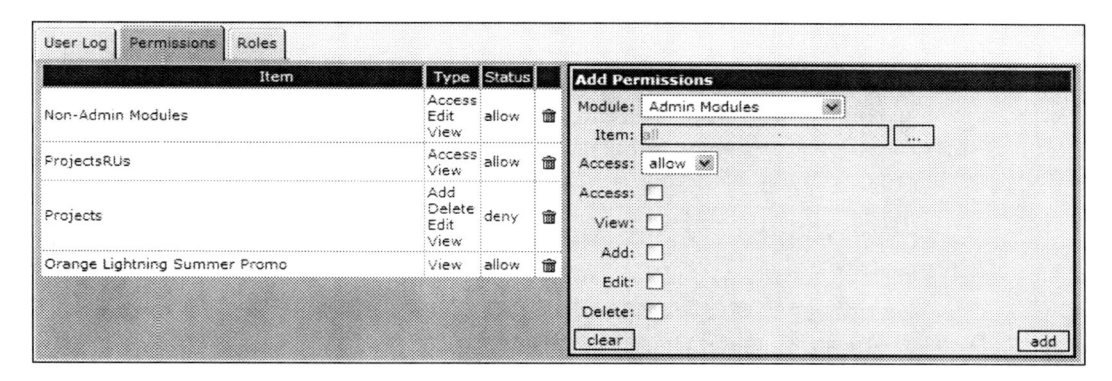

11. Finally we need to apply the **Project File Observer** role we created before to our user Ken Vandiver. Click on the **Roles** tab and select **Project File Observer** from the **Roles** drop-down list. Click the **add** button to apply the role to the user.

12. The new user role now appears on the left side of the screen under the **Role** column.

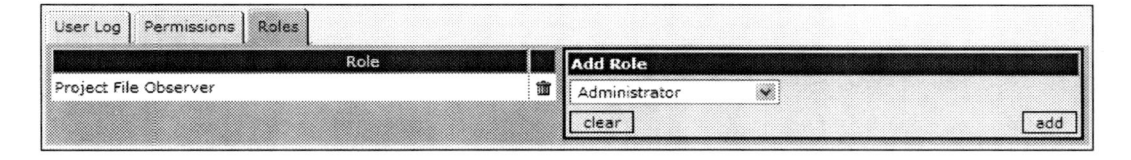

13. When we log out as an administrator and log in as Ken Vandiver, we can see the results of our work as shown in the following screenshot:

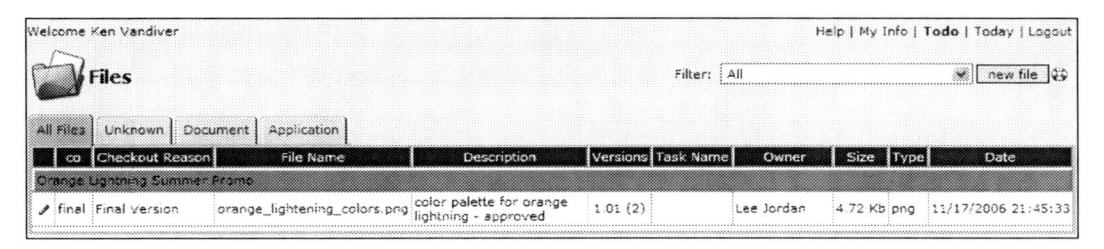

[149]

Restricted Company Access

A user may require access to projects only listed under a specific company or companies. The role created in this example will limit employees of the **ProjectRUs** client Enthusiastic Entrepreneurs to viewing their projects. They will not be able to edit or create new projects. This selective setup is relatively easy to do.

1. Click on **User Roles** under the **Administration** section of **System Administration**.
2. Type the unique role ID **companyproject**. Type **Company Project** in the **Description** field. Click the **add** button.

3. After the **Role** screen refreshes, click on the **view role** icon to set the permissions for the **Company Project** role. Select **Projects** from the **Module** dropdown. Leave **allow** selected on the **Access** dropdown. Check only the **Access** box. Save the changes.

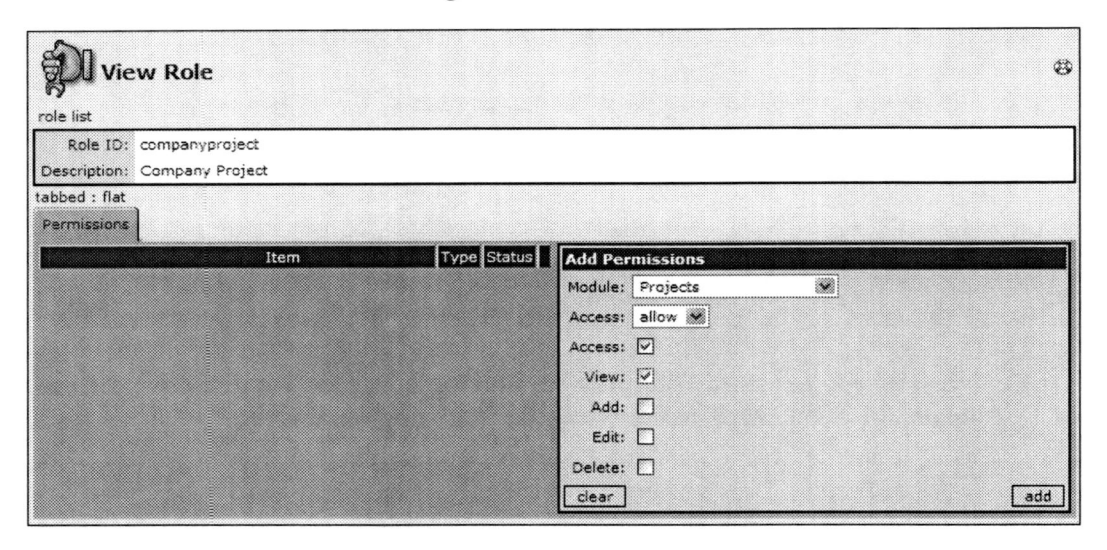

The new permission for the role can be seen now on the left side of the screen directly under the **Permissions** tab.

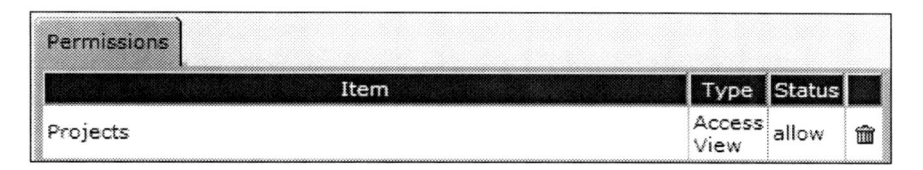

4. Go to **User Administration** and select a user who needs their access to projects and companies filtered. In this case it's Susan Frances.
5. Go to Susan Frances **View User** screen and click on the **Permissions** tab. Select **Companies** from the **Module** dropdown. Leave **allow** selected in the **Access** dropdown. Click the [...] button next to the **Item** selector. Choose the company to restrict access to. In this example we will choose **Enthusiastic Entrepreneurs**. When the screen returns to **View User**, check all boxes: **Access**, **View**, **Add**, **Edit**, and **Delete**. Click the **add** button to save the changes.

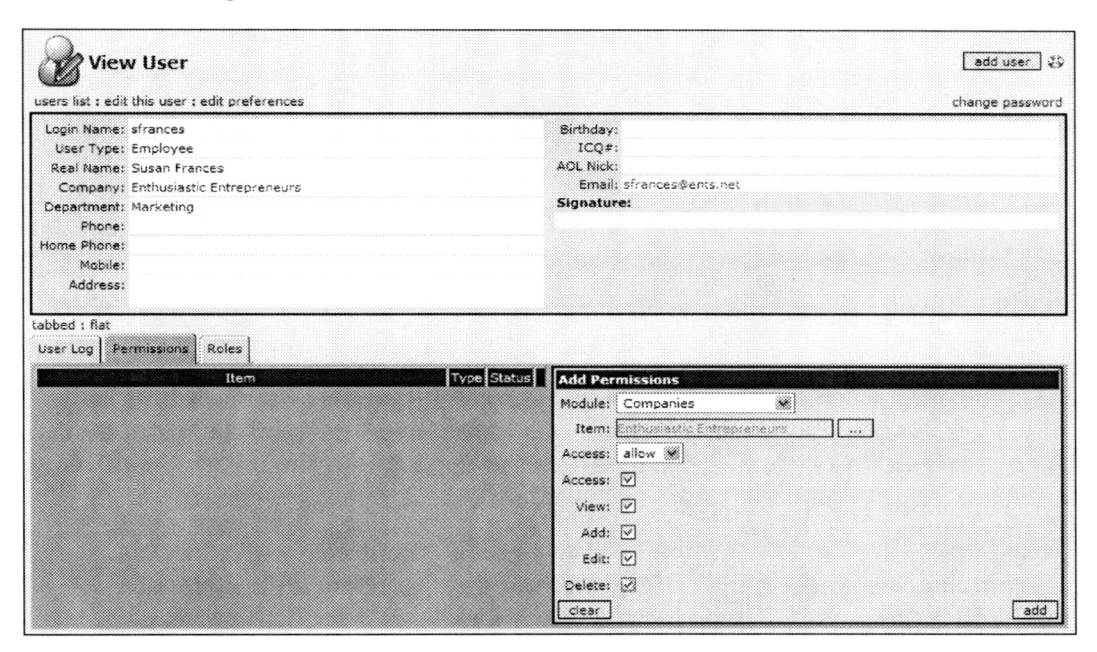

The new permission set for Susan Frances will appear directly under the **Permissions** tab.

Administering dotProject

6. The final step is to apply the **Company Project** role created earlier. Click on the **Roles** tab and select **Company Project** from the drop-down menu. Click the **add** button to save the role.

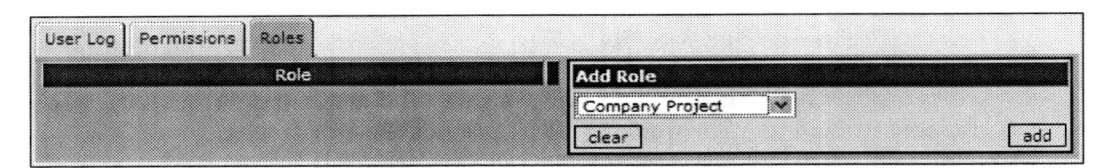

7. Susan Frances will now be able to view only projects for her company when she logs in to dotProject as shown in the following screenshot:

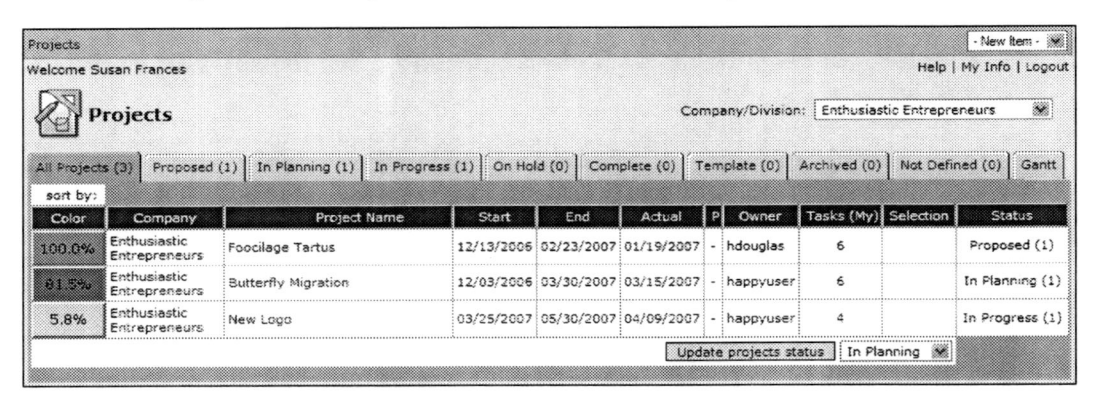

After assigning a role to a user, the administrator can further customize the user's access by going to the individual user's **View User** page and allowing or denying access generally or to specific modules. There are standard permissions setups that most organizations find useful. More information about permissions and roles, and other sample permissions setups can be found at the dotProject course on **Permissions for dotProject 2.x** at the URL http://sites.sakienvirotech.com/moodle/.

The permissions course is only ten USD and can be paid online with a PayPal account. This is a great way to directly support the creators of dotProject and have unlimited access to topical information. The information is well organized and written in a way that non-technical users can quickly get up to speed on permissions in dotProject.

Summary

We discussed many different areas of dotProject administration, including system configuration, user administration, setting up companies, and setting permissions.

dotProject uses a logical process for system configuration where modules can be in different states from disabled to active. dotProject's modular framework allows most modules to be turned on and off, giving the administrator great flexibility.

Administering users in dotProject is very simple. The most important point to remember is that users must be assigned a role or specialized permissions before they will be considered active in dotProject. Permissions in dotProject can be done with pre-set roles, or by using a very detailed rights system. Permissions must be set for each user of dotProject. Each user should have at least one role assigned to them. Users cannot log in to dotProject without a role assigned. dotProject uses a permissions philosophy that grants user access on a group or individual basis.

Changing the values in the **System Configuration** area can cause severe problems in the dotProject environment if not done carefully.

In the next chapter we will explore other ways to customize dotProject. We will examine themes, using different image icons and other methods of tweaking the look and feel of dotProject.

6
Customizing the Look-and-Feel

I like to think of this chapter as "trick my dotProject". This chapter focuses on the presentation layer of dotProject. We will explore different ways to customize the looks of dotProject. We will alter icons, change images, customize themes, and do other things to personalize the dotProject environment.

This chapter will include:

- Customizing themes
- Using different icons
- Stylesheet editing
- Customizing module text strings

By the end of this chapter you will be able to give your dotProject environment a look that blends in better with your website or business.

Setting User Preferences

User Preferences are found under the **System Administration** screen. We discussed them in detail, earlier in Chapter 5. They have the same structure as the personal user preferences available to each user. Even though these are global settings, they may not apply to current users. Determine and configure these settings before creating any additional users if at all possible. Let's take a closer look at the **User Interface Style** themes that can be set for users.

Customizing the Look-and-Feel

User Interface Style

dotProject installs with three available interface styles. These control the appearance of the tabs, the background colors, and the overall look of the dotProject environment. Which one to use is a matter of site requirements and user preference. Users can also change the style they see when they log in. I have not yet discovered a way to prevent users from changing their style except for blocking their access to **User Preferences** using permissions as shown in Chapter 5.

> Users created before the **User Interface Style** is changed in **System Administration** will not have the new theme instantly applied.

- **Grey Slimline Style**: Shiny, sleek, and silver, this style has a clean, modern look that mimics the `Apple.com` site.

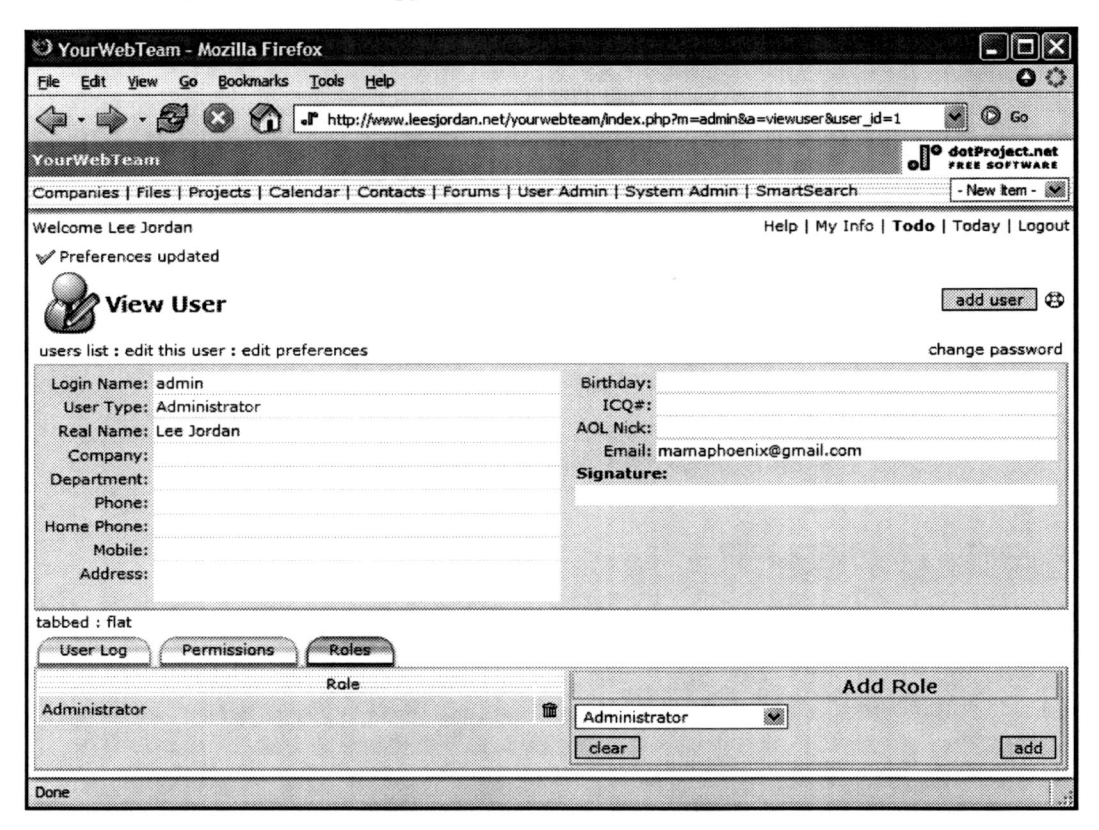

Chapter 6

- **Default Clean Style**: A blue and gray interface with minimal images. Screenshots of this theme have been used almost throughout this book.
- **Classic DotProject Style**: The original dotProject theme uses a left-hand menu system which has a mint green background. It has a clunky interface compared with the **Default Clean** style. It may not load properly on all installations. The following screenshot gives an overview of what the GUI would look like:

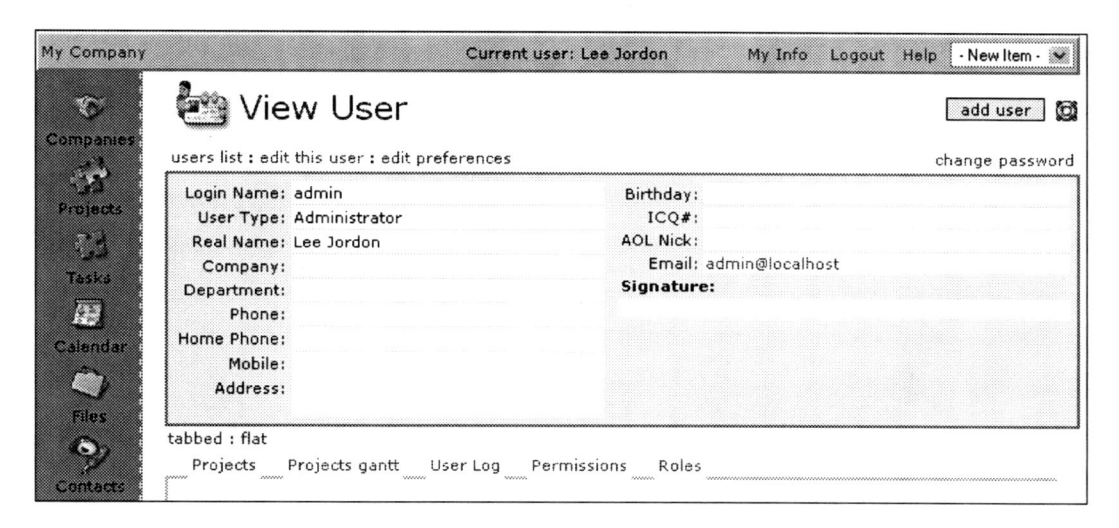

Finding Other Themes

There are other themes available to use with dotProject. Mats Djärf is a theme creating machine. He has several themes available for free download:

http://www.w8.se/dotproject/download

A variety of themes are available, including the popular **WPS-Redmond** theme shown in the screenshot overleaf:

Customizing the Look-and-Feel

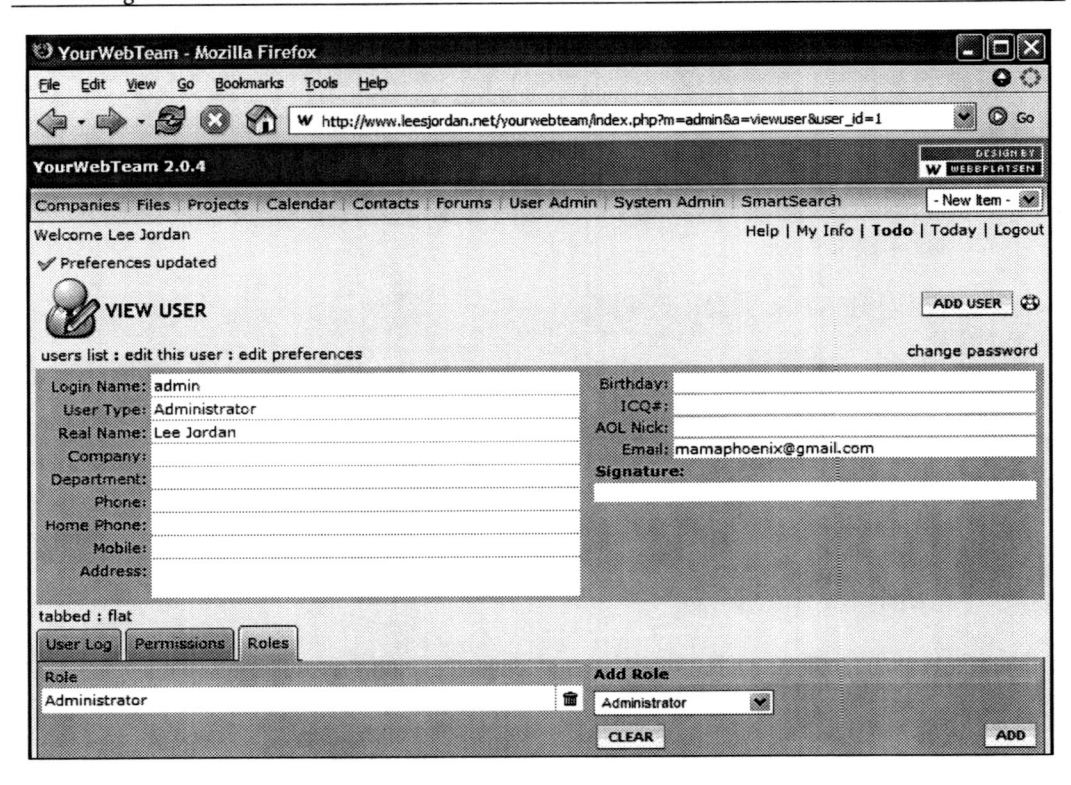

The **WPS-Light** theme has soft light gray 3-dimentional menu bars and tabs for a smooth, modern look.

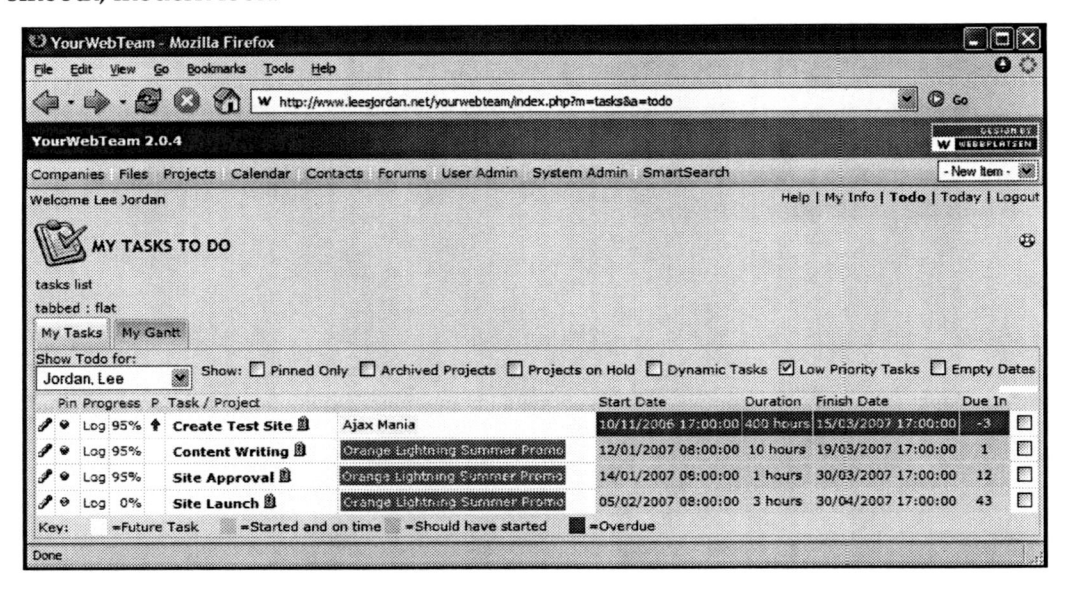

Custom Themes

In this section we will learn how to customize themes to suit our requirements.

Altering an Existing Theme

Altering an existing theme is a great way to become comfortable with the different presentation elements in dotProject.

1. Download an existing theme you want to alter.
2. Copy the theme. Use the original as a backup.
3. Rename the copy. Webteam_style is the name given for the **YourWebTeam** theme.
4. Make any changes you want. Do you not like the background color? Want to replace the dotProject logo with your own? Just want to add your logo? It can be done by altering the theme.
5. The next sections will include information on changing background colors, replacing fonts, and other aspects of customizing a theme. We will end up with an altered theme similar to the one shown in the following screenshot. It is a version of the WPS-Light theme with the background of the title header area and the logo area on the right altered using techniques learned in this chapter.

> **Is it a Style or a Theme?**
>
> Even though the skins or themes of dotProject are referred to as **User Interface Style** in the **User Preferences**, most people familiar with content management systems such as PostNuke are more comfortable with the term "Theme". Both the names refer to a centralized group of files that change the look-and-feel of dotProject.

Changing Images

Administrators often want to change the images to match a company style-guide or to create a customized look. How difficult it is to do will depend on what images need to be changed. Altering the icons of individual modules is a more involved task than altering the background behind the title of the entire dotProject environment.

Altering Icons

Icons are the small images usually stored in the images file of individual module folders or in a special icons folder within a dotProject style. The icons can be easily downloaded, altered in an image editing program, and then uploaded back to the original folder.

Replacing Icons

Mats Djärf has packaged up a slick set of icons labeled **Novola** for dotProject. This is available for download at `www.w8.se/dotProject`. The original author David Vignoni, also known as the Icon King, has many more icons available at `www.icon-king.com`.

Replacing icons involves a series of careful steps:

1. Download an icons package. They are usually available packaged in `tar.gz`.
2. Unpack the package in a new folder on your computer. Use a program such as WinRar.
3. Back up the original images folder of the dotProject installation located under the root folder of the dotProject installation (such as `/public_html/dotProject installation/images/`) and of every module subfolder.

    Example: The **YourWebTeam** dotProject installation is located in a subfolder. Its image path is as follows: `/public_html/yourwebteam/images/`.

    The images folders for the modules can be found under each module name in the modules subfolder. In the **YourWebTeam** installation, the `images` folder for the admin module can be found at this path: `/public_html/yourwebteam/modules/admin/images/`.

4. Upload the images folder within the icons package to the root of the dotProject installation. It should replace the original dotProject `installation/images/` folder.

> **A safer image files replacement method**
>
> To avoid deleting any other images, select all the image files in the new images folder, then drag and drop them to the dotProject images folder or select 'upload' using your FTP client to send them to the images folder.

5. Navigate to the sub folder of each individual module in the `core_images/modules/` folder of the icons package.
6. Upload the images folder of each individual module to the respective images subfolder of the module in the dotProject installation under `/modules/your module/`. This should replace the images folder of each module.

7. Clear your browser cache and examine the results.

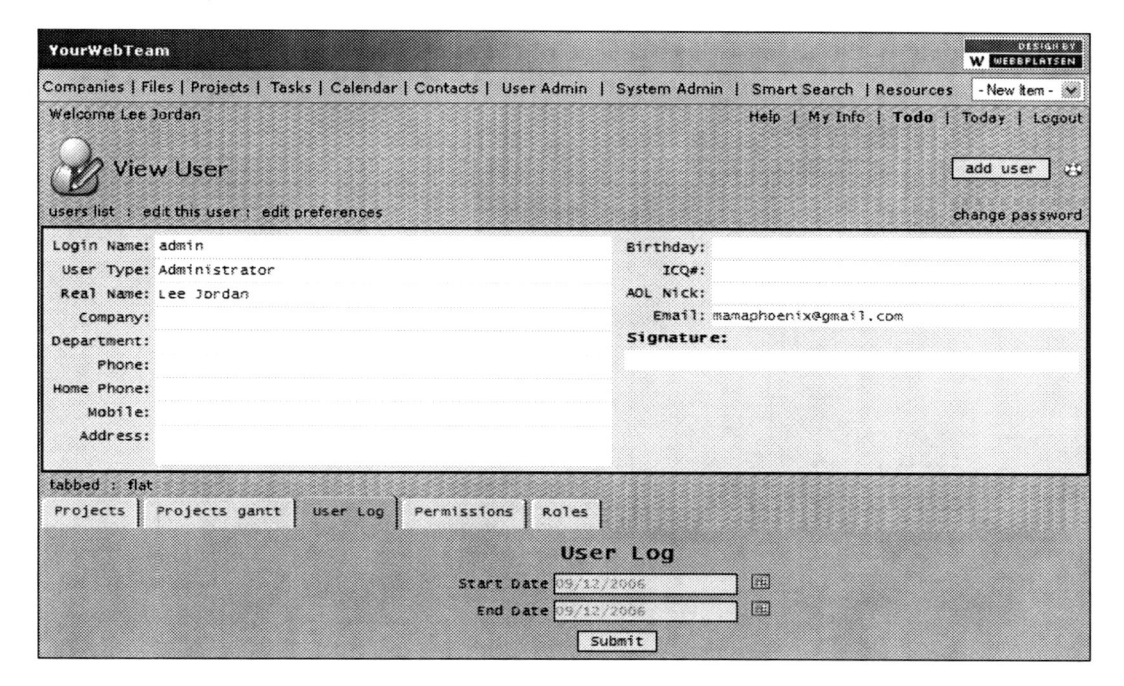

Replacing the dotProject Logo

The **YourWebTeam** administrator has been given a logo that is being used on every **YourWebTeam** site. The administrator decides the logo should go in the top right corner of the dotProject installation. This will replace the dotProject logo. The larger the logo is, the more space the header area will take up.

1. Back up the original logo. It can be found in the /dotProject installation/*theme name*/images/ as file dpicon.gif. Note that the size is 120 by 20 pixels in gif format.

    The **YourWebTeam** dotProject installation has the logo located at the following path:/public_html/yourwebteam/style/default/images/.

Customizing the Look-and-Feel

2. Crop the new logo to closely match the original size. The larger the logo is, the more space the header area will take up. The **YourWebTeam** logo will display without distorting at a size of 120 by 39 pixels.
3. Save the logo as `dp_icon.gif`.
4. Upload the new image to the `/style/your theme/images/` folder of the dotProject installation.
5. Refresh the browser and view the results.

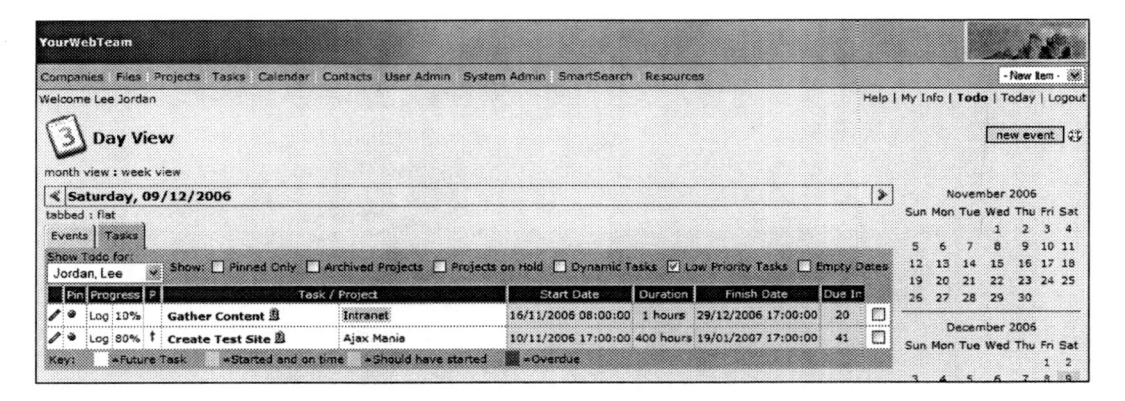

Replacing the Header Background

Is the dark blue gradient stripe of the default dotProject theme clashing with your company colors? Change the color of the title background in a few easy steps.

1. Create a new image file in an image editor such as Photoshop, Paint Shop Pro, or Gimp. Set the width to `2048 pixels` and the height to `2 pixels`. You can create an image with greater height, as long as you remember to reduce the height to 2 pixels later. The file will repeat horizontally in the header space once it is uploaded.
2. Fill the background image with any color or gradient. Save the image as `titlegrad.jpg` in your personal theme folder.
3. Upload the new image to the `images` folder of your dotProject theme (dotProject `installation/images/`). Refresh the screen. The new image will tile (repeat continuously) behind the dotProject Installation title in the header area as in the following screenshot:

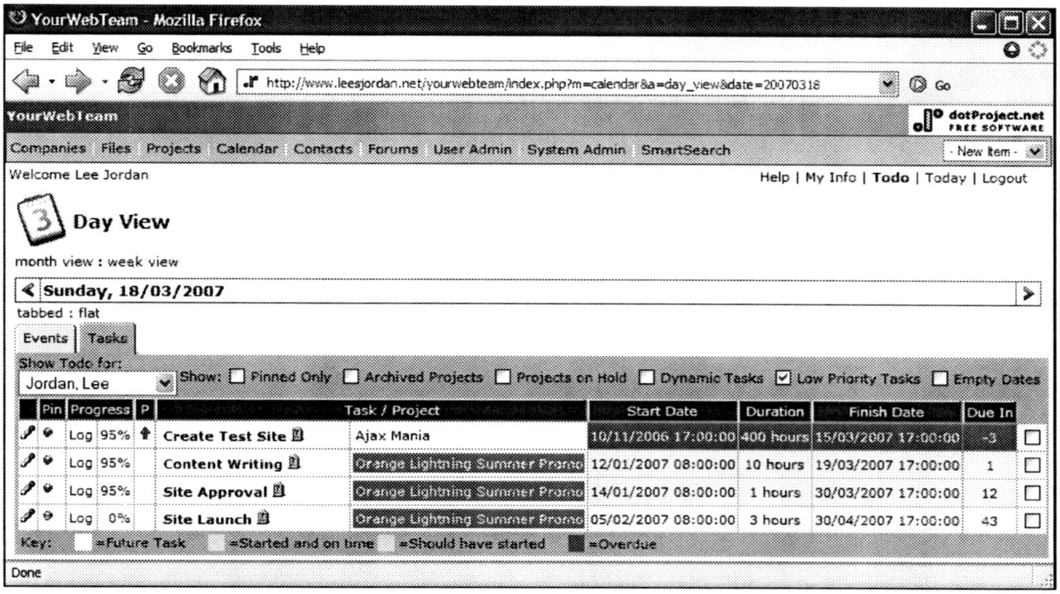

> **Easy Header Background**
>
> Download the `titlegrad.jpg` image. Open it in any image editing program. Make any cosmetic changes to the image file, including changing the color, adding patterns, or a different gradient. Save the changes in a new folder, and then upload the file to the dotProject installation as described above.

I Don't Want to See an Image There

If you do not want to see an image in a certain area at all, there is a simple hack to prevent an actual image from being seen. Any image in dotProject can be "hidden" this way. It is a smart idea to download a copy of the original image file and save it in case you change your mind later.

The easiest way:

1. Create a transparent background image with the same width and height as the original background image. Save it as the same type of file and with the same name.
2. Upload it into the image folder of the old image. This will replace the original image in the dotProject installation. The original image will no longer be visible. The placeholder image will take its place, acting as a clear film.

Editing the Style Sheet

dotProject uses style sheets extensively for design markup. Be sure to back up any files you want to change. Beware of changing the names of any existing style sheets as well. Comment changes you make. It will make things easier a month from now when you have forgotten what color the background used to be.

We will explore making changes to the existing styles in the style sheets, and perhaps adding a few of our own. If you already have styles from other web projects that you think would be a good fit, you can incorporate them into the altered style sheet.

Altering Existing Styles

Before any changes are made, the style sheet should be backed up. Being able to revert back to the original style sheet is a real-world necessity. Documenting changes made to style sheets is another good practice to use. Weeks or months later when the reasons why styles were changed have been forgotten, you will be glad the notes were made.

There are many styles and tags that can be altered in a style sheet. Describing each one in detail is beyond the scope of this book. Instead, several basic styles that frequently need to be altered will be explored.

Changing Fonts

Does your company use a preferred font? Do the fonts in dotProject need to closely match the fonts used on other company sites? Changing the font in the style sheet is a simple procedure that will reap big rewards. The default font of the dotProject **default** theme is Osaka. We will be replacing it with a different font in the following steps.

1. Save a backup version of the main.css style sheet. It is located in the *theme name* subfolder of your /styles/ folder of the dotProject installation. For example the stylesheet for the default theme of **YourWebTeam** is located at: /public_html/yourwebteam/style/default/main.css.

2. Open the style sheet in an editor such as HTML-Kit or even a basic text editor.

3. If you are using a Windows PC, click *Ctrl + H* to activate the find and replace function. Type Osaka in the find portion of the window and enter the font you want to use in replace. Click the **Replace All** button. All instances of the Osaka font will be replaced with the new font. There are only about thirteen occurrences of the font, so they can also be replaced by cutting and pasting.

4. Save the CSS file in a special folder.

5. Upload the file to the /styles/*theme name*/ folder of your dotProject installation.

6. Refresh the screen to see the change. Lucinda Console has a distinct look and is shown in the following screenshot. Any web-safe font such as Arial, Georgia, Courier, Trebuchet MS, and Verdana can be used.

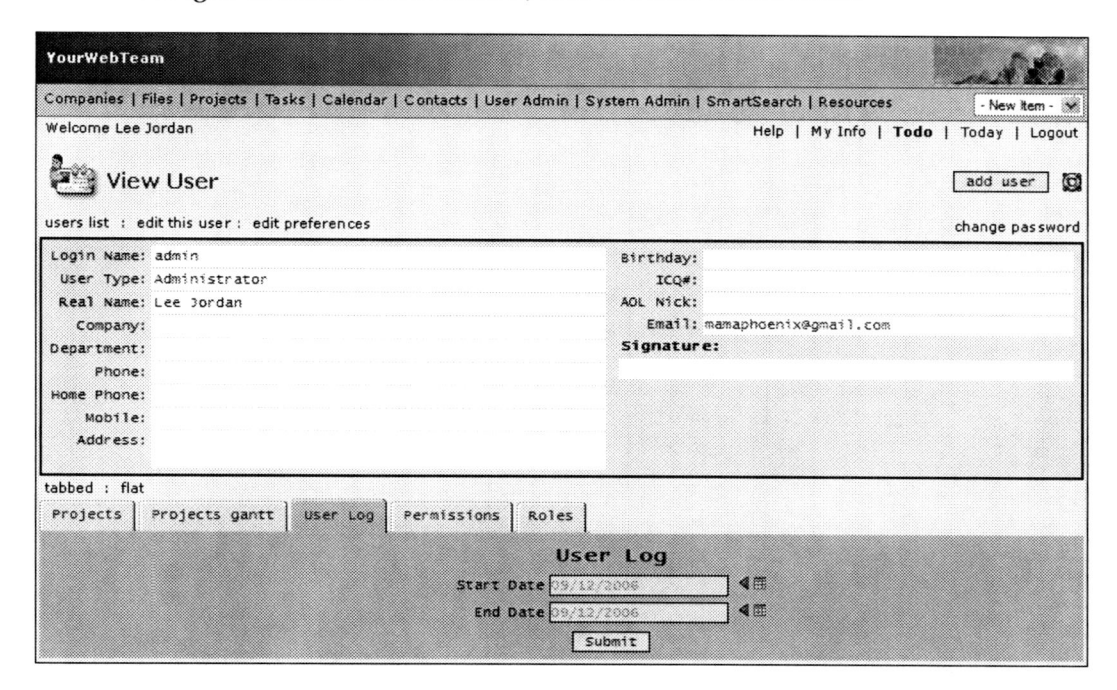

> **Why use a web-safe font?**
> Web-safe fonts can be boring, since there are only a few of them to choose from. Any font can be used, but be aware that not all users may have the font installed on their computers. Fonts such as Tahoma, Calisto MT, and Century Gothic are relatively safe alternatives.

Adjusting Links

We will change the color of the default link style and also set its text decoration element to underline. The default link style of the default dotProject theme uses a dark blue color with a hexadecimal value of 08245b:

1. To change the color, begin by opening the main.css style sheet in an editing program such as HTML-Kit.
2. Go to line number 36 and replace the current hexadecimal code 08245b with a new color. We will use #006600 in the following example 006600 — a bright web-safe green. Change the text decoration value from none to underline.

Customizing the Look-and-Feel

```
A:link{
    color: #006600;/*was 08245b*/
    text-decoration: underline;/*was none*/
}
```

3. Save the CSS file.
4. Upload the file to the `/style/your theme/` folder of the dotProject installation.
5. Refresh the browser. The calendar, links under the page title, and many other areas are affected by this change.

> **Commenting Style Sheets**
>
> Style sheets can be commented, and it is a best practice to add comments when changes are made, especially in development. The example above is commented. The forward slash and asterix symbols '/*' are typed in order begin a comment block. The asterix and forward slash symbols '*/' in reverse order together indicate the end of a comment block.

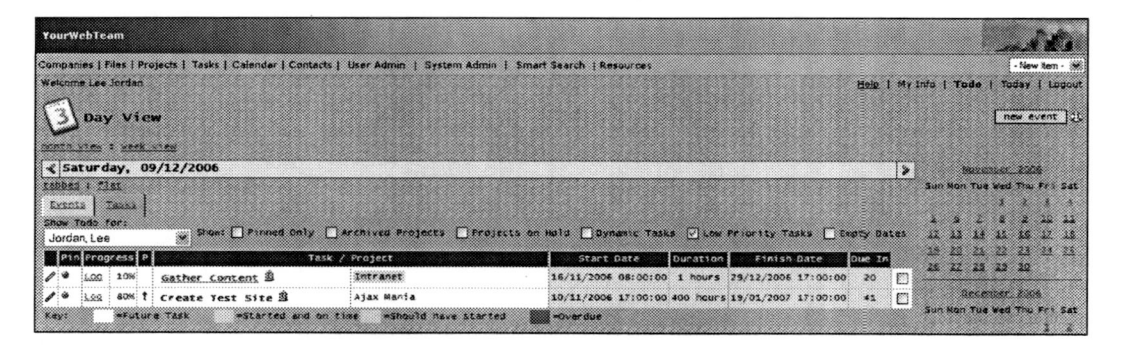

What Styles Should I Leave Alone?

If you have a test installation of dotProject, and you have backed up the style sheets, then go ahead and experiment. It is the best way to become comfortable with dotProject and CSS. Do not remove any of the required dotProject styles. All the original style names should be left in the dotProject `main.css` stylesheet. Any of the information within the styles contained in the brackets '{}'can be changed.

> The colors and other attributes such as background colors and margins can be altered, but beware that altering margins and other positioning elements can cause errors and disrupt the display of modules and information.

Currently I only have a production copy of dotProject (well several production copies) running on my web server, so I won't make any changes that cannot be fixed by uploading a copy of the backup file. Some of the styles in dotProject control the framework of the site itself. It is possible the site will break and strange things happen. Sounds fun. Let's try it.

Changing the Required Body Style

The background color, font, or other styles can easily be changed. A backup copy should be set aside in case the altered style sheet needs to be replaced. We will be replacing the background of the body tag.

1. Open up the `main.css` style sheet from the copied theme folder.
2. The required dotProject body style is located on line number 2 of the `main.css` file. The default dotProject body style has a light gray background color. Change the background color to a medium purple with the code `#cc66cc`. The bright hue of the color will be easy to see on the screen against the other objects in the dotProject environment.

    ```
    BODY {
            background-color: #cc66cc;/*was #f0f0f0*/
            margin-top: 0px;
            margin-left: 0px;
            margin-right: 0px;
            margin-bottom: 10px;
            font-family: Osaka,verdana,Sans-Serif;
            font-size: 10pt;
    }
    ```

3. Save the changes in a special folder labeled "altered" or in a new styles folder. I like to comment my changes in the CSS code as well to avoid confusion. If compression is an issue, save a special uncompressed version with comments for editing purposes.
4. Upload the changed style sheet and take a look. Wow! Even in black and white the change should look dramatic. It is easy to see what portions of the dotProject environment are affected by the background color style in the body tag. Any color can be used for the background, as long as it is in hexadecimal format.

Customizing the Look-and-Feel

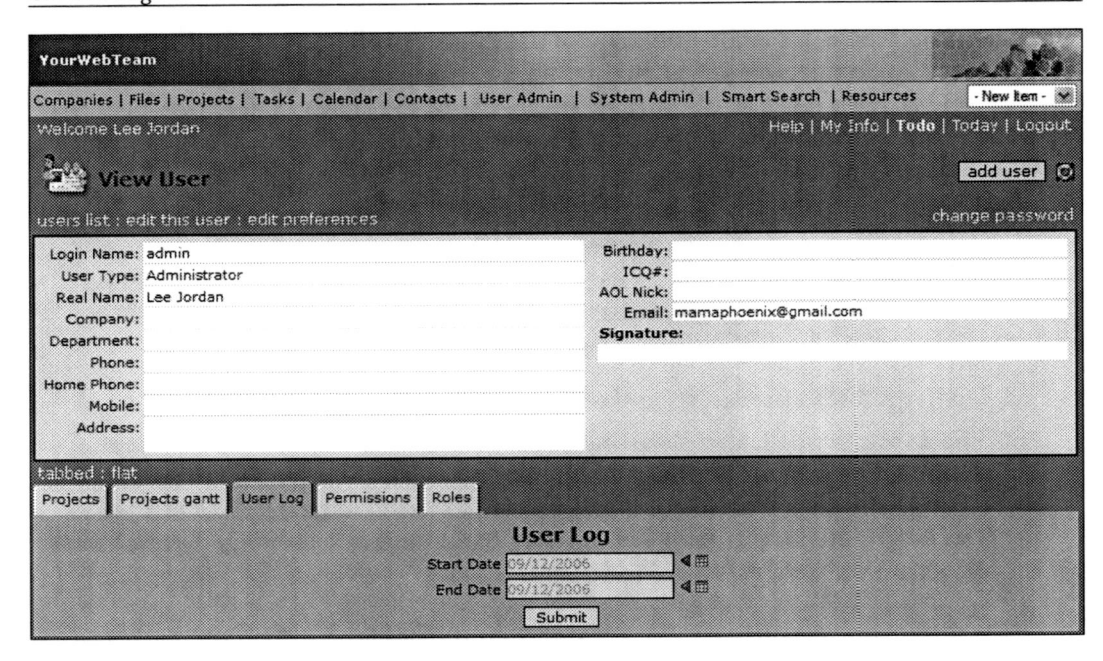

Replacing the Background Color with an Image

Images can also be used in the background style. Using a small image will work best. The same image is printed recursively on the background of the page. Images ideally should be no larger than 16 pixels by 16 pixels. Using larger images can cause display problems on the screen, including module information not displaying properly.

1. Alter background style in the body tag of the `main.css` file. We will replace the background-color attribute with the more general background attribute and add an image element to the background attribute.

   Replace the background-color attribute on line number 3:

   ```
   background-color: #f0f0f0;
   ```

   With this new background attribute:

   ```
   BODY {
        background-image:url(images/ywt_bg.png)
   }
   ```

2. Make sure the image path is to the images folder of the style. Save and upload the altered CSS file.

3. Upload the new image into the `style/`*`theme name`*`/images/` folder of the dotProject installation.

4. Refresh the page. This background image is dramatic so the change can be easily seen. A more subtle background would be easier on everyone's eyesight.

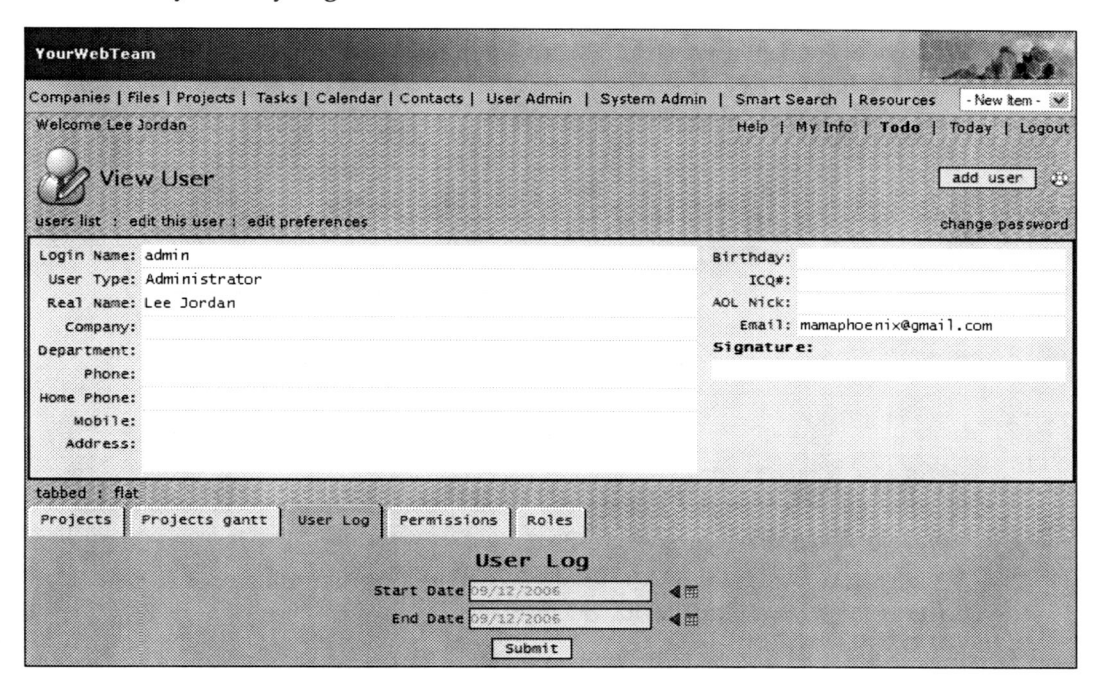

Adding New Styles

New styles can be added to affect the appearance of text, links, and other components that control the presentation of dotProject elements. Always back up the original style sheet before making any changes. Styles "cascade" in a style sheet, meaning if two styles are specified for the same element then style listed last will be used. This is important to remember when altering fonts or links in a style sheet.

Tips for Creating a New Theme

Creating a custom theme can be a difficult process. It is much easier to alter a copy of an existing theme. Before creating a custom theme, look at the files of other themes such as `wps_light` and `wps_redmond`. Make a note of the changes made by the theme author compared to the dotProject default theme.

If the different examples are followed in this chapter, the fundamentals of creating a new theme will already be in progress. Altering the icons, colors, fonts, and images of dotProject will create a unique look for your own dotProject environment.

Customizing the Look-and-Feel

Why am I making such a big issue of this? Creating a new theme or converting a dotProject theme to a complete CSS-driven one has several obstacles to overcome. There are images and other elements embedded into the code of the dotProject environment, making replacing certain colors difficult for theme creators. Theme creation can take a great deal of time. dotProject does a good job of using CSS, but it does use tables extensively. It may not be possible to have full control of how the environment looks without a great deal of effort.

Customizing Module Text Strings

When is a company not a company? When it is a group, government entity, club, or any other organized association of people. It is possible to change the titles, labels, messages, and other strings of text in modules to better suit the needs of an organization. Karen, an active dotProject developer originally proposed how to do this on the dotProject forums. We will walk through how to customize the company module as an example.

1. Log in to dotProject as an administrator and navigate to the **System Administration** screen. Click on the **Translation Management** link under **Language Support**.

2. The language dropdown should already have **English** selected. Choose **common** from the **Module** dropdown.

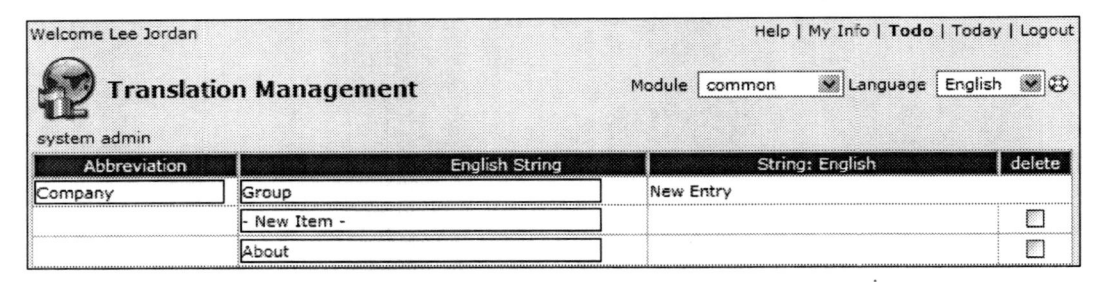

Abbreviation	English String	String: English	delete
Company	Group	New Entry	
	- New Item -		☐
	About		☐

3. Enter the word **Company** in the **Abbreviation** text field and the word **Group** in the **English String** text field.

   Scroll down the list of text strings until the word **Company** is found. Select the checkbox next to the word in **delete** column.

	Company		☑
	Complete		☐
	Completed Projects		☐

4. Click the **submit** button to finalize the change. The screen will refresh with the success message **Locales file saved** and the new English string displayed in the **English String** column.

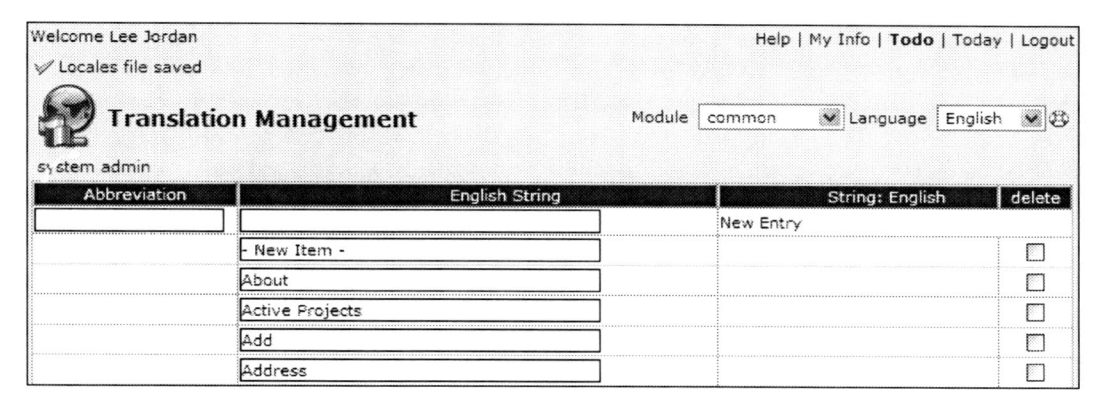

If there are multiple instances where a word, such as **Companies**, is combined with another string in a text field listing in the **English String** column, such as **Clients & Companies**, the text string **Companies** would be deleted from the text field listing leaving only the word **Clients** using the method described above.

To replace **English String** text field entries that contain more than one word, the full phrase must be entered in the **Abbreviation** field. So **Clients & Companies** would be typed into the **Abbreviation** field, and **Clients & Groups** would be typed into the **English String** field in the new entry location. The current text string entry would then be found by scrolling down the list and replaced by selecting the delete checkbox. Clicking the **submit** button would finish the process.

It is repetitive, but this must be done for each instance of an **English String** under the **common** selection of the **Module** drop-down where a text string such as **Companies** is combined with other words.

Summary

We explored many different ways to customize how dotProject looks. We went from using the default themes and settings to a new unique skin with customized settings. You can use your own images and icons with most of dotProject. Styles can be edited on the default dotProject style sheets to enhance existing themes. Customized looks can be created by copying the default folder, renaming it, and making changes to the new folder contents. The identifying text strings in modules such as **Company** can be altered and customized. Set default user preferences and customize your theme before adding any users.

The dotProject environment is very malleable. We have learned new ways to mold the dotProject environment so it matches our requirements as users and administrators. In the next chapter we will extend dotProject even further and learn more about dotProject reports and Gantt charts.

7
Beyond Projects: Charts, Reports, and Extensions

There is more to an effective project management application than managing projects. Managers rely on charts and reports in dotProject to capture high-level views of projects and tasks. Developers use a variety of modules to enhance and extend dotProject. We will go beyond projects in this chapter, exploring the charts, reports, and additional modules that extend the functionality of dotProject.

This chapter will include:

- Gantt Charts
- dotProject Reports
- Installing, configuring, and using add-on modules
- Do-It-For-Me modifications
- Resources for developers
- Information about module support and deprecation
- Support information

More Standard Modules

Standard modules are modules that are present in dotProject by default. We do not activate or configure these modules. We will discuss these modules in detail in the sections that follow.

Gantt Charts

Gantt Charts are provided as a default module in dotProject using the third-party extension JpGraph to process and display the Gantt Charts. There are two types of Gantt charts available. The combined view displays all project levels. The **Project Detail** view is accessible from within individual projects. The charts provide a visual graph of progression. Administrators occasionally experience errors with fonts and locales. These issues are well documented within the dotProject forums and on the JpGraph site `http://www.aditus.nu/jpgraph/` by volunteers, users, and developers. Most of the solutions will work fine for users who host their own installations of dotProject. Users with shared hosting may have additional difficulties with configuration. Those issues are covered in Appendix B of this book.

The Combined Projects View

The Combined Projects view is accessed by clicking on the **Gantt** tab in the **Projects** screen. Users can filter by date, projects shown, and other details. **Gantt Charts** show task progress over time. Making adjustments to the date range will "zoom in" on precise segments in the project timeline.

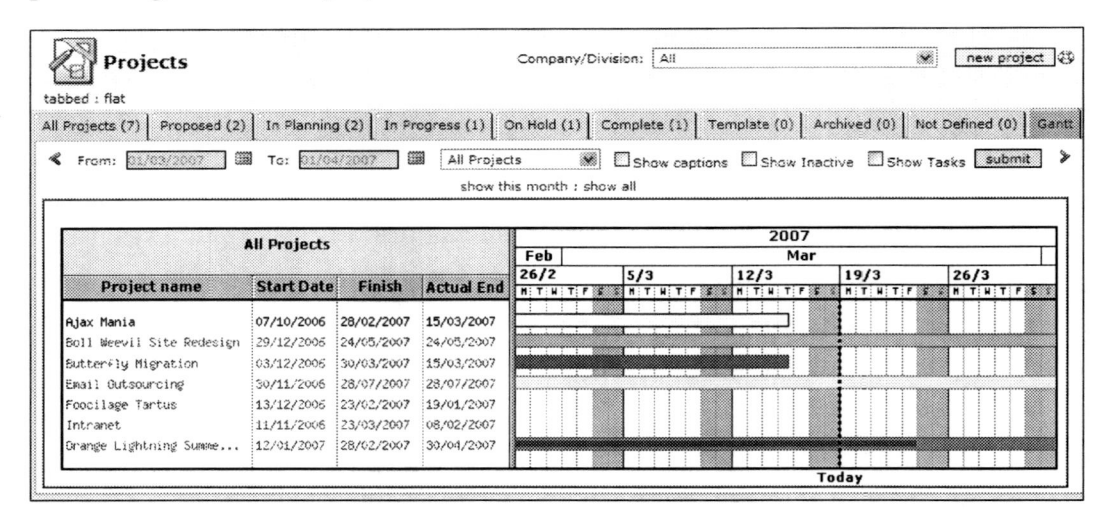

The Individual Project View

The Individual Project view is very similar to the combined view. The main difference is users can view overall progress at the task level. Task dates, durations, and activity for the whole project can be seen at a glance.

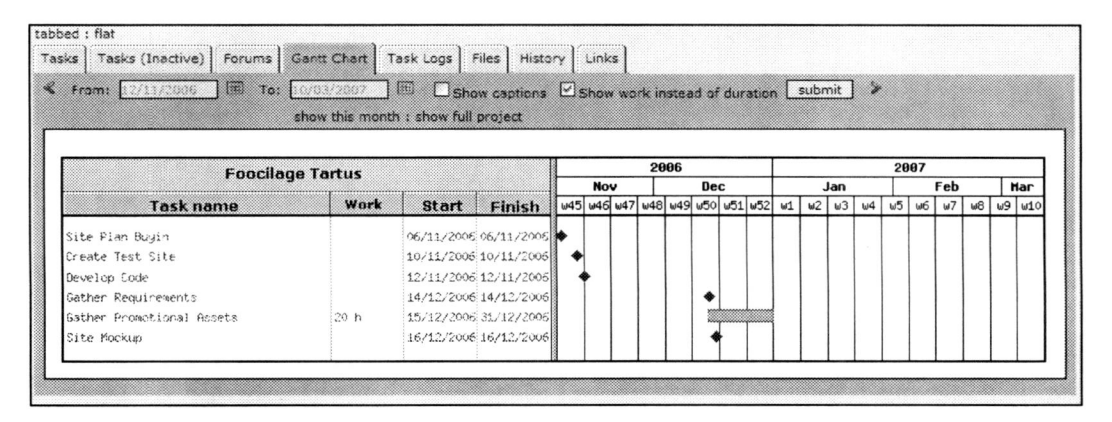

The ToDo View—New in Version 2.1.0

The newest version of dotProject released in February 2007 contains an additional Gantt Chart view for users. The **ToDo** view in version 2.1.0 includes a Gantt Chart for users.

Project Reports

The features of the **Project Reports** module are in a state of transition. The module is being updated in stages. What this means for users is that some reports are embedded within the code during the transition period.

> **Overall Report** and **Overdue** report are yet to be fully functional. dotProject is still working on it, and we hope to see the improvements in the near future.

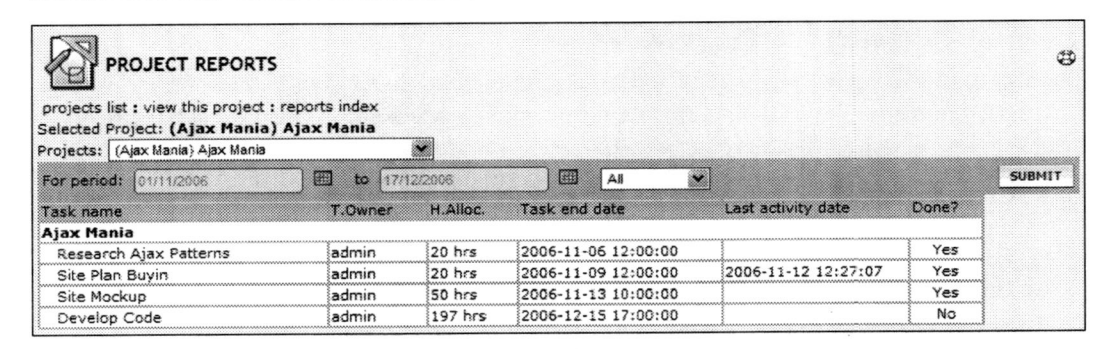

Beyond Projects: Charts, Reports, and Extensions

Reports are available for every project by clicking on the **Reports** link on the **View Project** screen. The **Project Reports** index screen will load and display a list of available reports as seen in the following screenshot:

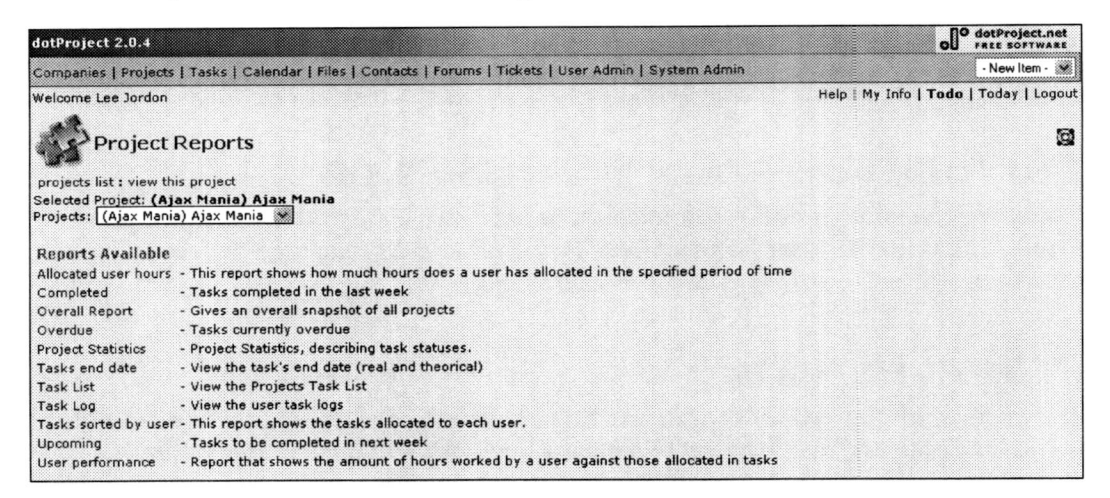

The reports do not all work consistently in version 2.04. The 2.1.0-rc1 version of dotProject has fixed several bugs including errors to do with the **Allocated User Hours** report not displaying consistently. As of version 2.04 the **Project Reports** module is *not* a fully functioning module.

A variety of reports are currently available on the **Project Reports** screen. Reports for different projects can be run from the **Project Reports** screen by selecting a project by name from the **Projects** drop-down list. Selecting a new project will cause the screen to reload and return to the reports index screen shown above. We will look at two very different and useful reports that show how most reports in dotProject can be generated and viewed.

Generating Reports

dotProject **Project Reports** are typically generated by clicking on the report name from the main **Project Reports** screen and then selecting a date range. Selecting the **Log All** checkbox will generate a report for all projects or tasks of that company, depending on the type of report chosen. The report results will appear in a table as seen in the screenshot below when the report requires a range of dates to be selected.

Not all reports require that choices be made before generation. The **Overdue**, **Upcoming** (tasks), and **Project Statistics** reports automatically generate output. While the first two reports create a PDF document to download, the **Project Statistics** generates a report with many distinct areas of information. We will take a closer look at it below in the following section.

Viewing Reports

Most of the **Project** reports display simple tabular results. The report title is usually displayed first on a dark background at the top of the table. The results of the report are shown in a grid format below the report title. The **Project Statistics** report displays multiple reports on one screen, both tabular and color coded. We will take a closer look at the results to learn more about viewing reports in dotProject.

> The PDF files for the **Overdue** and **Upcoming** reports may not display properly when downloaded. This appears to be an issue with the PDF generation tool within the dotProject code.

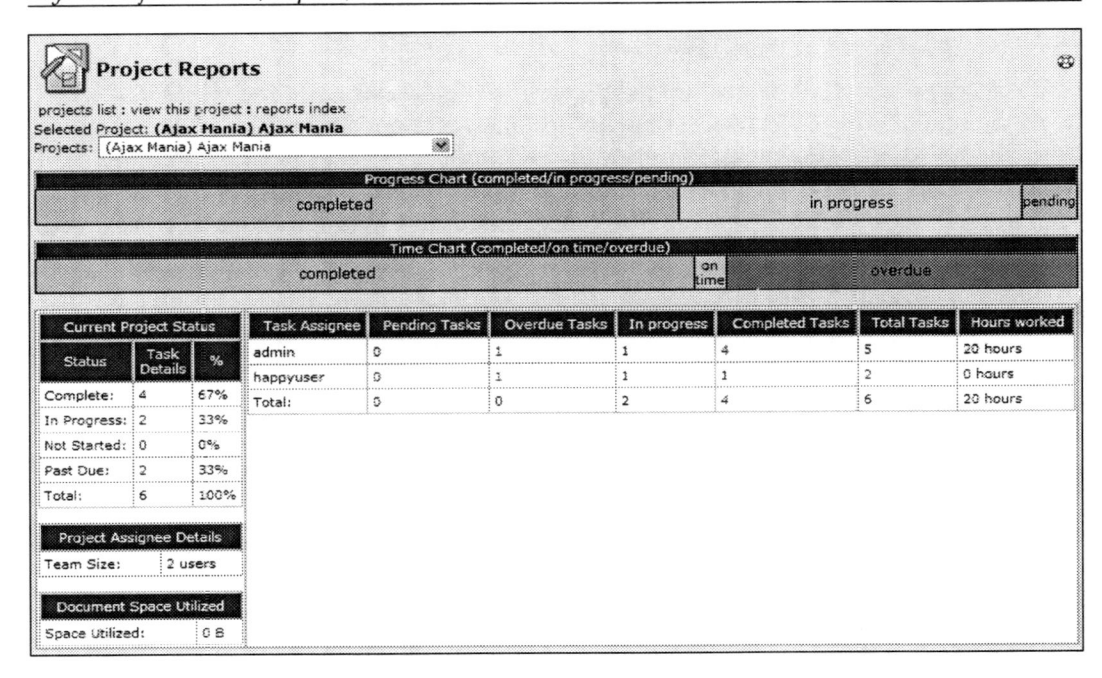

Beyond Projects: Charts, Reports, and Extensions

Project Reports							
projects list : view this project : reports index							
Selected Project: **(Ajax Mania) Ajax Mania**							
Projects: (Ajax Mania) Ajax Mania							

Progress Chart (completed/in progress/pending)		
completed	in progress	pending

Time Chart (completed/on time/overdue)		
completed	on time	overdue

Current Project Status			Task Assignee	Pending Tasks	Overdue Tasks	In progress	Completed Tasks	Total Tasks	Hours worked
Status	Task Details	%	admin	0	1	1	4	5	20 hours
			happyuser	0	1	1	1	2	0 hours
Complete:	4	67%	Total:	0	0	2	4	6	20 hours
In Progress:	2	33%							
Not Started:	0	0%							
Past Due:	2	33%							
Total:	6	100%							

Project Assignee Details	
Team Size:	2 users

Document Space Utilized	
Space Utilized:	0 B

The **Progress Chart** report displayed first shows the percentage of the project complete in green, the tasks in progress in blue, and tasks that should have started in orange. We can quickly see that over 60% of the project is complete by the large rectangle of green. The **Time Chart** has a disturbingly large rectangle of red. Over 30% of the tasks in the Ajax Mania project are past due.

Next a series of tables are displayed that include information on the **Current Project Status**, user task completion information, the number of people on the project team, and the file space used in the file repository. The different tables give a higher-level picture of how the project is doing when viewed together on one screen.

Resources

Resources in dotProject refer to furniture, equipment, rooms, and any other type of physical entity that may need to be allocated for a task. Resources must first be added in the **Resource** module before they can be associated with a task.

RESOURCES				NEW RESOURCE
tabbed : flat				

All Resources | Equipment | Tool | Venue

ID	Resource Name	Max Alloc %
121701	dell projector	100
121702	Iguana Meeting Room	100
121703	Persimmon Conference Room	100
121704	Full Color Printer	100
121705	Company Van	100
	Comfy Chair	100

Adding Resources

Resources are added by clicking on the **NEW RESOURCE** button on the **Resources** screen. They are classified as **All Resources**, **Equipment**, **Tools**, or **Venue**. The only required portion of the **Add Resource** screen is the name of the resource. Administrators may want to restrict access to this module to prevent users from clogging the resource list with clerical errors and inaccurate information.

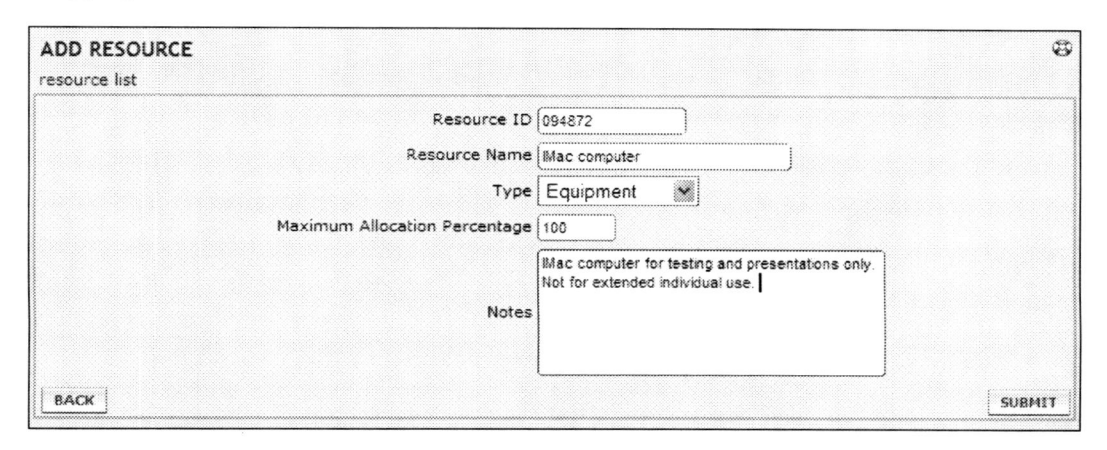

ADD RESOURCE
resource list

Resource ID: 094872
Resource Name: iMac computer
Type: Equipment
Maximum Allocation Percentage: 100
Notes: iMac computer for testing and presentations only. Not for extended individual use.

BACK   SUBMIT

Forums

The **Forums** module creates a basic discussion forum for use with individual projects. Users can use forums to record discussions, share notes, and distribute project news.

The forums module can be turned off if not being used by the system administrator in the modules area of the **System Administration** section of dotProject.

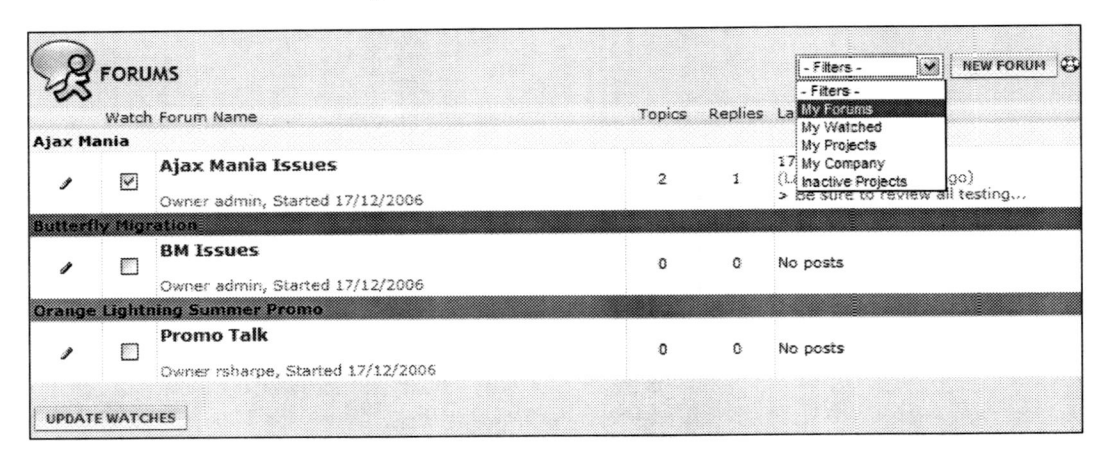

Those with access to the **Forums** module can view all the forums as their permissions allow. Forums can be added to a watch list so the user can be notified of any new posts or activity.

Forums for each project are accessible from that project's main screen on the tabbed section below the main display area.

Topics can be added to individual projects. Each topic can be watched for updates. Last posts, replies, and the post author are viewable from each forum's main screen.

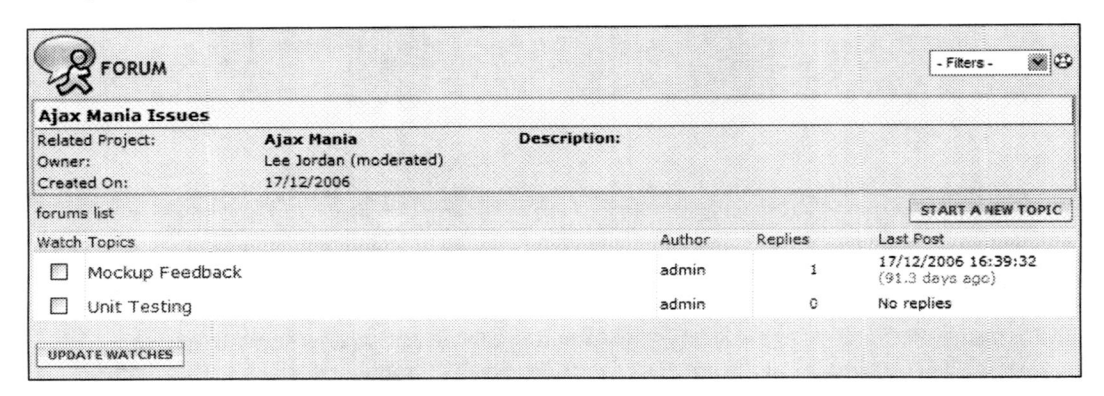

Calendar

The **Calendar** module displays different views depending on how it is accessed. A month view is the default view when accessed using the main navigation menu. The current day is shown on user login. A week view can be seen when users click on the icon of the numeral seven surrounded by a blue square at the beginning of each week.

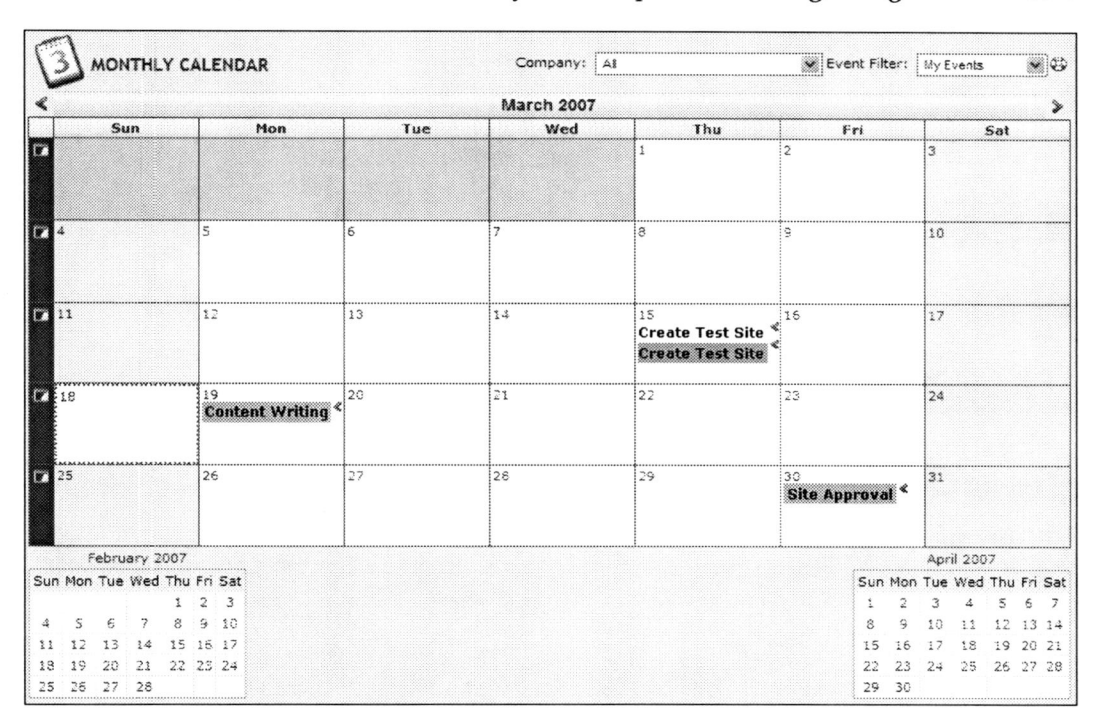

The **Week** view of the **Calendar** module gives users the option to filter the events seen. This reduces clutter when there are many tasks listed. The week and year are listed at the top of the view, but not the month. Hopefully future versions of the calendar will show the name of the month as well. Users can access the Month view underneath the Week view title. The **Today** view can be reached below the view. Each task can be directly reached by clicking on its listing.

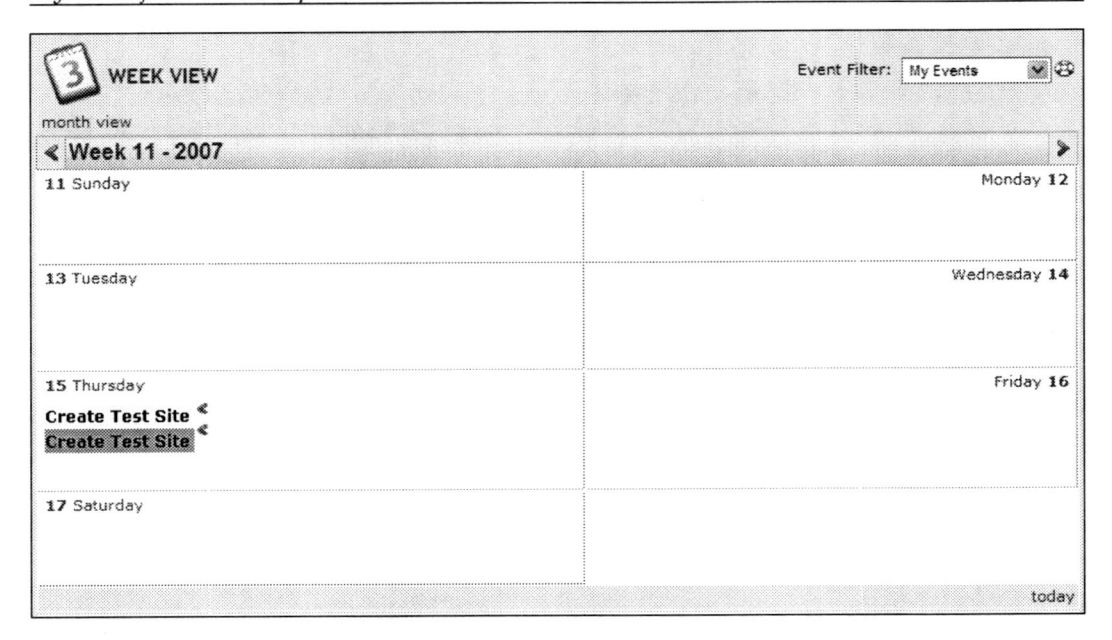

SmartSearch

The **SmartSearch** module allows users to search across all the modules within dotProject. Search features within individual modules are limited to their own module. This module can be activated within the module management area of the **System Admin** module.

To use **SmartSearch** on any available screen, type a word or phrase into the text box and click the **Search** button. The results will display once the page refreshes. Each active module is listed with links to any results returned from within it. Clicking on a result will take the user to a view of the result item. Users will have the option to search again as well.

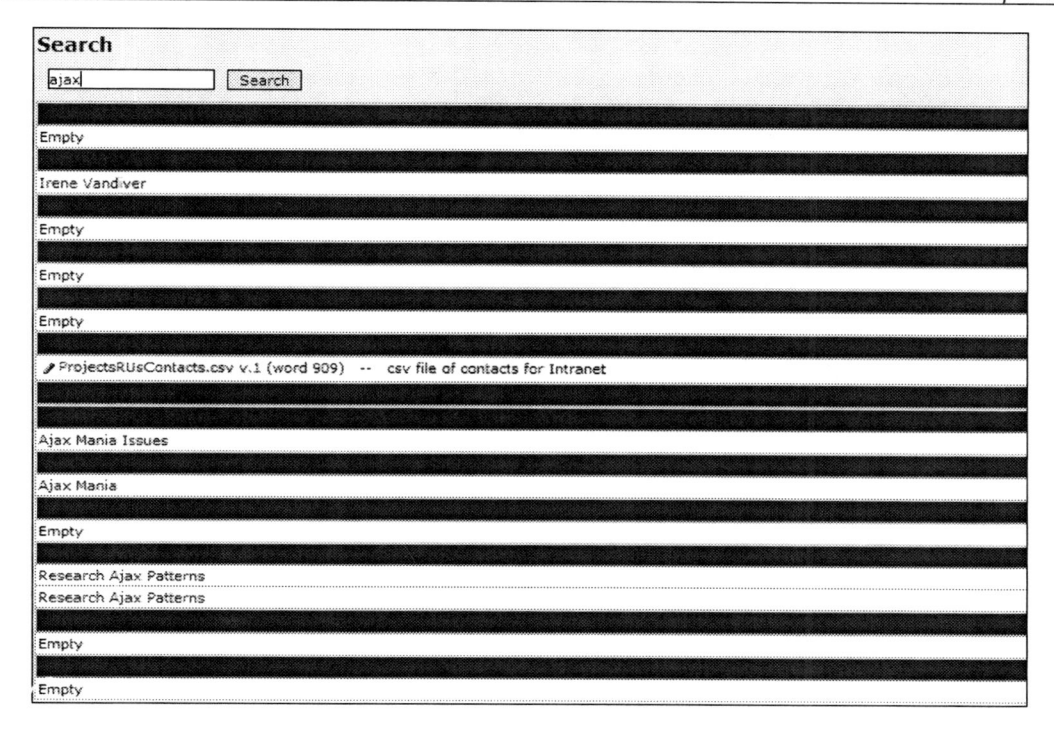

Backup

The **Backup** module is a new feature of dotProject 2.0. It gives administrators the option of creating an XML backup of the dotProject database. The files and other information of dotProject not stored in the database will not be backed up. Administrators should have a regularly scheduled backup system running in addition to the use of this module.

Backups are run from the **Backup** area within dotProject. The **Backup** module must first be installed before it can be used. **Backup** is considered to be both a standard module and an add-on. It can be downloaded from the dotProject mods on SourceForge.net at `http://sourceforge.net/project/showfiles.php?group_id=70930`.

Beyond Projects: Charts, Reports, and Extensions

To install the **Backup** module, unzip or un-tar the file then upload it to the modules subfolder of the dotProject installation. The module will then need to be installed just like all other modules. Once active it will appear on the main navigation menu. At this time it is only possible to back up the dotProject database. There is not a way to backup individual modules at this time.

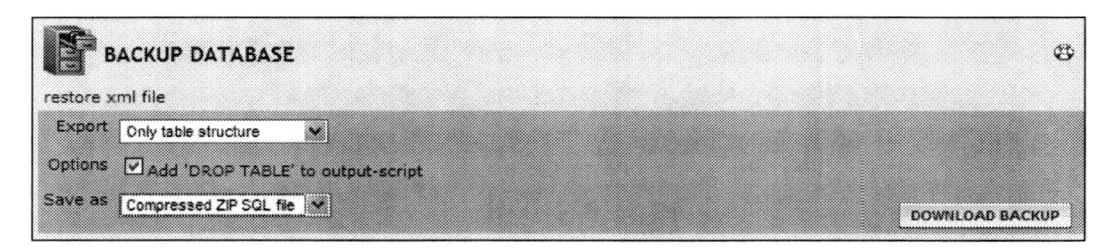

> **TicketSmith Module**
>
> **TicketSmith** is a depreciated legacy module. It will not be maintained past dotProject 3.0. It was originally included in dotProject to provide a helpdesk support feature. There are other add-on modules that provide the same functionality; we will discuss more about this in the later section about TicketSmith.

Add-On Modules

Have you wanted to add a ticketing or issue-tracking system into dotProject? Wondered where the risks assessment features were? The dotProject add-on modules are an easy way to extend dotProject to do all those things and more. Most of the add-on modules can be found at SourceForge.net at the dotProject mods project. Language packs can also be found at the same location: `http://sourceforge.net/projects/dotmods/`.

You can also search the Internet for other third-party modules. Before installing a module not listed on the SourceForge or dotProject sites, be sure to check the forums and see if anyone has posted any issues related to the module. Any third-party module is a potential security risk. Read any available documentation carefully. If the information is not clear, post on the forums or check the module creator's site for additional information.

Installing Add-Ons

dotProject modules can usually all be installed using exactly the same method. Be sure to check the `readme` file of a module before installation for any special instructions.

1. After the module is unzipped, upload it to the `/modules/` folder of the dotProject installation.

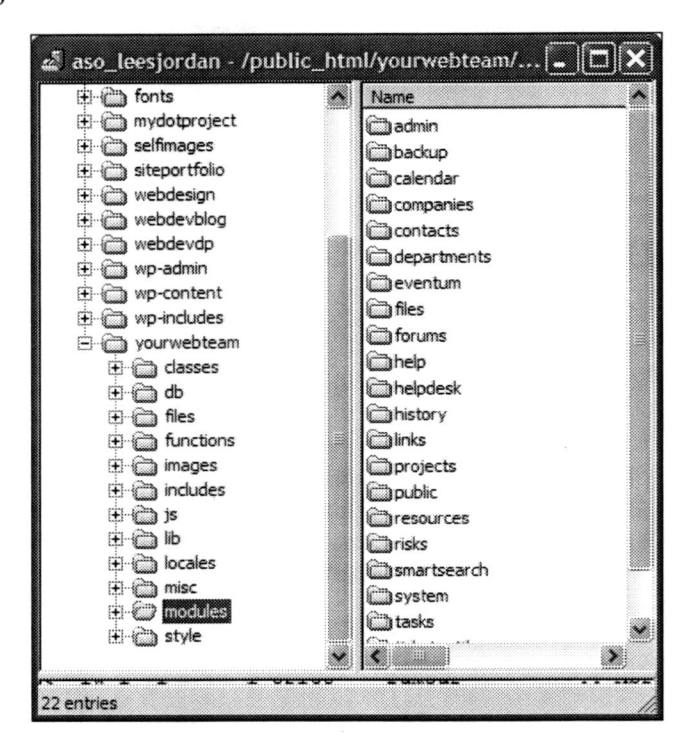

2. Log in to dotProject and go to the **System Administration** screen.
3. Click on the **View Modules** link.
4. The **View Modules** screen will appear. The module should now be displayed on the modules list. If the module is disabled, click on the **disabled** link to activate it. If the module has a **configure** link, click on it to make any additional changes. To make the module visible on the main navigation menu, click the **hidden** link in the **Menu Status** column.

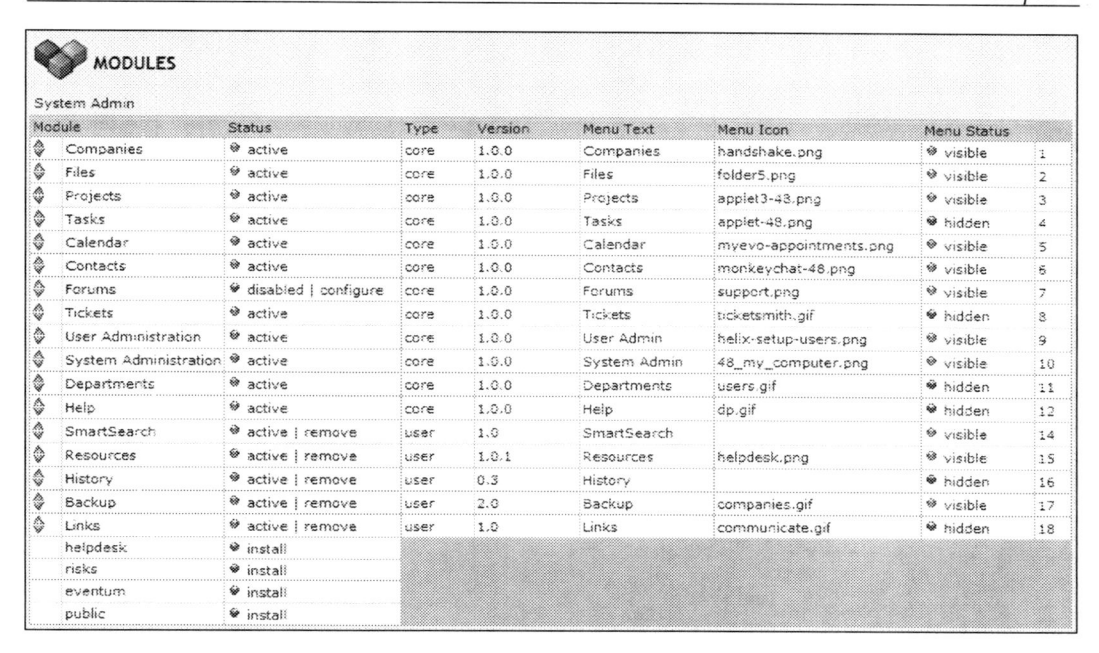

Module	Status	Type	Version	Menu Text	Menu Icon	Menu Status	
Companies	active	core	1.0.0	Companies	handshake.png	visible	1
Files	active	core	1.0.0	Files	folder5.png	visible	2
Projects	active	core	1.0.0	Projects	applet3-48.png	visible	3
Tasks	active	core	1.0.0	Tasks	applet-48.png	hidden	4
Calendar	active	core	1.0.0	Calendar	myevo-appointments.png	visible	5
Contacts	active	core	1.0.0	Contacts	monkeychat-48.png	visible	6
Forums	disabled	configure	core	1.0.0	Forums	support.png	visible	7
Tickets	active	core	1.0.0	Tickets	ticketsmith.gif	hidden	8
User Administration	active	core	1.0.0	User Admin	helix-setup-users.png	visible	9
System Administration	active	core	1.0.0	System Admin	48_my_computer.png	visible	10
Departments	active	core	1.0.0	Departments	users.gif	hidden	11
Help	active	core	1.0.0	Help	dp.gif	hidden	12
SmartSearch	active	remove	user	1.0	SmartSearch		visible	14
Resources	active	remove	user	1.0.1	Resources	helpdesk.png	visible	15
History	active	remove	user	0.3	History		hidden	16
Backup	active	remove	user	2.0	Backup	companies.gif	visible	17
Links	active	remove	user	1.0	Links	communicate.gif	hidden	18
helpdesk	install						
risks	install						
eventum	install						
public	install						

Eventum

Eventum is an enterprise-level ticketing and issue tracking system. The dotProject developers created an add-on module that integrates **Eventum** with dotProject. **Eventum** should be installed before the dotProject module (also known as **Eventum**) is added to your dotProject installation.

> Eventum being a very useful feature has been covered in this book. However, it will be worth noting that this feature is redundant in dotProject 2.0.4 and is applicable in 2.0.1.

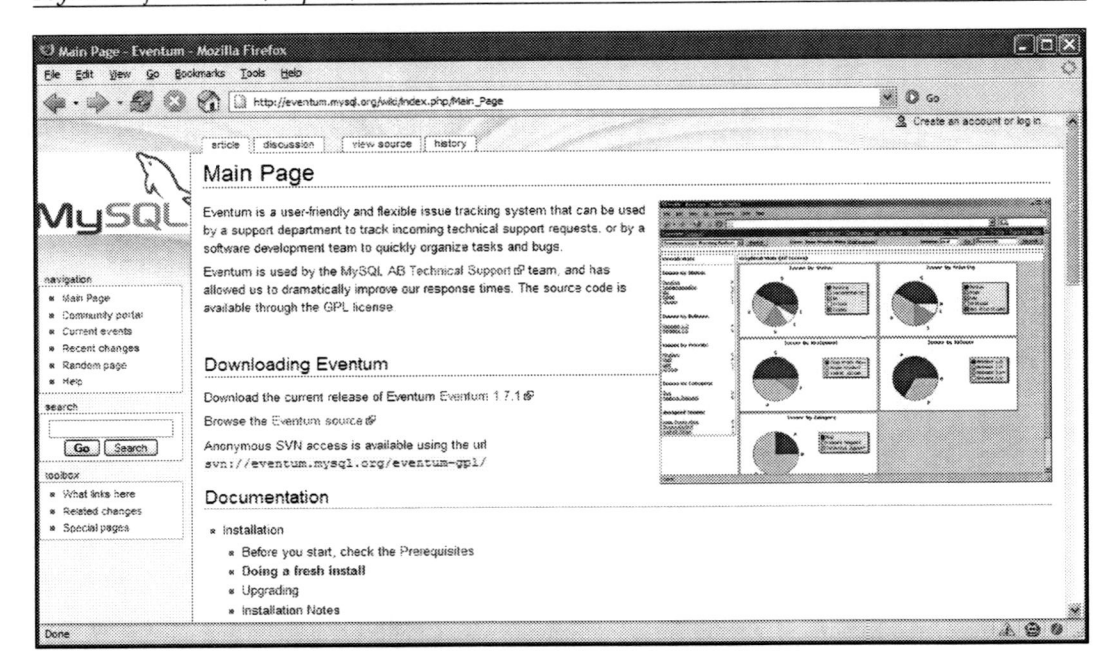

Eventum is available for download from the MySQL.org site:

```
http://dev.mysql.com/get/Downloads/eventum/eventum-1.7.1.tar.gz/from/pick
```

Read Eventum's documentation wiki at MySQL.org:

```
http://eventum.mysql.org/wiki/index.php/Main_Page
```

Installing the Eventum Module

After the **Eventum** integration folder has been uploaded to the dotProject installation, additional steps need to be taken to configure it to work properly in dotProject.

Chapter 7

1. Install the module by clicking on the **disabled** link next to **Eventum** on the modules list.

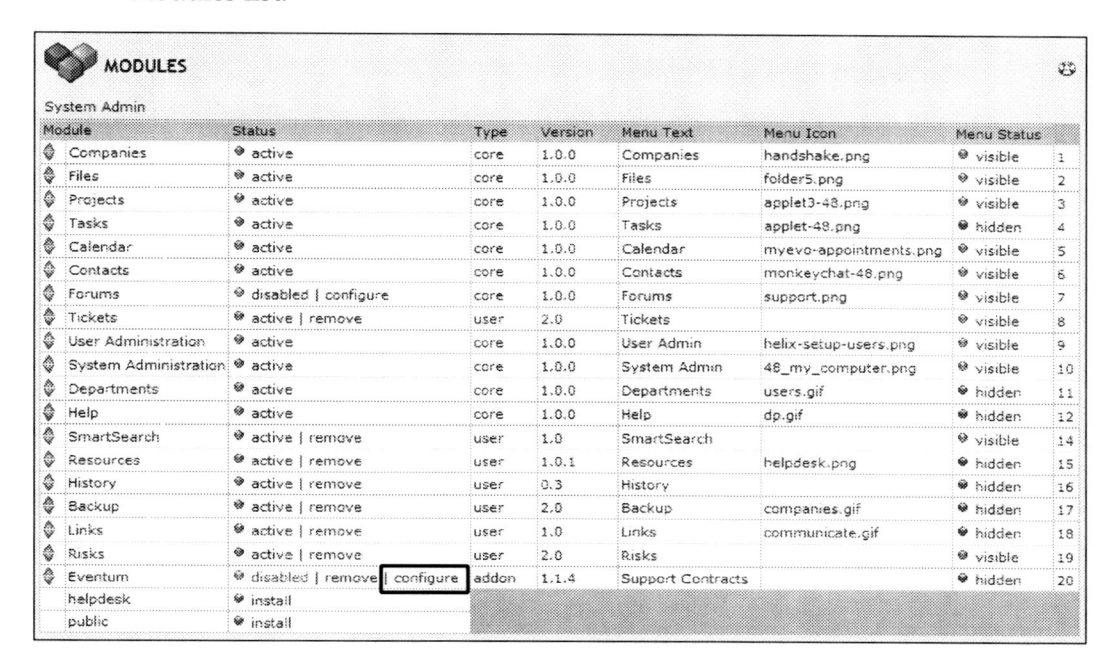

Module	Status	Type	Version	Menu Text	Menu Icon	Menu Status	
Companies	active	core	1.0.0	Companies	handshake.png	visible	1
Files	active	core	1.0.0	Files	folder5.png	visible	2
Projects	active	core	1.0.0	Projects	applet3-48.png	visible	3
Tasks	active	core	1.0.0	Tasks	applet-48.png	hidden	4
Calendar	active	core	1.0.0	Calendar	myevo-appointments.png	visible	5
Contacts	active	core	1.0.0	Contacts	monkeychat-48.png	visible	6
Forums	disabled	configure	core	1.0.0	Forums	support.png	visible	7
Tickets	active	remove	user	2.0	Tickets		visible	8
User Administration	active	core	1.0.0	User Admin	helix-setup-users.png	visible	9
System Administration	active	core	1.0.0	System Admin	48_my_computer.png	visible	10
Departments	active	core	1.0.0	Departments	users.gif	hidden	11
Help	active	core	1.0.0	Help	dp.gif	hidden	12
SmartSearch	active	remove	user	1.0	SmartSearch		visible	14
Resources	active	remove	user	1.0.1	Resources	helpdesk.png	hidden	15
History	active	remove	user	0.3	History		hidden	16
Backup	active	remove	user	2.0	Backup	companies.gif	hidden	17
Links	active	remove	user	1.0	Links	communicate.gif	hidden	18
Risks	active	remove	user	2.0	Risks		visible	19
Eventum	disabled	remove	configure	addon	1.1.4	Support Contracts		hidden	20
helpdesk	install						
public	install						

2. Click the **configure** link and you will see the following screenshot:

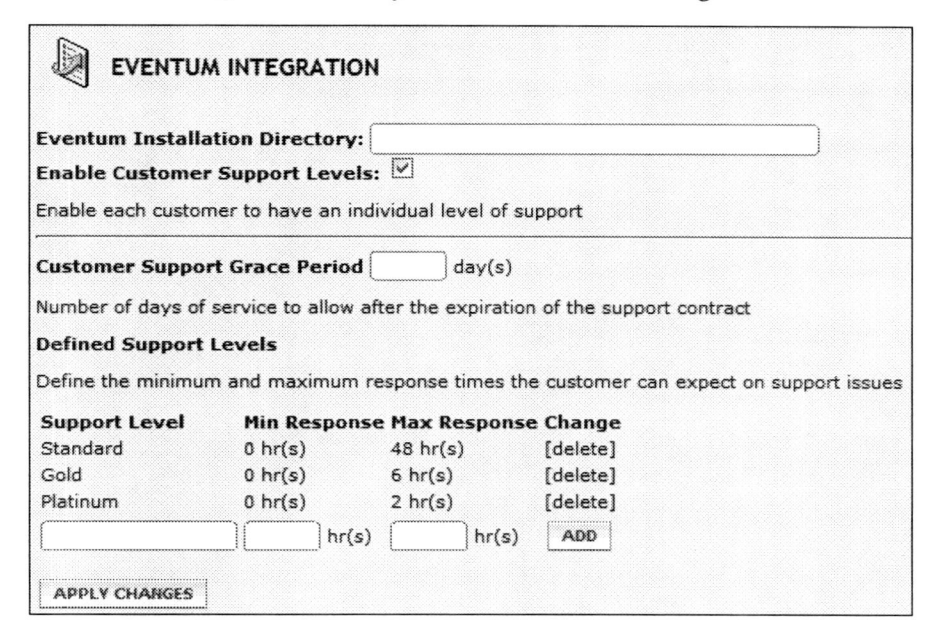

EVENTUM INTEGRATION

Eventum Installation Directory: [   ]
Enable Customer Support Levels: ☑
Enable each customer to have an individual level of support

Customer Support Grace Period [   ] day(s)
Number of days of service to allow after the expiration of the support contract

Defined Support Levels
Define the minimum and maximum response times the customer can expect on support issues

Support Level	Min Response	Max Response	Change
Standard	0 hr(s)	48 hr(s)	[delete]
Gold	0 hr(s)	6 hr(s)	[delete]
Platinum	0 hr(s)	2 hr(s)	[delete]
	[ ] hr(s)	[ ] hr(s)	ADD

APPLY CHANGES

3. Type the installation directory into the **Eventum Installation Directory** text field.
4. Check **Enable Customer Support Levels** if the module will be used to help track customer issues and tickets.
5. A new series of choices will appear if the **Enable Customer Support Levels** checkbox is selected. The **Customer Support Grace Period** can be set by day(s).
6. The **Defined Support Levels** section sets up various levels of response time for support issues. **Custom levels** can be added using the form fields.
7. When configuration is completed click the **Apply Changes** button.
8. A final configuration screen will appear with links to `.zip` and `.tar gz` compressed versions of the `evlink` folder. Download the folder, then upload it to the **Eventum** installation and unzip it to complete the integration. The files can also be unzipped locally and then uploaded according to the folder paths.
9. If the **Eventum** configuration file is not writable from the dotProject installation, a text file to copy and then paste at the end of the **Eventum** `config.inc.php` file will be displayed as shown in the following screenshot:

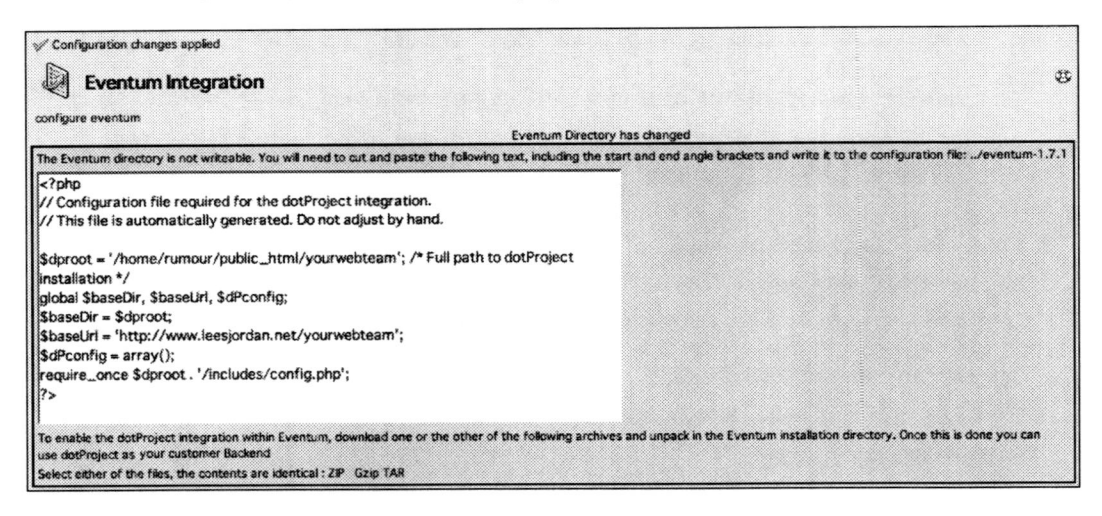

![Eventum Integration screenshot]

10. Log out of dotProject and log back in. An **Issues** tab should appear in the **ToDo** area and in the bottom tab section of individual project screens.

Using Eventum

Once **Eventum** has been successfully installed and the dotProject **Eventum** module has been configured, the combined support contracts system should be ready to use. The integration works by sharing dotProject companies and contacts who have a support contract defined with the **Eventum** installation. **Projects** in **Eventum** and dotProject can be linked to each other individually, but not in a group. Users who have a login set up for **Eventum** that is the same as their dotProject login can view issues assigned to them on the **Today** tab in dotProject.

> **Eventum** is currently available only for version 2.01 of dotProject.

Eventum is primarily used for bug tracking and support ticket issues. It provides additional functionality to dotProject users who need a ticketing solution.

Enabling Support Contracts in dotProject

Support contracts can be enabled for each company on the **Eventum Support Contracts** screen. Click on **Support Contracts** from the main navigation menu. The **Eventum Support Contracts** screen will be displayed as in the following screenshot:

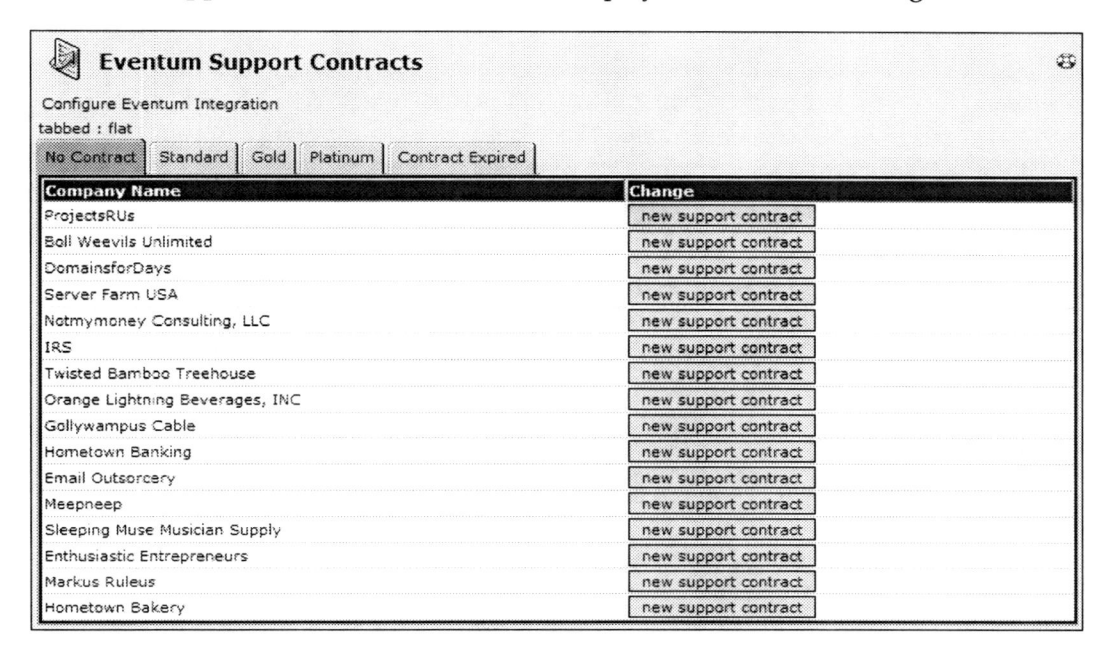

Eventum Support Contracts

Configure Eventum Integration
tabbed : flat

No Contract | Standard | Gold | Platinum | Contract Expired

Company Name	Change
ProjectsRUs	new support contract
Boll Weevils Unlimited	new support contract
DomainsforDays	new support contract
Server Farm USA	new support contract
Notmymoney Consulting, LLC	new support contract
IRS	new support contract
Twisted Bamboo Treehouse	new support contract
Orange Lightning Beverages, INC	new support contract
Gollywampus Cable	new support contract
Hometown Banking	new support contract
Email Outsorcery	new support contract
Meepneep	new support contract
Sleeping Muse Musician Supply	new support contract
Enthusiastic Entrepreneurs	new support contract
Markus Ruleus	new support contract
Hometown Bakery	new support contract

Five tab choices are displayed by default: **No Contract, Standard, Gold, Platinum**, and **Contract Expired**. Until support contracts are added, all companies will be listed under the **No Contract** tab. There is currently no way to assign contracts to multiple companies at the same time.

1. To add a support contract to a company, click on the **new support contract** button in the **Change** column next to the **Company Name**. The **Add/Edit Eventum Support Contract** screen is shown in the following screenshot:

2. Select a date range for the company by clicking on the calendar next to each date field. Select a contract type from the drop-down list then click the **save** button to apply the support contract to the company.

Helpdesk

Helpdesk is a ticketing and support desk module. It is recommended as a replacement for TicketSmith by the developers of dotProject. There is still a great deal of work being done on **Helpdesk**. It is recommended that users download the latest version or individual code patches from the CVS on SourceForge.net, which can be found here: `http://sourceforge.net/project/showfiles.php?group_id=70930`.

To download, click on the **HelpDesk** link on the page. It will take you to the **HelpDesk** download screen. Choose which compressed file format you prefer and click the file name to begin the download—`helpdesk_20040507.tar.gz` or `helpdesk_20040507.zip`.

If there are problems users can update files from the CVS: `http://dotmods.cvs.sourceforge.net/dotmods/helpdesk/` or visit `http://www.packtpub.com/support`, and select this book from the list of titles to download.

Attempting to install the `tar.gz` version on the main portion of the dotmods project will most likely result in a blank content area of the dotProject installation.

Installation and Configuration

The module should install normally. It can be configured before being activated by clicking on the **configure** link. Make sure that the `config.php` file is writable before making any changes.

The **Helpdesk** module is highly configurable. It is a more advanced ticketing tool than TicketSmith. Administrators have many choices that tailor the module to suit the needs of the users.

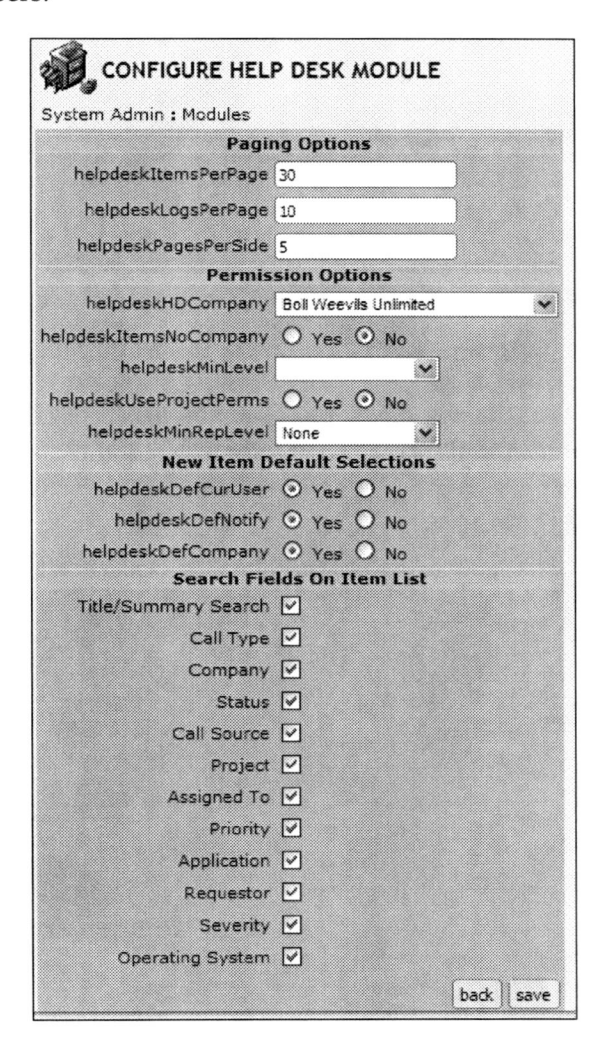

Beyond Projects: Charts, Reports, and Extensions

Using Help Desk

The user view is much cleaner than TicketSmith and has many options of bug tracking software such as **Bugzilla** that users should be familiar with. The types of tickets are clearly organized and contain useful icons. The tickets are categorized by status, when opened, closed, and if watched on the progress of the solution. New items can be added by clicking on the **NEW ITEM** button.

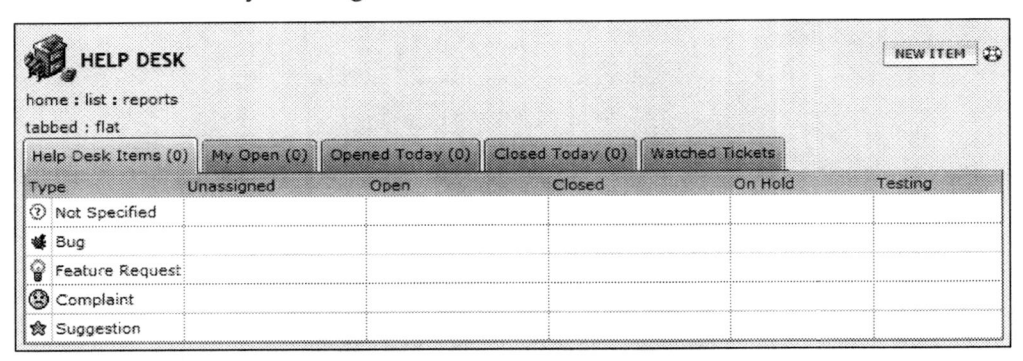

Clicking the **NEW ITEM** button will take users to the **ADDING HELP DESK ITEM** screen. Users creating new items have many options to choose from. All required fields are clearly marked. Once the ticket has been created, clicking the **SUBMIT** button will return the user to the **Help Desk** screen.

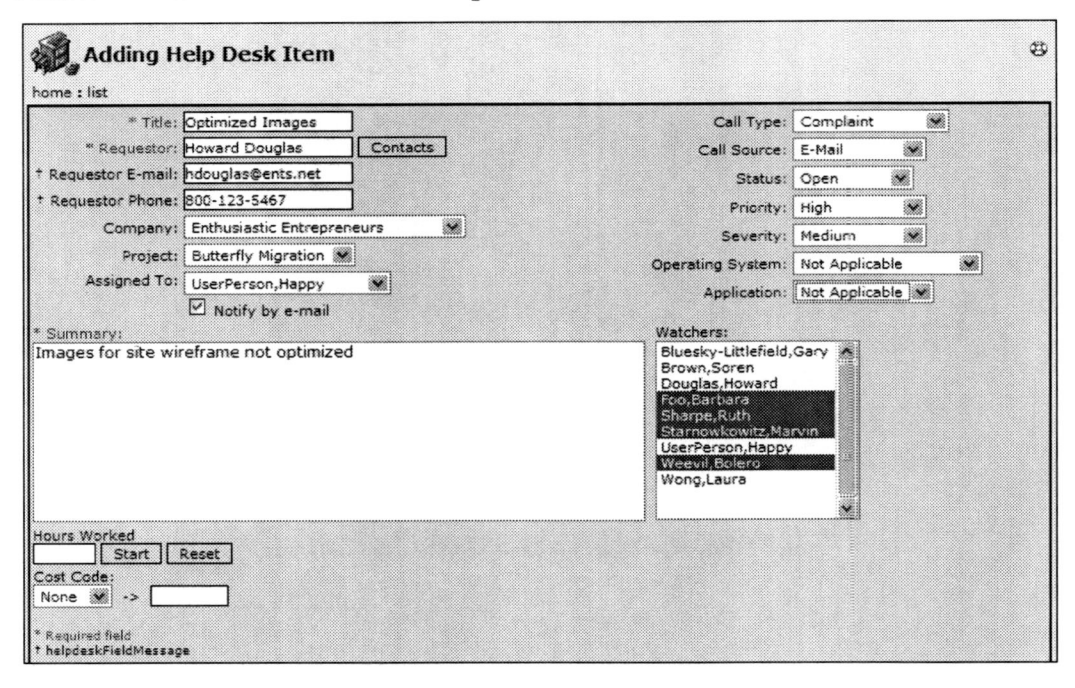

Invoice

The **Invoice** module was designed for everyday users to have a way to create invoices from within dotProject. Professional accountants may find it lacking in features. If you are having trouble with the **Invoice** module, the latest version may need to be installed (`invoice_alpha2.tar.gz` as of May 2007) from SourceForge.net.

Installing the **Invoice** module follows the basic installation method given at the beginning of this chapter. The **Invoice** module is designed differently than many other dotProject modules. Invoices can only be created from within a project. Users are not able to create invoices from the main **Invoice** screen. Invoices can only be sorted and viewed from that location.

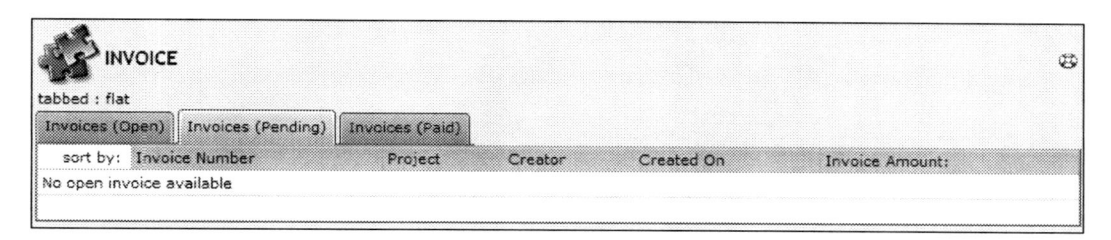

Using Invoice

New invoices can be created from the individual project screens by clicking on the **new invoice** button underneath the **Invoice** tab. Users will then be taken to a **New Invoice** screen. After filling out the invoice information, clicking the **submit** button will save the invoice.

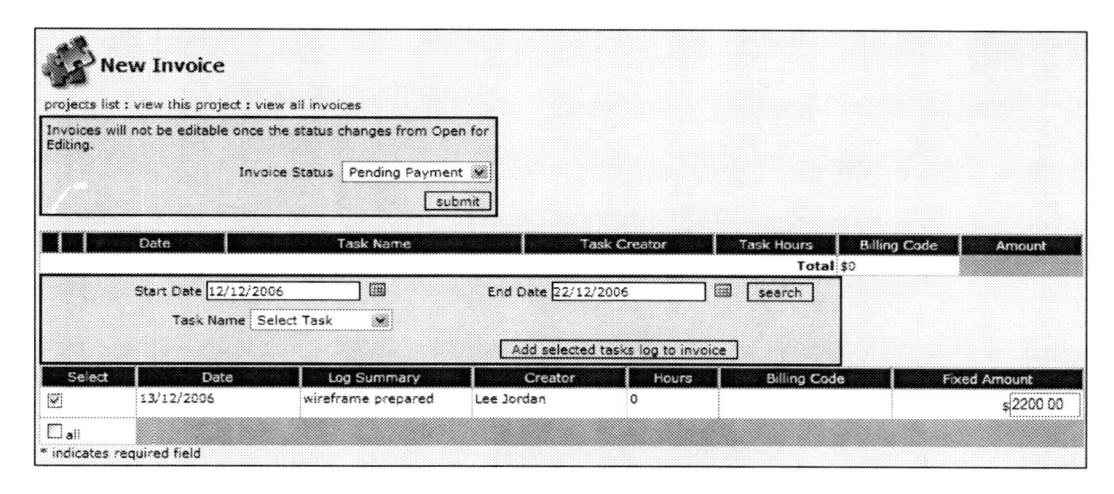

TicketSmith

TicketSmith is a basic ticketing system which is expected to be replaced by **Helpdesk** in version 3.0 of dotProject. The developers will not be updating TicketSmith for versions of dotProject 3.0 and above. If you are going to commit to using dotProject for any length of time, **Helpdesk** is a better investment of time.

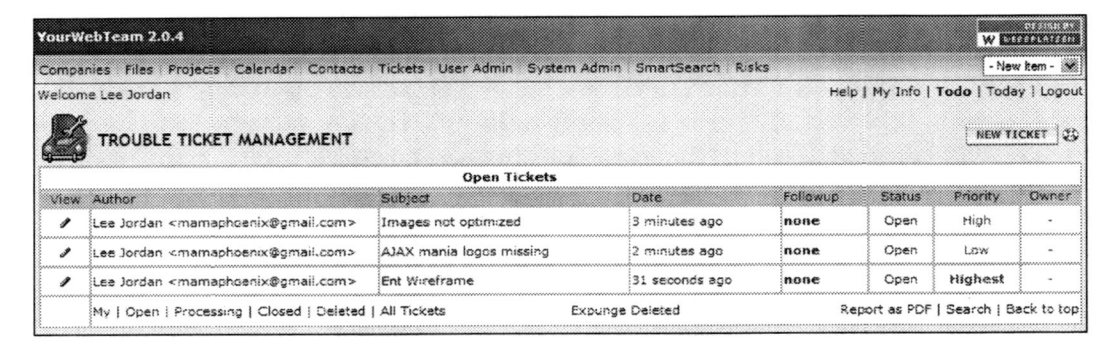

TicketSmith installs easily. Upload the unzipped folder to the modules folder of your dotProject environment. The module will display as **Tickets** on the **View Modules** list. Click the **update** link if necessary and then make the module visible by clicking on the **hidden** link.

Using TicketSmith

TicketSmith uses a simple form to add issue tickets in a forum style format. More details can be set for a ticket after it is created. Tickets do not have to be associated with a project, but they can only be assigned to a person who as a dotProject user account.

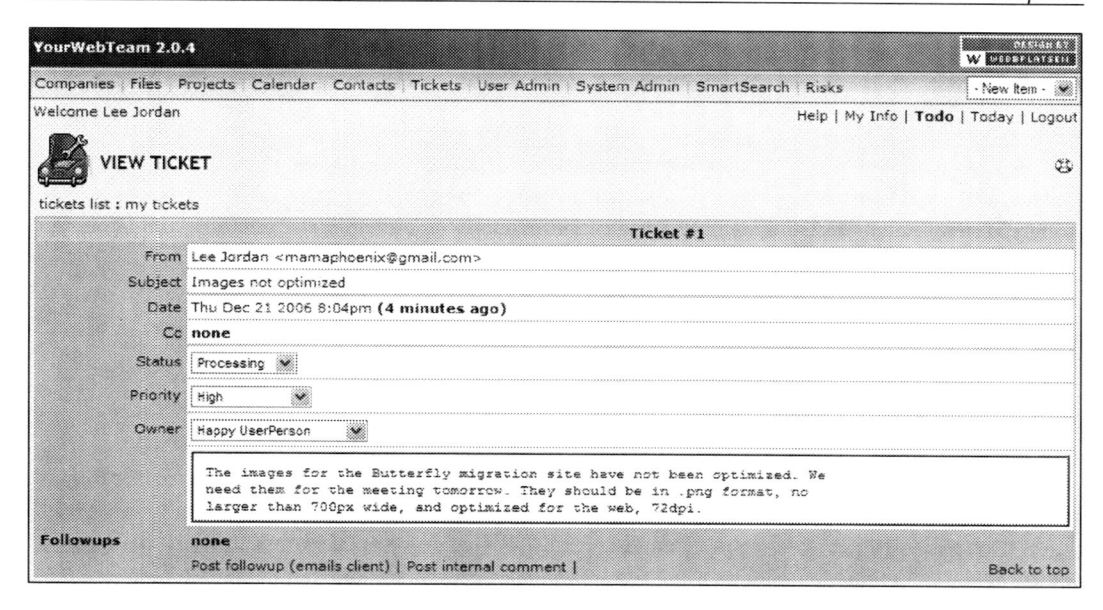

Internal notes can be added to tickets. They will appear with a blue background in their own box below the ticket notes. The actual ticket information is kept separate from staff notes. Follow-up information can also be posted. Posting follow-up information will automatically email the client.

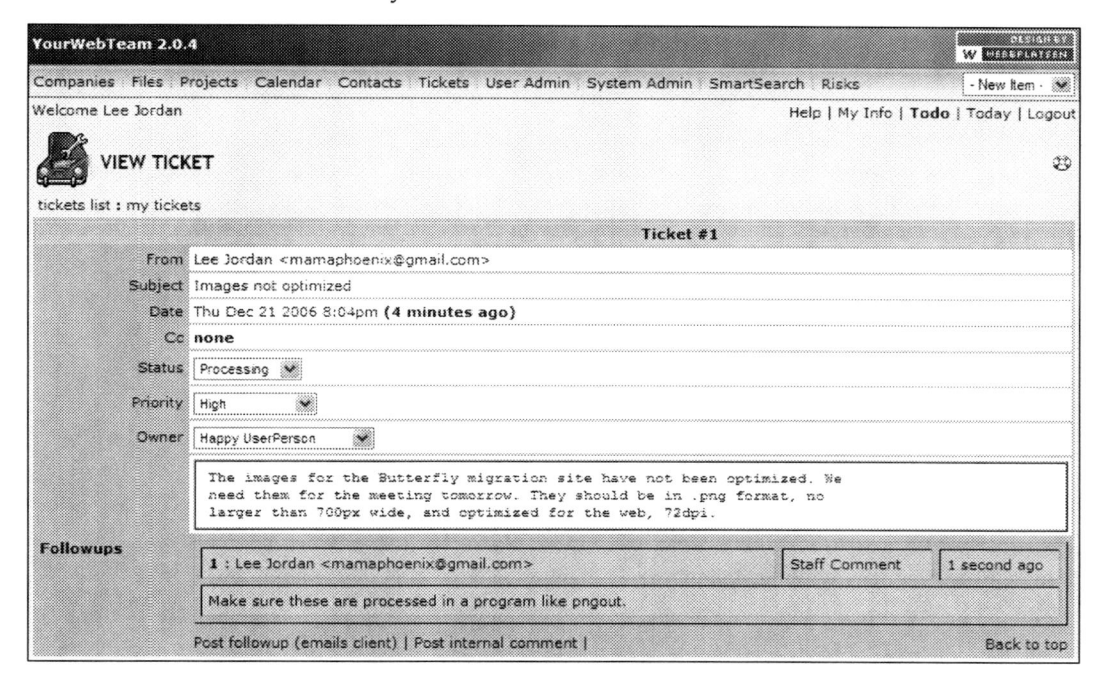

Custom Modification and Integrations

Short on time or developer resources? Think dotProject would be a great solution for your situation if you could just change a particular thing about it? Customized modification may be for you. Developers and support resources are available to customize dotProject at a price. Customization projects are priced individually according to complexity and the developer's rate.

What are the advantages?

- A developer who is experienced with dotProject code
- Specialized programming resources
- Quick development time

Another option to having a dotProject-approved developer work on your installation is to purchase courses through dotProject for your own developers or consultants. The courses were created by key dotProject developers and cover a variety of topics.

Developer Resources

There are many types of developer resources available for dotProject. Programmers can find extensive information about contributing to dotProject on the documentation wiki in the Programmer docs section. Information about the framework, module creation, CVS access, as well as other in-depth documentation is provided.

How do I Volunteer?

If you are looking to volunteer with dotProject, there are three key areas where you can contribute that may eventually lead to being able to directly contribute to core development:

1. Become and active contributor on the forum (http://www.dotproject.net/vbulletin/).
2. Report bugs and submit patches or suggestions.
3. Create a useful module for everyone to use.
4. Translate dotProject into another language.

Being listed as a Professional Developer on the dotProject site is limited to authorized core developers. Showing commitment to the project as a whole is the first step to becoming a trusted contributor.

The dotProject community is international and made up of users from a variety of backgrounds and levels of experience. The primary location of community activity is the dotProject forum site. No issue is too big or too small to answer. Registering as a member of the dotProject forum gives participants access to email notifications when threads are updated, different statuses based on posting frequency and helpfulness, and free membership in a global community of dotProject users.

What should I Know?

Developers should be familiar with PHP, MySQL, JavaScript, XHTML 1.1, and CSS 2.0. Documentation of changes made and version control is a must. They should be willing to follow the basics of code contribution as described in the Contribution Basics section of `http://docs.dotproject.net`. dotProject is coded in a platform-independent methodology.

If you cannot find a language pack for your particular dialect or language, consider translating dotProject and contributing the language pack.

Summary

Having a basic understanding of their purpose allows users and administrators to make informed decisions about what modules are necessary in their dotProject environment.

The twelve core modules can be disabled but not removed. There are four main types of modules: **Issue Tracking**, **Project Enhancements**, **Business Modules**, and **Language Packs**. Not all modules will continue to be supported by dotProject in version 3.0. Modules such as the **Department** and **Reports** are not yet fully functional. Third-party tools such as JpGraph enable the dotProject developers to spend more time focusing on improving the core modules. A new version of dotProject is available as a public beta: 2.1 RC1. It is not ready for production use. Review the documentation at `http://docs.dotproject.net/index.php/Release_Notes_-_2.1.0_-_rc1`.

In addition to installing ready-made modules, users can hire experienced dotProject developers for "Do-It-For-Me" customization and integration. Users can take a variety of courses that will show them how to further extend dotProject. Serious developers can use the many resources available to delve into the back-end functionality of dotProject to make further modifications.

The dotProject team has always been committed to the project functionality of dotProject. They continue to focus on improving the core features.

A
Upgrading dotProject

The core developers regularly update dotProject. If your version of dotProject is 2.03 or below, upgrading to version 2.04 will make your installation more secure. Version 2.04 contains a major security patch. The process of upgrading dotProject is usually routine. There are several precautions that should always be taken with any upgrade:

- Back up the dotProject database.
- Back up the dotProject files.
- Review the release notes for the planned upgrade.
- Have a rollback plan in place.
- Test the upgrade in a development "sandbox" first.

The most recent public version of dotProject is available at:

```
http://sourceforge.net/projects/dotproject/
```

Those who want the very latest stable version can download it from the CVS, which is also located at the above URL.

If you are already using a control-panel-based tool such as Fantastico, you will automatically be prompted to upgrade when you visit the Fantastico tool.

Other users will need to upload the new files to their dotProject installation. Always download the most recent version possible to avoid conflicts with modules and possible security risks.

Backing Up dotProject

Things don't always go according to plan. Natural disasters, hardware failures, and other unforeseen circumstances occur. Risk management is a crucial part of any project. A dotProject administrator who prefers to manage and minimize potential risk takes measures to safeguard data against loss, whether from a planned upgrade or a random disaster.

> Backing up environment files and database is a best practice, no matter what application you use.

The actual process followed to back up files and databases will depend upon what system architecture dotProject is installed on. That is a fancy way of saying, if a control panel such as **cPanel** or **Plesk** is used, then backing up is fairly easy. Both the popular control panel environments have applications that do the hard work for administrators and have a friendly GUI environment. Advanced administrators can use command-line interfaces to create automatic backups. Using a command-line interface is beyond the scope of this book. We will instead cover how to back up files and databases using cPanel, a popular control-panel environment provided by most Internet Service Providers who host domains.

The screenshot opposite shows the three tools of cPanel we will discuss in this appendix: Backups, Cron jobs, and Fantastico.

Appendix A

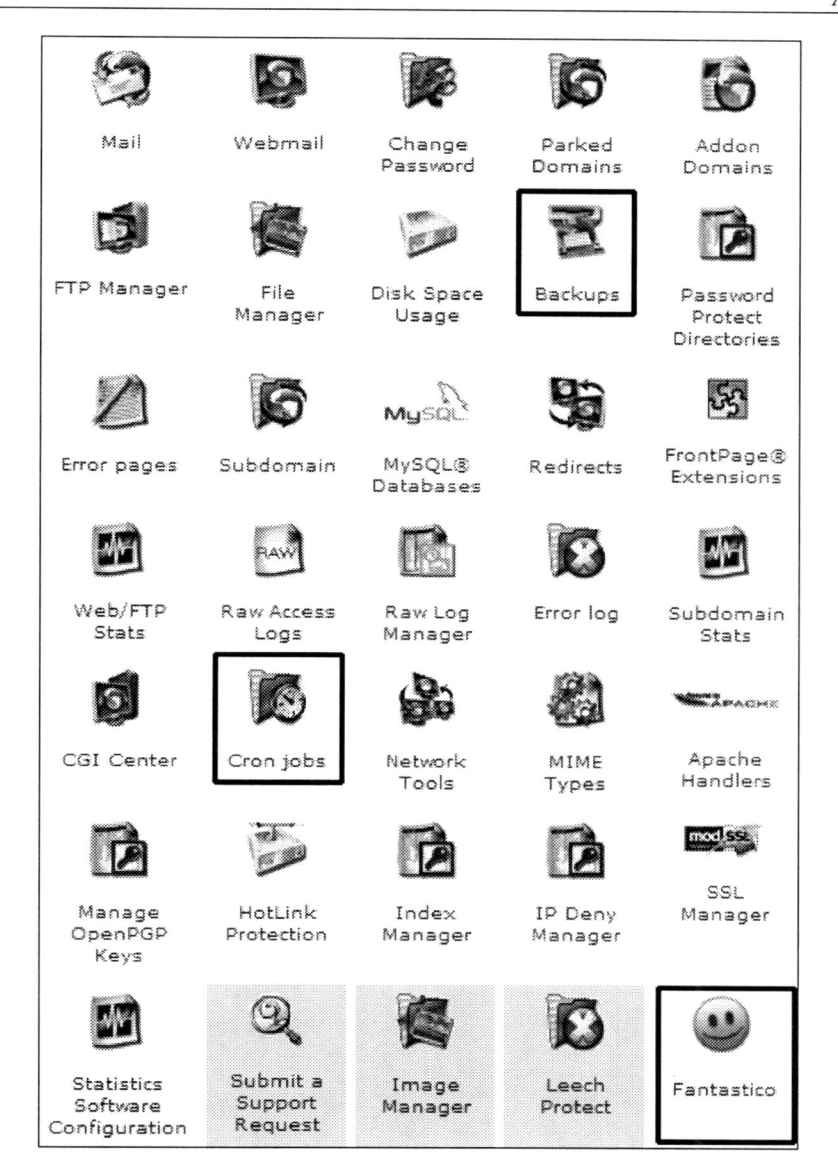

Mail	Webmail	Change Password	Parked Domains	Addon Domains
FTP Manager	File Manager	Disk Space Usage	**Backups**	Password Protect Directories
Error pages	Subdomain	MySQL® Databases	Redirects	FrontPage® Extensions
Web/FTP Stats	Raw Access Logs	Raw Log Manager	Error log	Subdomain Stats
CGI Center	**Cron jobs**	Network Tools	MIME Types	Apache Handlers
Manage OpenPGP Keys	HotLink Protection	Index Manager	IP Deny Manager	SSL Manager
Statistics Software Configuration	Submit a Support Request	Image Manager	Leech Protect	**Fantastico**

[203]

Upgrading dotProject

Using cPanel Backups for Easy Manual Backups

It is easy to create and restore manual backups of databases and files using the **Backups** tool in cPanel X. No coding or messing with databases or FTP is required. The screenshot below shows the **Backups** tool as it appears in a browser window.

Clicking on the **Download a home directory Backup** link under the **Home Directory** heading creates a manual backup of the dotProject installation. Restore the backup under the **Restore a Home Directory Backup** heading by browsing and then uploading the backup file.

Manually back up a MySQL database by clicking on the name of the database under the **Download a MySQL Database Backup** heading. The **Restore a MySQL Database** area is where a backup copy of a database can be restored by browsing to the backup file and then uploading it.

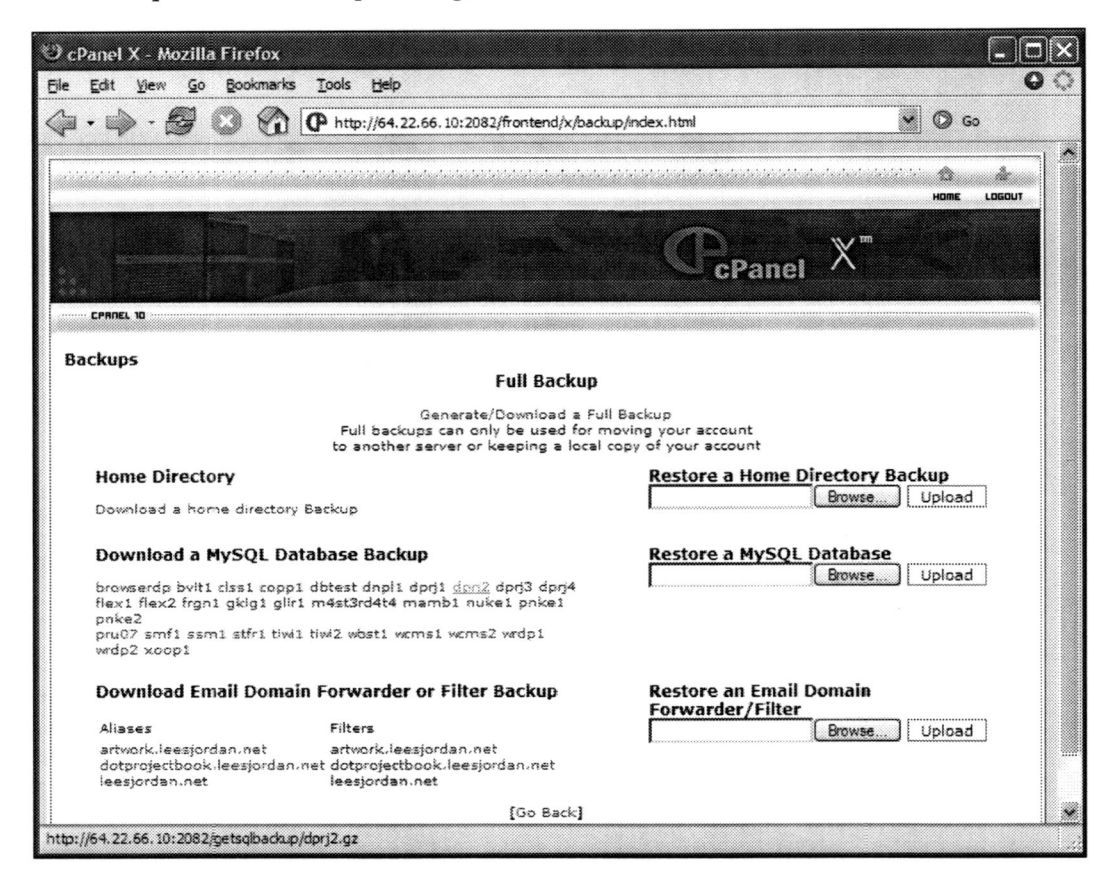

Back Up the dotProject Database Automatically with Cron Jobs

Knowing how to back up the dotProject database manually and automatically gives administrators flexibility. Even though we can restore the dotProject database using the Backup module discussed in Chapter 7, being able to back up a database is a crucial administrative skill. It is the same process no matter what application is using the database. The fictitious ProjectsRUs company uses MySQL for its dotProject database. We will walk through setting up an automatic back up for a MySQL database since that is the database most users are likely to use.

1. Create a folder for the dotProject backups. It should be just under the `/home/root name/` (the site root) folder on the server, and not in the `/public_html/` folder. In the following screenshot, a folder for the ProjectsRUs backups called **dotProject_backups** has been created and placed just under the root folder of the site.

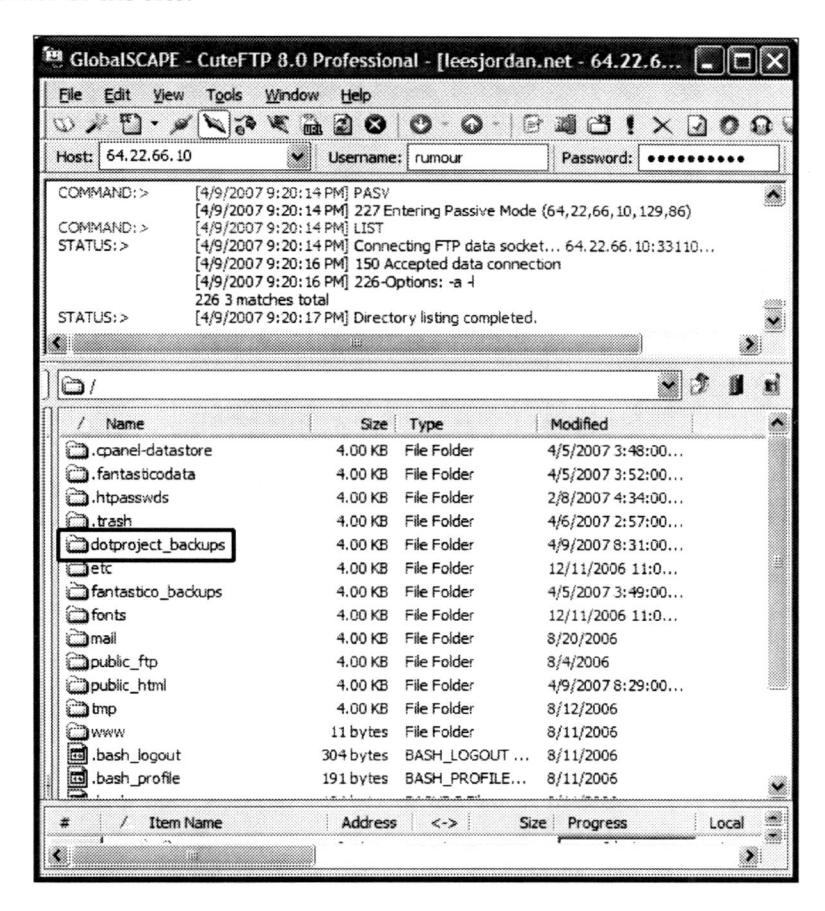

Upgrading dotProject

> Placing any backup file in the `public_html` folder is a security risk. It is much easier for unscrupulous people or malicious Internet bots to snatch sensitive database files if they are left in the `public_html` folder.

2. Log in to cPanel and click on the Cron Jobs icon. It looks like a folder with a clock leaning against it. The Cron Jobs experience menu will appear. Click on the **Standard** button to open the Cron Jobs screen.

> The word **Cron** is a shortened version of the term "chronological". Cron Jobs are tasks done within a specified time frame. They are often repeated on a regular schedule.

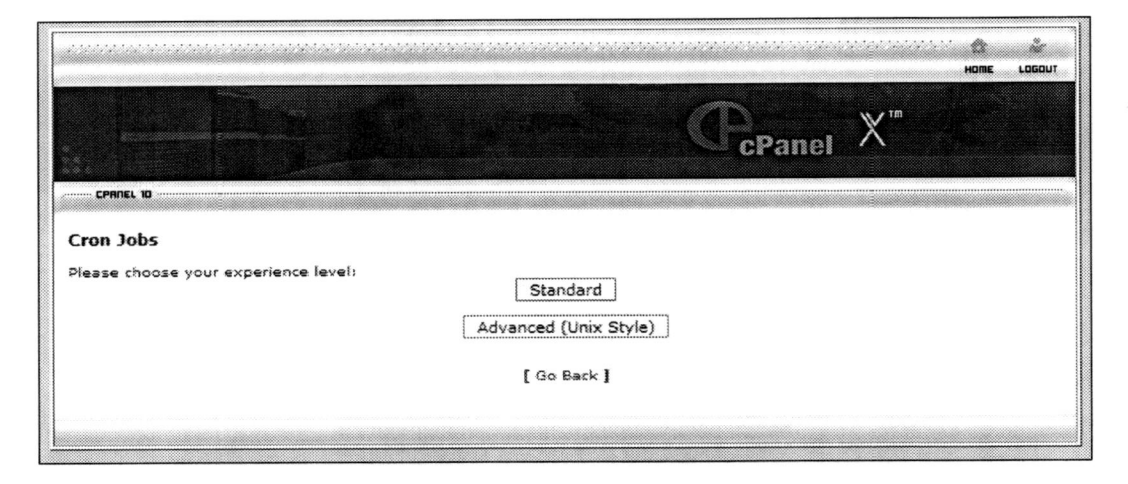

3. The Cron Jobs screen will display a form with a text field entry for commands as seen on the screenshot on the page opposite. This may look intimidating for administrators who have never run a Cron Job before. cPanel environments use UNIX terms for Cron Job commands. If you have never used UNIX before, don't worry, we will discuss each step in detail. First, enter an email address where Cron Jobs can send information about the backup.

Appendix A

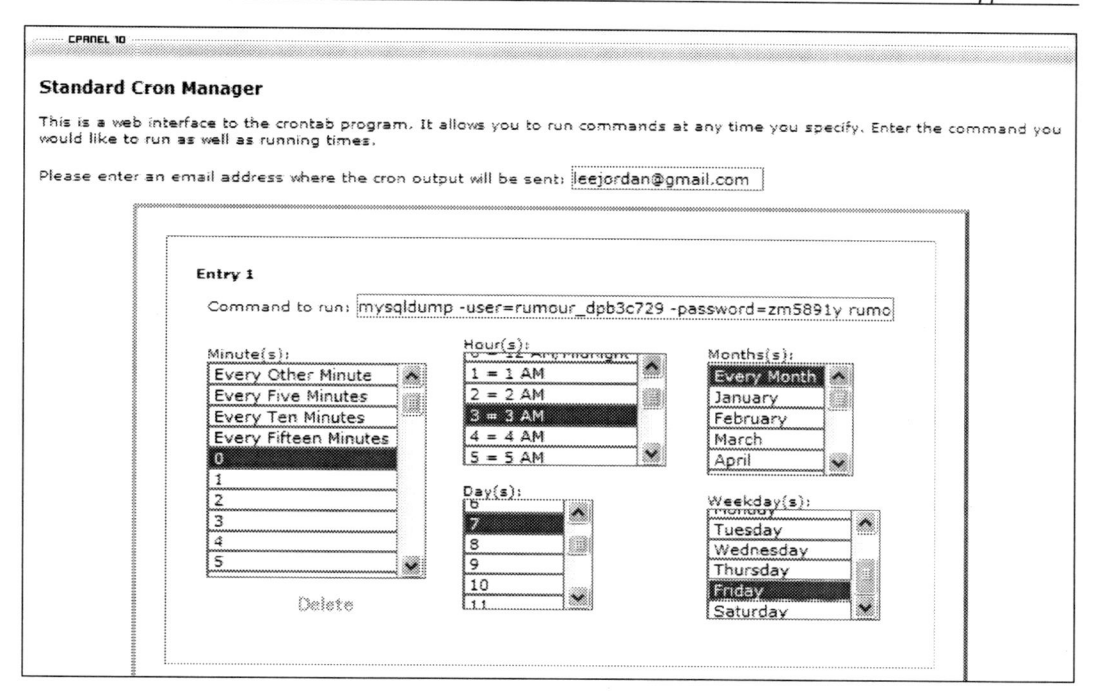

Standard Cron Manager

This is a web interface to the crontab program. It allows you to run commands at any time you specify. Enter the command you would like to run as well as running times.

Please enter an email address where the cron output will be sent: leejordan@gmail.com

Entry 1

Command to run: mysqldump -user=rumour_dpb3c729 -password=zm5891y rumo

Minute(s): 0
Hour(s): 3 = 3 AM
Months(s): Every Month
Day(s): 7
Weekday(s): Friday

4. The **mysqldump** is a special MySQL command to backup databases. We will enter a string of text that will tell Cron Job to back up the dotProject database every month on Friday mornings at 3 AM. Type the following text into the **Command to Run** text field:

   ```
   mysqldump -user=rumour_dpb3c729 -password=zm5891y rumour_dprj2 | gzip>/home/rumour/dotproject_backups/weekly_backup.sql.gz
   ```

   What did it all mean? The mysqldump command comes first, followed by -u or -user. The username for a database user who has full permissions to the database is listed, followed by -p or -password for that user's password. The next information entered is the database name. In the example above the database name is rumour_dprj2. A pipe symbol separates the database name from the gzip function. The gzip function will compress the database to reduce bandwidth and storage costs. The final information listed is the path and name of the backup file. Notice the file will be created by the gzip program and then given the name weekly_backup.sql.gz. It will be stored in the dotProject_backups folder we created in step 1.

5. The time settings are next. Each selection will highlight when it is chosen. Following the screenshot above, set the **Minute(s)** to **0**, **Hour(s)** to **3- 3AM**, **Month(s)** to **Every Month**, **Day(s)** to **7** and **Weekdays(s)** to **Friday** for the Cron Job.

[207]

6. Scroll down and click the **Save Crontab** button at the bottom of the browser window when the set up is complete. The compressed backup file will automatically be sent to the backup folder on the scheduled date and time.

> Knowing UNIX is not required to use Cron Jobs. I do recommend that you learn more about Cron Jobs if you are new to the tool. Visit the cPanel site for more in depth information: http://www.cPanel.net/docs/cPanel/Cron_jobs.htm.

Backing Up the dotProject Installation Files for Automatic Upgrades

cPanel makes it easy to back up files before an automatic upgrade. If it is an upgrade suggested by a cPanel tool such as Fantastico, the administrator will be prompted on the main Fantastico screen to upgrade the installation when a new version of the program is available. All upgrades for programs listed in the Fantastico tool follow the same procedure. The current installation can be updated by clicking on the 'Upgrade to…' link.

Before clicking the **Upgrade** button on the **Upgrade** screen, make sure that copies of any modules or modifications added after the installation are available or documented. The **Upgrade** screen will back up the files automatically as part of the upgrade process.

Fantastico will run an upgrade script for the installed program. When the installation is complete the screen will refresh with updated information about the upgrade. It is important to document the file names and restoration process in case there are any problems with the new upgrade.

cPanel also enables administrators to back up their files and directories using the **Backup** tool as described earlier. A third way to backup the installation files is to download a copy of the installation using FTP.

> **Review the Release Notes for the Planned Upgrade**
> dotProject upgrades usually come with release notes or readme files. If it is an automatic upgrade using a control panel such as cPanel, review the upgrade notes on the dotProject site before upgrading. Most releases such as 2.04, the most recent version, provide important security patches and bug fixes.

Have a Rollback Plan in Place

The files and database were backed up, the release notes were read, but something went wrong. Returning to the way the environment was previously is a time-saving method to recover from problems. Before any upgrades are done, plan what should happen if there is a critical failure.

A simple plan might involve:

- Backing up the database and files
- Deploying the upgrade
- Testing the upgrade
- Applying any patches, additional files, or other fixes as described in the troubleshooting documentation for the upgrade
- Rolling back to a previous database and/or set of installation files if there is a critical failure

Test the Upgrade in a Development "Sandbox"

A development environment, also often referred to as a sandbox, is a safe way to test how upgrades will affect the current dotProject environment. The process for creating a development is the same as for installing a production version of dotProject. Set aside a subfolder or sub domain where the environment will exist, then proceed with the installation as described earlier in this book.

Troubleshooting Upgrades

The main errors seen during an upgrade are database or `installscript` errors. Even if you are upgrading by clicking a button on a control panel such as Fantastico, take the time to document and back up your database files and information. If the installation fails, your Internet Service Provider may be able to help you if you have saved information such as the database names, and other backup information. You should be prompted during a Fantastico upgrade to copy the backup information.

Database and Install Errors After Upgrade

First roll back the changes to the previous installation. You did back up the database and files, right? If you are upgrading from dotProject 2.0.2 to 2.0.4, just upload the new 2.0.4 files. Do not run the upgrade scripts in the `install` folder. The same problems will just occur again. If you grabbed your upgrade from the dotProject CVS, check Sourceforge.net and make sure you are using the most recent version from the stable_2 branch. The other dotProject branch is for development only.

It is important to upgrade dotProject to version 2.04 to patch security issues. Full details can be found at the dotProject.net website and on the user forums.

Contacts Issues or User Details Lost During an Upgrade

If you have a small number of users, you can connect them to their information on the contacts list. Connecting the users to their contact information should correct the issue. dotProject installations serving a large number of users will require an SQL script. If the database was backed up, as discussed earlier in this appendix, then it should be possible to upload the correct information to the new database. Administrators may need to insert a backed-up copy of the user table rows into the dotProject database if user information is missing. User and contact information can also be loaded and exported using CVS formats. Further details about resolving this issue can be found in the dotProject forums.

B
Troubleshooting

There are many different types of errors that can be encountered during installation or use of a program. Always take the time to test the installation before deploying it into production. Appendix B will cover the most common type of error users experience after dotProject has been installed—Gantt Chart error. A variety of patches, fixes, and other solutions are available in the dotProject user forums at http://dotProject.net/vbulletin/. They will contain the most up-to-date information about errors and other issues.

Resolving Gantt Chart Errors

Font Error is experienced when users click on the Gantt chart tab on the **Projects** screen or within individual projects. It is a source of great frustration for users and administrators.

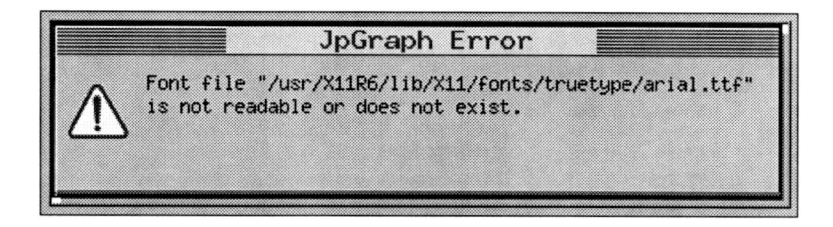

```
JpGraph Error
⚠  Font file "/usr/X11R6/lib/X11/fonts/truetype/arial.ttf"
    is not readable or does not exist.
```

If you see an error as shown in the previous screenshot there are two fixes for this. Well three if you do a combination of the two.

Troubleshooting

Method 1

You will need to upload a new fonts folder with the Arial fonts into the `locales/language/` folder of your dotProject installation.

Then, update the `jpGraph_config.inc` file located in the `/lib/jpGraph/src/` folder by adding the following line after the cache definition:

```
//----------------------------------------------------------------
// DEFINE("CACHE_DIR","/tmp/jpgraph_cache/");
// DEFINE("TTF_DIR","/usr/X11R6/lib/X11/fonts/truetype/");
//edited font source
DEFINE("TTF_DIR","/home/leesjordan.net/public_html/yourwebteam/locales/en/fonts/");
// end edited font source
// DEFINE("MBTTF_DIR","/usr/share/fonts/ja/TrueType/");
```

For most hosted solutions the generic format would be:

```
DEFINE("TTF_DIR","/home/mydomainname/public_html/mydotprojectinstallation/locales/en/fonts/");
```

Save the file and upload it back to the original `jpGraph/src` directory. Log in to the dotProject installation and attempt to view a Gantt chart on the projects list and on an individual project. You should see a result similar to the following screenshot:

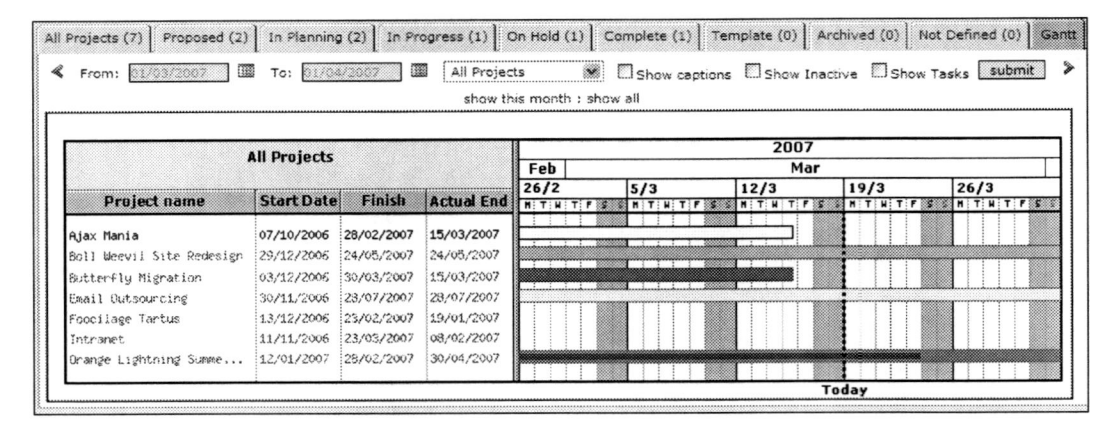

Method 2

If the combined view of all the projects is *not displayed* and you do not want to download font files, then do the following.

Download the `gantt.php` file from the `modules/projects/` folder in the dotProject installation. Save it as a backup. Create a test folder, then find and replace `FF_ARIAL` with `FF_FONT1`. This will replace `Arial` with the internal system font and we need to upload the file. The combined projects Gantt chart should now display.

Individual Project/Task Gantt Display Error (Fonts)

If your projects list combined view displays fine but you get an error similar to the following screenshot:

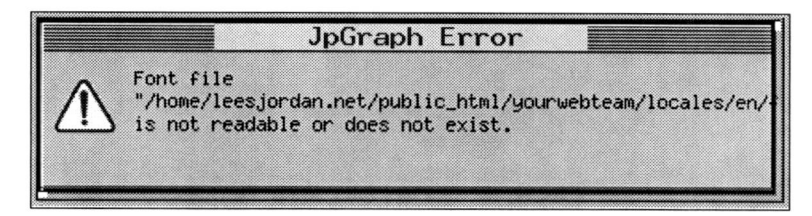

Then do the following:

Download the `gantt.php` file from the `modules/tasks/` folder in the dotProject installation. Save it as a backup. Create a test folder, then find and replace `FF_ARIAL` with `FF_FONT1`. This will replace Arial with the internal system font. To see the changes we have to upload the file. This is what I had to do for individual Gantt charts to display properly.

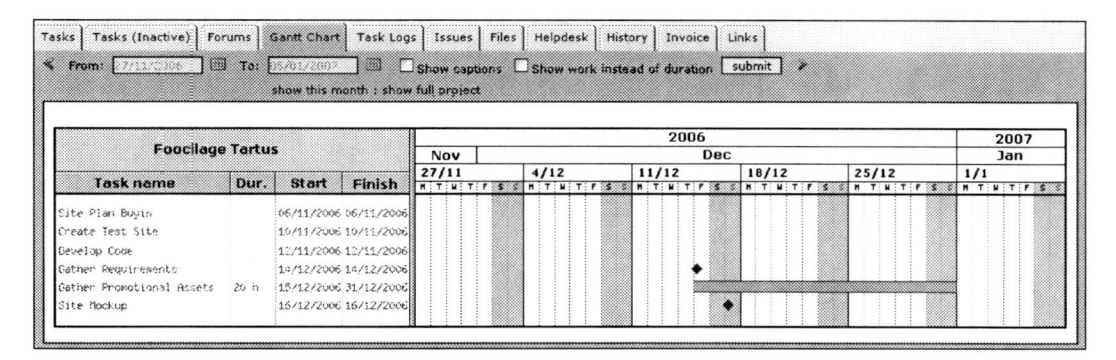

Index

A

add-on modules *See also* **standard modules**
  about 184
  custom modifications 198
  developer resources 198
  Eventum 187
  helpdesk 192
  installing 186
  integrating 198
  invoice 195
  TicketSmith 196
administrative roles
  about 139
  creating 139-141
  restricted administrator 142, 143
  restricted company access 150-152
  restricted file access 144-149

B

backup module 183
backups, dotProject
  about 202
  cPanel used, for manual backups 204
  Cron jobs used, for automatic backups 205-208
  installation files, for automatic upgrades 208
  roll back plan 209
  upgrade, testing 209
billing code table 121

C

calendar 181
companies
  about 54
  adding 55
  department, adding 60-62
  editing, preparing for 59
  general information, updating 59
  internal companies 57
  managing 53
  tabs, viewing 58
  updating 58
  viewing 56, 57
contacts
  adding 64
  adding as vCard 65-67
  downloading as CSV 62-64
  managing 62
  updating 68
  viewing 68
custom fields
  about 118
  adding 119, 120

D

default user preferences
  about 114
  options 115
dotProject
  about 5, 7
  add-on modules 184
  administering 87
  backing up 202
  companies, managing 53

contacts, managing 62
core features 9-12
customizing 155
environment, for installing 16
features 8
file management 77
installing 15, 18
interface 35
LAMP, server setups 16
language support, adding 89
license 7
limitations 13
main navigation bar 46
modules, managing 123
need for 12
password, changing 39
PMA 5
preferences setting 98
prerequisites 15
projects, managing 69
server setups 16
standard modules 173
style sheet, editing 164
support contracts, enabling 191, 192
system, administrating 87
task view, filtering 44
troubleshooting 31, 211
upgrading 201
user interface 35
users, administrating 126
version control 77
volunteering to 198
WAMP, server setups 16
WIMP, server setups 16
dotProject, customizing
theme, altering 159
user interface style 156-158
user preferences, setting 155
dotProject, installing
backups 19
browser, using 24-30
environment 16
online control panel, using 19-23
prerequisites 15
server setups 16
SSL, secured installation 30
types 18

E

email settings
email transport 111
host requires login 111
queue email for later sending 112
SMTP host 111
SMTP password 111
SMTP port 111
SMTP server timeout 112
SMTP username 111
environment, for installing dotProject
browser 18
fonts 18
mail server 18
memory limit 18
MySQL 17
PHP 17
web server 17
Windows 17
Eventum
about 187
installing 188-190
support contracts, enabling 191, 192
using 191

F

file management
current files, updating 82
file checkin 82
file checkout 82, 83
file repository terms 78-80
files, editing 84, 85
files, viewing 81, 82
new files, adding 78
forums 179

G

Gantt chart error 211
Gantt charts
about 174
combined projects view 174
error 211
individual project view 175
todo view 175

general settings
  admin username 101
  all task assignees, showing 103
  calendar end hour 104
  calendar minute increment 104
  calendar start hour 104
  calendar working days 104
  check task dates 102
  company name 101
  currency symbol 100
  daily working hours 103
  debug level 105
  debug messages, showing 103
  default file indexing parser 105
  default module 104
  default submodule 105
  default tabbed subview 105
  default user interface style 101
  editing of prevous versions, allowing 106
  email prefix 101
  file settings on CI, preserving 106
  gantt charts, enabling 102
  host locale 99
  HTML file indexing parser 105
  jpGraph locale 102
  log changes 102
  maximum file size for indexing 105
  memory limit for Gantt 106
  minicals in day view, showing 104
  minimum password length 102
  minimum username length 102
  MS Word indexing parser 105
  multiple task assignments, editing 104
  overall checking 100
  page title 101
  PDF indexing parser 105
  project colour selection, restricting 104
  site domain 101
  task relinking, allowing 103
  task time editing, restricting 104
  translation alert string 102
  translation warning 102

H

helpdesk module
  about 192
  Bugzilla 194
  configuring 193
  installing 193
  using 194

I

interface, dotProject
  about 35
  help screen 39
  main navigation bar 46
  my info screen 40
  password, changing 39
  task view, filtering 44
  today section 45
  todo list 44, 45
  user menu 38
  user preferences, editing 42, 43
invoice module
  about 195
  using 195

L

language support
  about 88
  dotProject, adding to 89-97
LDAP settings
  about 109
  distinguished name 110
  SMTP 111
  special variables 110
  variables 110
lookup values 116

M

main navigation bar
  about 46
  companies 47
  company, changing 47
  contacts 51, 52
  files 50, 51
  projects 48
  project status 49
  tasks 49

[217]

modules
    activating 124
    installing 123
    managing 123
    ordering 126

P

PMA
    about 5
    dotProject 5
    features 6
PostNuke
    authentication 106-109
    login for standard login 106
preferences
    general settings 98
    system, configuring 98
Project Management Application. *See* PMA
project reports
    about 175, 176
    generating 177
    viewing 177, 178
projects
    adding 70-72
    best practices, for creating 72
    editing 70-72
    managing 69
    project screen, altering 69
    task, creating 73-77
    task dates tab 75
    task dependencies tab 76
    task human resources tab 77
    task logs 77

R

resources
    about 178
    adding 179
roles
    about 132
    adding 134-137
    administrative roles 139
    creating 134
    full access 137-139
    permissions, setting up 137

S

session handling settings
    about 112
    scan event queue on session garbage
        collection 113
    session handler 112
    session idle time 112
    session maximum lifetime 113
SmartSearch 182
standard modules *See also* add-on modules
    about 173
    backup 183
    calendar 181
    companies 47
    contacts 51, 52
    files 50, 51
    forums 179
    Gantt charts 174
    projects 48
    project reports 175
    resources 178
    SmartSearch 182
    TicketSmith 196
style sheet
    body style, changing 167
    editing 164
    fonts, changing 164
    image as background 168, 169
    links, adjusting 165, 166
    module text strings, customizing 170, 171
    new styles, adding 169
    new theme, creating tips 169
    styles, altering 164
system, configuring
    billing code table 121
    custom field notes 121
    custom fields 118
    default user preferences 114
    email settings 111
    general settings 99
    LDAP settings 109
    lookup values 116
    session handling settings 112
    task reminder settings 113
    user authentication settings 106

[218]

system administration
 contacts, administrating 88
 language support 88
 modules 88
 preferences 88, 98
 user roles, administrating 88

T

task reminder settings
 maximum number of reminders to send 114
 number of days warning for due tasks 113
 task reminders, sending 113
theme
 altering 159
 dotProject logo, replacing 161
 header background, replacing 162
 icons, altering 159
 icons, replacing 160
 images, changing 159
 new theme, creating tips 169, 170
TicketSmith
 about 196
 using 196
troubleshooting, dotProject
 database, installing failed 31, 33
 different OS used 33
 different page, displaying 33
 different setup used 33
 different web server used 33
 Gantt chart font error 33, 211-213
 JpGraph font error 33

U

upgrading, dotProject
 backing up 202
 contact issues, troubleshooting 210
 database errors, troubleshooting 210
 install errors, troubleshooting 210
 roll back plan 209
 sandbox testing 209
 testing 209
 troubleshooting 209

user authentication settings
 PostNuke authentication 106-109
 PostNuke login also allows standard loging 106
 user authentication method 106
user menu
 help on forums, finding 39
 help screen 39
 my info screen 40
 today section 45
 todo list 44, 45
 user preferences, editing 42, 43
users
 adding 129
 administrating 126, 127
 deleting 130, 131
 editing 130
 permissions, setting 131
 roles 132
 roles, adding 134-137
 roles, creating 134
 viewing 128

V

vCards
 about 62
 contact, adding as 65
version control 77

[219]

[PACKT PUBLISHING] Thank you for buying Project Management with dotProject

Packt Open Source Project Royalties

When we sell a book written on an Open Source project, we pay a royalty directly to that project. Therefore by purchasing Project Management with dotProject, Packt will have given some of the money received to the dotProject project.

In the long term, we see ourselves and you—customers and readers of our books—as part of the Open Source ecosystem, providing sustainable revenue for the projects we publish on. Our aim at Packt is to establish publishing royalties as an essential part of the service and support a business model that sustains Open Source.

If you're working with an Open Source project that you would like us to publish on, and subsequently pay royalties to, please get in touch with us.

Writing for Packt

We welcome all inquiries from people who are interested in authoring. Book proposals should be sent to authors@packtpub.com. If your book idea is still at an early stage and you would like to discuss it first before writing a formal book proposal, contact us; one of our commissioning editors will get in touch with you.

We're not just looking for published authors; if you have strong technical skills but no writing experience, our experienced editors can help you develop a writing career, or simply get some additional reward for your expertise.

About Packt Publishing

Packt, pronounced 'packed', published its first book "Mastering phpMyAdmin for Effective MySQL Management" in April 2004 and subsequently continued to specialize in publishing highly focused books on specific technologies and solutions.

Our books and publications share the experiences of your fellow IT professionals in adapting and customizing today's systems, applications, and frameworks. Our solution-based books give you the knowledge and power to customize the software and technologies you're using to get the job done. Packt books are more specific and less general than the IT books you have seen in the past. Our unique business model allows us to bring you more focused information, giving you more of what you need to know, and less of what you don't.

Packt is a modern, yet unique publishing company, which focuses on producing quality, cutting-edge books for communities of developers, administrators, and newbies alike. For more information, please visit our website: www.PacktPub.com.

Creating your MySQL Database:
Practical Design Tips and Techniques

ISBN: 1-904811-30-2   Paperback: 108 pages

A short guide for everyone on how to structure your data and set-up your MySQL database tables efficiently and easily.

1. How best to collect, name, group, and structure your data.
2. Design your data with future growth in mind.
3. Practical examples from initial ideas to final designs.

cPanel User Guide and Tutorial

ISBN: 1-904811-92-2   Paperback: 208 pages

Get the most from cPanel with this easy to follow guide

1. Everything you need to manage files, email, and databases using cPanel.
2. Organise your website and create subdomains, custom error messages, and password protected areas.
3. Analyse site logs, ensure your site and data remain secure, and learn how to create and restore data back ups.
4. Use advanced features, find powerful cPanel add ons, and install web scripts from within cPanel: osCommerce, Mambo, phpBB, and more.

Please visit www.PacktPub.com for information on our titles

Printed in the United States
77441LV00004B/13-18